ON BEING WITH OTHERS

'Glendinning's is a highly original approach, one that draws responsibly from both the analytic and continental traditions to present an important alternative to the usual epistemological approach to the problem of other minds. The argument is a forceful and coherent one that not only shows the usefulness of bringing continental and analytic perspectives together on a problem of fundamental significance but also points towards avenues for future work on similar "hard cases" in philosophy. I enjoyed reading *On Being With Others* and found I learned a good deal from the author's way of posing the problem of other minds.'

Steve Crowell, Rice University

'*On Being With Others* picks an unwavering and controlled line through a mass of difficult material. It is highly thought-provoking and opens up a lot of areas of investigation. It will attract a lot of attention and generate much discussion – this is the way I think that philosophy should be going. It makes Heidegger and Derrida intelligible to an analytic audience without losing their distinctive "flavour"; it treats analytic literature sensitively but without getting bogged down in the fine detail. I liked this book very much.'

Jane Howarth, University of Lancaster

ON BEING WITH OTHERS

OTHERS

Heidegger – Derrida – Wittgenstein

Simon Glendinning

London and New York

First published 1998
by Routledge
2 Park Square, Milton Park, Abingdon, Oxon, OX14 4RN

Simultaneously published in the USA and Canada
by Routledge
270 Madison Ave, New York NY 10016

Transferred to Digital Printing 2006

© 1998 Simon Glendinning

Typeset in Baskerville by Routledge

British Library Cataloguing in Publication Data
A catalogue record for this book is available from the British Library.

Library of Congress Cataloging in Publication Data
Glendinning, Simon
On Being With Others: Heidegger, Derrida, Wittgenstein / Simon
Glendinning
Includes bibliographical references and index.
1. Other minds (Theory of knowledge) I. Title.
BD213.G57 1996
121'.2—dc21 97-24111

ISBN 0–415–17123–7 (hbk)
ISBN 0–415–17124–5 (pbk)

CONTENTS

CONTENTS

PREFACE

In 1986, I found a copy of Wittgenstein's *Philosophical Investigations* in a box in the loft at my father's house. My eldest brother had had enough of it, it seems. Five years later I was still reading it. For about two years after that, however, I found it hard to pick up at all, and it was in fact readings of Heidegger's *Being and Time* and Derrida's *Limited Inc* that rediscovered it for me. That rediscovery is what this book, in a formal way, recites.

As a result of this personal history, academic friends tell me that 'the central and distinctive characteristic of my work' is the way in which it bridges the current gulf between analytical philosophy and Continental philosophy. I might continue: this pretty much guarantees that some readers will think my work insufficiently analytical and others insufficiently Continental. So, to take a crude example, some readers of this book might worry about the omission of detailed treatments of the standard approaches to the problem of other minds – the argument from analogy and the argument from best explanation; other readers might be equally concerned that it omits detailed readings of the thought of Levinas or Merleau-Ponty. To such complaints I could simply and honestly reply that this book is not intended to present a descriptive survey of the central arguments from the analytical and/or Continental traditions. But what that answer would conceal is the fact that this work does not aim to 'bridge the current gulf' either. Of course, given the current gulf, the fact that my work ignores it is bound to give the impression that it aims to bridge it.

I don't intend here to go into why I think the division deserves ignoring. Suffice it to say that what I have found characteristic about my work is that it only gets along at all by getting along without it. Thus, my readings of the philosophers who figure in this book are constantly, and of course I hope responsibly, informed by each other. For example, the treatment of 'Wittgensteinian criteria' with which this book concludes develops from and out of the examination of Heidegger and Derrida which precedes it.

I think that this sheds new light on Wittgenstein's position. As I have indicated, however, my first encounter with both Heidegger and Derrida was, in fact, subsequent to devouring and repeated readings of Wittgenstein. This historical ordering perhaps explains what some will consider to be an 'under-reading' of

Heidegger's and perhaps especially of Derrida's work. There may be some justice to this concern. I am particularly aware that my take (or at least my currently printable take) on Derrida's work focuses on what one might roughly call its 'theoretical' content – its demonstrations and arguments. And I am aware that this falls short of the riches of his extraordinary writings. But perhaps this narrowness on my part can reap some unintended rewards. For my considered view is that there are at least two sorts of top-notch nonsense connected to Derrida's work, nonsense for which he is not, or should not be held, personally responsible. The first appears as the upshot of partial and selective readings. Passages are cited as a badge of radicalism or of theoretical mastery. Motifs of 'deconstruction'; the 'reversal and displacement' of traditional binary opposi-tions, the aim at 'effective intervention', the broad notion of a 'text', the sometimes barely parsable sentences . . . all this has been pounced on like sweets from a jar. Or, perhaps, people have failed to see the jar for the sweets. This is the situation recognisable in (but not 'everywhere in') literary studies today. And it is faintly embarrassing. The second sort of nonsense arises as the upshot not of partial or selective reading but of simple non-reading. Here one is happy to make do with free-floating opinions, confident that deconstruction is mere bonnet-polishing, cant dressed up as serious thought. Everyone knows, it will be said, that deconstruction is charlatanry, obscure sophistry. And so everyone knows that it is not worth spending (wasting) time actually reading it. This is the situation recognisable in (but not 'everywhere in') English-speaking philosophy today. And, strictly speaking, it is worse than embarrassing: it is a disgrace. One of my hopes in writing the Derrida sections of this book is that I can make a contribution to setting the records straighter on the (yes, not-very-straight) paths of Derrida's thought. I think some will feel that the resulting reading of Derrida is insufficiently rich. That's almost certainly right. Full stop.

As I say, I hope I have not been unfairly unfaithful to any of the writers who enter this book's embrace. But I know, too, that, quite late in the day, I found a story to tell and that it is not entirely theirs. Many people not mentioned (or not mentioned much) in this book have helped me a great deal in finding this. While they shouldn't take the blame for what I have done either, I am particularly grateful to Anita Avramides, Matthew Bell, Max de Gaynesford, John Hyman, Stephen Law, Marie McGinn, Alan Montefiore, Stephen Mulhall, Jennie Walmsley and my former colleagues at the University of Kent at Canterbury.

All of these people, and many others too, have been helpfully there at various stages and in various ways during the development of this book. I dedicate it, however, to those who were there first: my father, Nigel, my mother, Victoria, my three big brothers, Paul, Hugo and Matthew; and to the cats and dogs who were there with us too.

S.B.G.
London, October 1997

ABBREVIATIONS

AC   Baker, G. P. and Hacker, P. M. S. (1983) *Analytical Commentary on the 'Philosophical Investigations': Wittgenstein: Meaning and Understanding*, vol. I, Basil Blackwell, Oxford.

AL   Derrida, Jacques (1992) *Acts of Literature*, Routledge, London and New York.

BB   Wittgenstein, Ludwig (1969) *The Blue and Brown Books*, Basil Blackwell, Oxford.

BT   Heidegger, Martin (1962) *Being and Time*, trans. John Macquarrie and Edward Robinson, Basil Blackwell, Oxford.

EW   Derrida, Jacques (1991) 'Eating Well', in E. Cadava *et al.* (eds) *Who Comes After the Subject*, Routledge, London and New York.

FCM   Heidegger, Martin (1995) *The Fundamental Concepts of Metaphysics*, trans. W. McNeill and N. Walker, Indiana University Press, Bloomington.

LH   Heidegger, Martin (1977) 'Letter on Humanism', in *Basic Writings*, trans. David Farrell Krell, Routledge, London.

LI   Derrida, Jacques (1988a) *Limited Inc*, North Western University Press, Evanston.

LWI   Wittgenstein, Ludwig (1982) *Last Writings On The Philosophy of Psychology*, vol. I, trans. C. G. Luckhardt and M. A. E. Aue, Basil Blackwell, Oxford.

NB   Wittgenstein, Ludwig (1961a) *Notebooks: 1914–1916*, trans. G. E. M. Anscombe, Basil Blackwell, Oxford.

OC   Wittgenstein, Ludwig (1979) *On Certainty*, trans. D. Paul and G. E. M. Anscombe, Basil Blackwell, Oxford.

OM   Austin, J. L. (1979) 'Other Minds', in *Philosophical Papers*, Oxford University Press, Oxford.

OS   Derrida, Jacques (1987) *Of Spirit: Heidegger and the Question*, trans. Geoffrey Bennington and Rachel Bowlby, The University of Chicago Press, Chicago.

PG   Wittgenstein, Ludwig (1974) *Philosophical Grammar*, trans. A. Kenny, Basil Blackwell, Oxford.

PI   Wittgenstein, Ludwig (1968a) *Philosophical Investigations*, trans. G. E. M.

Anscombe, Basil Blackwell, Oxford.

PP   Merleau-Ponty, Maurice (1962) *Phenomenology of Perception*, trans. Colin Smith, Routledge, London.

PR   Wittgenstein, Ludwig (1975) *Philosophical Remarks*, trans. R. Hargreaves and R. White, Basil Blackwell, Oxford.

RFM   Wittgenstein, Ludwig (1978) *Remarks on the Foundations of Mathematics*, trans. G. E. M. Anscombe, Basil Blackwell, Oxford.

RPPI   Wittgenstein, Ludwig (1980a) *Remarks on the Philosophy of Psychology*, vol. I, trans. G. E. M. Anscombe, Basil Blackwell, Oxford.

RPPII   Wittgenstein, Ludwig (1980b) *Remarks on the Philosophy of Psychology*, vol. II, trans. C. G. Luckhardt and M. A. E. Aue, Basil Blackwell, Oxford.

S&S   Austin, J. L. (1962) *Sense and Sensibilia*, Oxford University Press, Oxford.

TLP   Wittgenstein, Ludwig (1961b) *Tractatus Logico-Philosophicus*, trans. D. F. Pears and B. F. McGuinness, Routledge & Kegan Paul, London.

Z   Wittgenstein, Ludwig (1981) *Zettel*, trans. G. E. M. Anscombe, Basil Blackwell, Oxford.

INTRODUCTION

I

When philosophers talk about the external world, they typically populate it with small-to-medium-sized dry-goods: chairs, pens, desks, sticks, and so on. So our perceptual openness to the world is conceived, primarily, in terms of the disclosure of facts about such things. Yet much of our lives is occupied with far more exotic creatures, namely, *living* things, and particularly, living human beings. I think it would be misleading to conceive our being with others simply in terms of the perceptual disclosure of a thing of some kind, a thing among things. We characteristically talk of many living things as *having* and not merely *being* a body – or, even more strikingly, as having a soul. Whatever stance one takes with respect to notions like the soul, it seems clear that a satisfactory account of our being with others must do justice to its distinctive and familiar phenomenology. That is, it must do justice to the fact that, in everyday life, certain entities are disclosed not as mere environmental bodies but as *others*.

In this book I try to provide such an account. The aim is to explain how it can be that what is disclosed in our perception of certain things in the world does not fall short of facts about *others*. Others: that is, living things which are not merely *in* the world, but which are *there too* and *there with* oneself.

Hot on the heels of bent-looking sticks, this topic is normally treated under the title of the problem of scepticism concerning other minds. However, as I will try to explain in this introduction, the critical focus of this book is not simply scepticism but, casting the net more widely, the conceptual or metaphysical framework within which the threat of scepticism is a live one. In virtue of the special emphasis and elevated position that it accords human beings, I will come to call this framework 'humanism'.

In a certain way humanism begins where I, too, want to begin – namely, with a rejection of the idea that others are simply a kind of thing in the world among other things. It thus rejects what can be called the baldly naturalistic assumption that a human being is merely an environmentally occurring organism.[1] What distinguishes humanism, however, is the proposal that this insufficient definition can be overcome or offset by outfitting such organisms with immortal souls or by

1

adjoining minds to their bodies. Thus, in its most familiar modern form, humanism outlines a dualistically conceived account of (what it calls) 'man' as a 'self-conscious subject'. My initial (and I hope not-too-controversial) suggestion will be that such a conception cannot but sustain the threat of scepticism.

The focus on humanism introduces a complication in the characterisation of the response to the problem of other minds outlined in this book. The questions I pursue are not of the form: 'How can we bridge the gap between a man's observable behaviour and the experiences of which only he is conscious?' Rather, turning this question around, the attempt is made to explore questions of the form: 'What is it about human beings which makes them maintain an interpretation of themselves that sustains the threat of scepticism?' I call this approach a reframing of scepticism, and in the first part of the book I explore how such an approach is developed in the work of J. L. Austin and Martin Heidegger.

While I think that a reframing of scepticism is the only way of avoiding, once and for all, its threat, I argue that the positions defended by both Austin and Heidegger are, in different ways, unsatisfactory. In Austin's case this is because, at a submerged level, his account of being with others retains the problematic conception of the self-conscious subject which, in my view, sustains the threat of scepticism. The difficulties I will identify in Heidegger's account are harder to summarise neatly. In part, this is because his approach to human existence (the analytic of Dasein) does, fairly obviously, escape the threat of scepticism. The trouble as I see it is rather that, in common with the humanism against which he also recoils, his rejection of bald naturalism constitutes a wholesale rejection of naturalism *per se*. In this sense the humanist background remains largely in place. Heidegger's conception of Dasein, as Derrida puts it, 'comes to occupy the place of the "subject", the *cogito* or the classical "Ich denke". From these it retains certain essential traits.' I argue that this retention underlies and informs a deep lack of clarity in the Heideggerian account of being with others (*Mitsein*). It will then begin to emerge that a satisfactory reframing of scepticism must pursue a critique of humanism as anti-naturalism.

II

The claim is that Heidegger, too, attempts to supplant bald naturalism by outfitting human beings with a uniquely distinctive trait. That is, Heidegger shares the classical humanist's tendency to suppose human beings as separated by an 'abyss' from what are conceived as mere animals. This tendency is, I will suggest, motivated by an interpretation of the (admittedly distinctive) phenomenon of human language. As will become clear, I hope to show why, *pace* humanism, what is distinctive in human life does not lead us away or separate us from our natural, animal history. So while I have great sympathy with Heidegger's recoil from classical humanism, I conclude that, ultimately, it does not pursue the critique of humanism *far enough*.

Heidegger's recoil from classical humanism is characterised by a claim which, when taken *au pied de la lettre*, exactly contradicts the position I want to defend, namely, his claim that the classical humanist is *insufficiently* anti-naturalistic, that the 'rational animal' remains *too much* an animal. Heidegger's basis for this claim is his view that a human body is quite other than an 'organic thing' which occurs in the world and which turns out to be (in a more or less mysterious way) the point of occupancy for a subjectivity or personality. It will bear stressing that I think that Heidegger's argument against classical humanism on this point is profoundly correct. What seems quite wrong to me, however, is that we should see it as posing a challenge to our thinking about human beings alone. We have to rethink what it is to be an animal. And rethink this, not 'as well', but, and now including human beings, *simpliciter*.

What, I submit, is essential is to re-evaluate the baldly naturalistic assumption, rejected by both classical and Heideggerian humanism, that 'the essence of man consists in being an animal organism'. Such a re-evaluation would have to target the idea that the sub-personal (or, say, sub-canine) accounts offered by the sciences in this area exhaust what can sensibly be said of the life of an *animal*; as if all attributions of psychological states to the behaviour of living things was just a way of talking (or reacting) and not a response to the facts. For it is precisely when we do conceive an animal organism, and animality in general, in a baldly naturalistic way that, when it comes to considerations about human beings, the humanist's supplement, whether in its classical or Heideggerian form, seems almost unavoidable. But freed from this narrow conception of animality we will not find it problematic to reject the humanist assumption that human life is separated from animal nature by an 'abyss'. As before we will reject conceptions of human behaviour which reduce it to the complex workings of an anatomical apparatus. But this will no longer force us to conceive even our most distinctive form of behaviour, our use of language, as separate from (or as separating us from) the life of an animal. Indeed, on this view, human life can be comfortably acknowledged as being itself a manifestation of nature; relatively distinctive, no doubt, but not absolutely so. The result is a conception of behaviour which will enable us to affirm quite generally that, as Wittgenstein puts it, 'to see the behaviour of a living thing is to see its soul'.

To realise this possibility amounts to achieving the basic aim of the book. So my basic claim is that what stands in the way of a fully satisfactory account of being with others is not simply (as Heidegger supposes) the conception of 'man' as the entity with self-consciousness but, more generally, the humanist rejection of naturalism.

In virtue of its conception of animality, humanism, whether in its classical or its Heideggerian form, presumes that the distinction between the human and non-human must, at least at certain crucial points, constitute an absolute break or pure cut. 'Man', as the *zoon logon echon* or rational animal or thinking thing or Dasein, is credited with a uniquely distinctive capacity which affords it alone access to the world *as* world. Against this conception my claim is not that the traits which are usually reserved only for human beings (language, reason, conceptual thought, self-consciousness, etc.) are, in any developed way, actually possessed by other animals. It is rather that accounts of these distinctive traits which begin with or posit a radical break between humanity and animality cannot be other than idealised and distorted.

III

What is needed, then, is a conception of human existence which eschews bald naturalism but which does not simply affirm a new humanism. Achieving this, I am suggesting, will perforce require a new account of human behaviour in general; an account which explains how something manifest in that behaviour might be (*pace* humanism) 'immanent to the behaviour as such' and yet (*pace* bald naturalism) 'transcendent in relation to the anatomical apparatus' (Merleau-Ponty).

Presenting and defending such an account is the task of the second part of the book, in which I undertake a renewed treatment of behavioural events which involve the use of signs. By making perspicuous structural features internal to all such behaviour (speech, writing, sign-language, expressive gesture, etc.) it is shown that the general space of their possibility can be described in terms traditionally thought to be applicable only to *writing*. This demonstration makes plausible a strategic generalisation of the concept of writing to cover significant behaviour in general – and with that a novel account of our openness to others.

The basic line of argument is that the intelligibility or significance that belongs to 'writing' is intrinsic to it, but that this can be so only on condition that it is capable of functioning again, and so has an independence from any single context of its production or 'inscription'. For this reason, an event of 'writing' must, in a certain way, detach itself from every empirically determined 'inscriber'. This account nicely captures the sought-for immanent/transcendent structure, and in the last part of the book I explain how it provides the basis for a fundamentally non-sceptical and non-humanist approach to openness to others.

Openness implies that what is disclosed in non-deceptive perception does not stop short of the facts. With respect to this thought, the case of one's access to minds other than one's own seems particularly problematic. I hope to show that, by conceiving significant behaviour in general as 'writing', we can overcome this difficulty: the perception of a soul, being open to a living thing *as* an other, is a matter of 'reading the behaviour' of a living thing. On this conception, how things are for an other is indeed something that can be manifest. But what is manifest here is not something that can be manifest to just anyone; someone might fully perceive the outward behaviour of an organism (*qua* movements of an anatomical apparatus) and yet not see, for example, a human being encouraging herself, asking herself a question, or winking to her mother.

This account is developed through an investigation of the later Wittgenstein's notion of 'criteria'. In the literature, criteria are often conceived as behavioural conditions of some type. And in a sense that is correct. However, I argue that what is in question here is never simply a case of the presence of some typical condition which then elicits some typical response. On the contrary, the behavioural condition in question is not something that can be established to obtain independently of such a response. That is, the identification or recognition of such a behavioural condition is *already* a response.

This suggests that one is implicated in the 'what' of what is recalled when one recalls criteria. As Wittgenstein puts it, 'my relation to the appearance here is part of my concept.' On this account, in each case, what one recognises (for example, a wink or a wince) is not a 'merely behavioural' feature of the behaviour of a living thing; not something which is accessible to just anyone. Here again it seems compelling to elaborate this thought with the suggestion that, in order to be open to a living thing *as* an other, one must be able to read its behaviour.

Two basic claims are developed with respect to this notion of reading the behaviour of a living thing. First, a claim concerning the identity, the 'what', of inner states and processes; and second, a claim concerning the identity, the 'who', of their owner or possessor. The first claim is that the ways in which we read–respond to the behaviour of a living thing are integral to the 'what' of inner states and processes themselves. As Wittgenstein puts it, 'an "inner process" stands in need of outward criteria.' The second claim is more difficult to articulate in an unproblematic way. We can approach it through consideration of the thought that 'writing' (a readable identity) must, in virtue of its essential detachability from every context and from every 'inscriber', possess a structural anonymity. The trouble is that, far from supporting it, this feature seems to destroy the very possibility of being with others.

In my view, this anonymity is ineliminable, and any reading must pass through it. However, as will become clear, such anonymity is also essentially limited. There is no absolutely anonymous trait because its reading–response entails a singularity of its own (a 'this time', even if one structured by internal relations to other times). And my claim is that, for this reason, such a response is best conceived as presuming, in each case, a spontaneous or originary apostrophe. That is, it is a turn to a living thing *as* an other in advance of evidence or reasons which might ground it. Responding to the behaviour of a living thing in this distinctive way is, here and now, to leap to a 'we'. This leap does not, however, constitute the other as other. Rather, it is what first assigns to a living thing the *position* of a subject. This, then, is the second claim: that the individuation of a subject, the 'who', like the 'what', stands in need of a reading–response.

It is with these points in view that I develop a new approach to being with others. Others, I argue, are like myself not because I know that there is *one of these* (a mind) which is not my own and is *over there* (or, somehow, *in that*). Rather, as living things at home with the 'writing' of living things, they are, in

Heidegger's words, 'those from whom, for the most part, one does *not* distinguish oneself – those among whom one is too.' With this conclusion we arrive where we want to be, namely, where we already were. For now there remains no special obstacle to affirming that 'if one sees the behaviour of a living thing, one sees its soul.' Indeed, one can even say it, as Wittgenstein does, of a dog.

1

THE THREAT OF SCEPTICISM

INTRODUCTION

The problem of other minds

In the somewhat bizarre context of a question concerning the nature of our acquaintance with the soul of a dog, Wittgenstein advances the following suggestion: 'one might say this: If one sees the behaviour of a living thing, one sees its soul' (PI, §357). Some might fight shy of the folk-psychological or even theological implications of using the word 'soul'. 'Souls' are, surely, highly suspect entities: ethereal, gaseous and occult; or simply a fiction '*lyingly invented* in order to destroy the body' (Nietzsche, 1992, p. 102). Not the stuff that a realistic and sober philosophy is made of. And is not resistance to positing such 'queer' entities something that Wittgenstein himself insists on?[1] Can one speak of 'seeing the soul of another' without embarrassment? And the soul of a *dog*?

In a rather ungainly translation, I want to transpose these questions into the rather more formal terms of the topic of other minds. The question is: How are we to understand the fact that each one of us, without special embarrassment, normally attributes psychological properties to living things other than oneself? This is the central question of this book. The aim is to provide an approach to the topic of other minds which enables us to affirm the suggestion that to see the behaviour of a living thing is to see its soul.

As my initial *fil conducteur* I will explore the problem which most dramatically stands in the way of this affirmation: the classical problem of scepticism concerning other minds. The outstanding feature of the problem of other minds is that it throws into relief the fact that one does *not* normally hold in suspense all attribution of psychological properties to living things other than oneself. Each of us relates to many living things as being *like oneself* in the respect that psychological properties are attributed to them. My overarching assumption will be that any response to the problem of other minds which can be shown to lead us to compromise or retreat from this position cannot be satisfactory. The task, then, is to do justice to the phenomena of being with others. And this implies that the inquiry must, in a certain way, leave us where we already are (only, as it were, more clearly). As I hope to show, however, this task is not as straightforward as it sounds.

The problem of other minds is best conceived as a conceptual problem motivated by epistemological doubts. That is, a concern with the possibility of *making sense* of the idea of inner states and processes which are not one's own inner states and processes arises out of reflections on *claims to know* minds other than one's own. I will briefly explain this.

The sceptical argument about other minds is intended to show that the attribution of psychological properties to beings other than oneself is always presumptuous. There is, it seems, an unbridgeable gulf between one's evidence for and the reality of the inner states and processes of another. The sceptic concludes that his epistemic standing can never justify saying, for example, 'N.N. is in pain', but only, for example, 'N.N. is behaving as I behave when I am in pain'.

While the sceptic may try to remain agnostic as to the actual facts concerning the minds of others ('I know what it would be for there to be other minds, I just don't know if there are any'), his position can quickly collapse into a more substantive solipsism ('I cannot conceive of there being a mind other than my own'). The reason for this is that, if it is accepted that one's experience always falls short of the facts concerning the inner states and processes of others, it becomes questionable whether what one *does* experience can, logically, have the status of *evidence* for them? Citing Wittgenstein, P. M. S. Hacker (1986, p. 220) makes the point in the following way: 'How can something be established as good inductive evidence for an inner state if the inner state is not an object of possible experience? And "how could I ever come by the idea of another's experience if there is no possibility of any evidence for it" (BB, p. 46).' So, once it is concluded with the sceptic that the attribution of psychological properties to beings other than oneself must always pass through the detour of one's experience of one's own inner states, even the possibility of *conceiving* (coming by the very idea of) inner states that are not one's own is called into question. It is not merely that 'for all one knows others are automatons' but that having even the remotest idea of an inner state that is not one's own inner state is impossible. The affirmation of this impossibility is solipsism. The retreat from the ordinary practice of attributing psychological properties to things other than oneself that this involves is what I will call *the threat of scepticism*. In this chapter I hope to shed light on the nature and source of this threat.

The metaphysics of the subject

Why is it, then, that we do not normally hold in suspense all attribution of psychological properties to things other than oneself? Contemporary thought on this issue is characterised by the suggestion that the reason for this, at least in the case of other human beings, is because what is at issue is the behaviour of a *person*. And the concept of a person is here taken to imply, for example and in particular, 'the possession of consciousness on the part of that to which [such properties] are ascribed' (Strawson, 1959, p. 105). A person is a subject of experience, an 'I'. And, as Strawson acknowledges, even Descartes held ('was well aware') that 'I am *not* lodged in my body like a pilot in a vessel' (Descartes, cited *ibid.*, p. 90).

This route of response aims to avoid what John McDowell has called 'our proneness to extend an objectifying mode of conceiving reality to human beings' (McDowell, 1983, p. 478). In the next chapter I will explore this thought in more detail through an examination of J. L. Austin's writings on the problem of other minds. However, as will become clear, my suspicion is that this route of response does not really escape the field of force of the sceptical problematic. Specifically, I will argue that it sustains an objectifying mode of conceiving not the human body but what it is to be a subject; the 'subject' character of a human being. And I will suggest that this objectifying conception cannot but sustain the threat of scepticism.

What I mean by an objectifying conception of what it is to be a subject is one that defines this in terms of a human being's *self-presence*. On such a conception, persons are accorded the special status of being entities which are, or are capable of being, in a special way, and in each case, present to their own states and operations. A person is, that is to say, an entity which is not simply present but is, essentially, present to itself. Heidegger captures this conception in the following image: on the problematic conception the 'subject' character of a human being lies in its being, to itself 'something which is in each case already constantly present-at-hand, both in and for a closed realm' (BT, p. 114).[2] In what follows I will call this conception *the metaphysics of the subject*.

A whole series of attempts to resolve the problem of other minds have been developed within the framework of the metaphysics of the subject. These are approaches which take the persisting self-presence of a subject as their matter-of-course point of departure in an inquiry into being with others. My claim is that commitment to this metaphysics cannot but sustain the threat of scepticism: attempts to overcome scepticism which maintain the metaphysics of the subject do not pursue their criticisms of the sceptic's position *far enough*.

Thomas Nagel's work on other minds presents a clear example of the distinctive way in which the metaphysics of the subject informs approaches to the problem of others:

> To understand that there are other people in the world as well [as oneself], one must be able to conceive of experiences of which one is not the subject: *experiences that are not present to oneself*. To do this it is necessary to have a general conception of subjects of experience and to place oneself under it as an instance.
>
> (Nagel, 1986, p. 20, my emphasis)

This approach to the problem of other minds treats as self-evident the metaphysics which, in my view, sustains the threat of scepticism. That is, it implicitly accepts that what I am trying to prove of *others* is unproblematically and obviously true of *myself*, namely, that, as a subject of experience, I am present to my own experiences and states, present to myself.

While the focus will shift and develop somewhat as the argument proceeds, the metaphysics of the subject will be a target of investigation throughout this book. A significant upshot of this orientation and focus is that the investigation which follows does not set out to *refute* scepticism concerning other minds – to show that I can know what the sceptic doubts I can know; namely, that there are 'other minds' in Nagel's sense – but to consider ways in which one might reframe it. My assumption here is that, if we are to find our way through and beyond the problem of other minds, the metaphysics which sustains and informs both the problem and its attempted resolutions must first be undermined. So the questions I pursue are not of the form: 'How can we bridge the gulf between a person's observable behaviour and the experiences of which only he or she is conscious?' Rather, turning this question around, the attempt is made to explore questions of the form: 'What is it about human beings which makes them maintain an interpretation of themselves that sustains the threat of scepticism?'

Writing

By following this strategy I will be able to sidestep – at least for some time and I hope with sufficient justification – direct examination of the traditional arguments from 'analogy', 'best explanation', and 'satisfied criteria' which dominate contemporary discussions of the problem of other minds. However, targeting what I am calling the metaphysics of the subject must also raise the bathwater suspicion that my general approach to the problem of other minds is tantamount to the absurd denial of the existence of consciousness. Am I saying, for example, that everything except events of behaviour of living things is a fiction?

Anticipating the arguments which follow, two basic responses to this question can be sketched, two responses which will provide an overview of the central line of thought that I will develop in this book. First, if the concept of a 'behavioural event' is defined in terms of physical movements or singular and dateable occurrences (what is sometimes called 'mere behaviour') then, like the person-centred approaches to the problem of other minds such as Nagel's, I will say: 'No, it is not the case that everything except events of behaviour of living things is a fiction.'

However, in response to a philosopher who attempts to 'thicken' mere behaviour by reference to the presence 'in' or 'behind' it of a self-present subject, asking the same question as before, I will say: 'Your "subject" cannot do the work of "thickening" that you suppose it can. It is a fiction.'

The basic thesis of this book is that both ways of conceiving the behaviour of a living thing rejected here – the 'thin' and 'thickened' notions of behaviour – rely on a deep lack of clarity on the logical status of events of behaviour with respect to which we do not hold in suspense all attribution of psychological properties. Conversely, if we do achieve clarity on this matter we will also achieve a fundamentally non-sceptical and non-behaviourist conception of being with others.

No doubt this is highly opaque at present. No less so will be my alternative. I will argue that an event of behaviour with respect to which we do not hold in suspense all attribution of psychological properties must have the same logical structure as writing, and so is something which, as such, must be read. This may not seem to get us any further. Surely the significance of writing derives from, or at least stands in need of, a writer, an author who, at least at the time of writing, was present to and intended what he or she wrote? Such an author would be the 'thickening' source of the 'inscribing' behaviour. While I will not deny that writings have a context of inscription which includes what we call 'the presence of the writer', I will argue that the 'thickening' solution (which is simply the metaphysics of the subject *qua* author) involves a misunderstanding of this presence. That is, again, it construes such presence in terms of self-presence.

Appeal to the phenomenon of writing can help us remove the felt need to make recourse to such a subject because, patently, writing can *do without* the presence of the writer and still function. One of the central arguments of this book is that this feature can be generalised to all significant behaviour. If this can be achieved, then the assumption that the behaviour of living things stands in need of 'thickening' by reference to something (a 'subject') which is co-present-at-hand 'in' or 'behind' it will be removed. To paraphrase Wittgenstein: on the line of thought that I aim to defend, whatever accompanies the writing would just be more writing.[3] This analysis will then be used to show how we can affirm the suggestion that to see the behaviour of a living thing is to see its soul. First, however, we must examine the thinking which most dramatically stands in the way of such an affirmation: scepticism.

A SCEPTICAL ARGUMENT

What follows is an example of a sceptical meditation. It is not a reconstruction of any particular philosopher's argument. Nor, however, is it a philosophically naive voice. While the meditation may appear innocent, and to begin at the beginning, in reality the sceptic will have begun at the end and aims to entice us to follow.[4]

Ordinarily I am quite ready to make claims to know about the most diverse range of facts. And in doing so I am not ordinarily aware of having performed an especially striking or remarkable feat. It seems to come quite naturally. However, sometimes when I sit back and look around me, this capacity to know external facts can give rise to a real sense of wonder. At such times the thought of my mind's ability to grasp reality in its net, the possibility of my mind reaching out to the world outside me, is an occasion for genuine astonishment. It is simply astonishing that this most ordinary thing is possible at all.

When I am thinking in this way, the fact that I am a being who can know things does not seem to be one fact among others about me. Rather, I want to say that it is the fundamental characteristic of the kind of being that I am. In order to explore this characteristic I will begin by considering what kinds of entities I normally purport to know.

I said that I normally make claims to know about a diverse range of facts. But what kinds of entities enter into such claims? To start with we might distinguish two basic types: (1) claims which make reference to myself and (2) claims which make reference to entities other than myself.

(1) Claims which make reference to myself. This class of cases can be further divided into two types:[5]

(1a) Claims in which 'I' refers to myself-as-an-object. Examples of this use of 'I' include: 'I've got clean finger nails', 'I am still as tall as I was last week', 'I have just had my hair cut'.

(1b) Claims in which 'I' refers to myself-as-a-subject. Examples of this use of 'I' include: 'I see a blue bird', 'I think it will rain', 'I hope it's better now', 'I understand that it's late'.

(2) Claims which make reference to entities other than myself. This class can also be divided into two important types:

(2a) Claims which make reference to entities which are *not* of the same or a remotely similar kind as I myself am. By this I mean an object with respect to which one *only* attributes physical and chemical properties and characteristics. Examples here include: stones ('That stone is too heavy'), telephones ('The telephone hasn't stopped ringing'), plants ('A rose by any other name would smell as sweet') and certain animals ('There's a spider in the bath').

(2b) Claims which make reference to entities which are of the same or a similar kind as I myself am. By this I primarily mean entities that purport to know things of the same kind and in the same way as I do (i.e., entities that can make claims of type (1) and (2) themselves). Examples here include: Jeffrey Archer ('J.A. saw the fax'), Nelson Mandela ('N.M. felt utterly safe during the bomb scare'), Mary

Warnock ('M.W. thinks deeply about moral questions'), and, perhaps in an attenuated way, human infants ('My niece is a bit of a flirt') and certain animals ('Sophie is a friendly dog').[6]

That the distinction between (1) and (2) is somewhat rough can be seen if we consider that the references to myself in cases (1a) can be conceived as a special sub-set of (2). That is, references to myself-as-an-object *can* be conceived simply as references to an object in the world. Indeed, to just one object in the outside world among other objects.

What this consideration shows is that cases (1b) are quite unlike any other. In a certain way, a stone, a lion, a human being, all stand on the same level. They are all objects in the outside world. But the 'I' that refers to myself-as-a-subject does not refer to such an object. I objectively confront every object, but not the I.[7] What is referred to in cases of claims (1b) is never simply an *object* in the world. Rather, it is the *subject* that makes and is presupposed by claims of every kind. This presupposition can be seen in the fact that it is always possible to prefix claims of every other type with 'I judge . . . ' or 'I think . . . '.

What is distinctive about reference in cases (1b) is that what is referred to is what does the referring. Such coincidence does not denote the recognition of an entity in the world called 'I'. There is no *distance* between what is referred to and what does the referring. What is at issue here is not the recognition of an object by a subject but what might be called the *presence to itself* of a subject. For this reason, reference in (1b), unlike any other type of reference, is immune to error through misidentification.[8] This is not because it is an encounter with an unmistakeable thing, but because reference in such a case does not denote an encounter at all. It does not denote a self-encounter but self-presence.

In the light of this analysis, a further development of the initial schema suggests itself. Specifically, the referents distinguished in (2) can be re-described, by substitution, in the following ways:

(2a) Claims which make reference to entities which cannot make any claims of type (1b).

(2b) Claims which make reference to entities which can make claims of type (1b) (or at least can, in some way, be the subject of claims of type (1b) in the third person).

Having drawn up this schema, I want to think for a moment about the entities referred to by my claims of the type (2b), for these seem especially problematic. I have said that such claims refer to entities which are of the same (or a similar) kind as I myself am. Specifically, therefore, for the most part they are entities of a kind which make the types of claim that I can make in the same way as I do. If entities of this kind really exist, then, like myself, they are not simply objects or things in the world; they are not simply present but, like myself, present to themselves. Such entities are not simply objects but what I will call Others.

It is a fact that I have very often claimed to know that certain entities I encounter in the world think, perceive and feel. That is, very often I have been sure that certain entities in the world are Others. And this also means: In their own case Others would be prepared to say the same themselves.

However, it is also true that in the course of my life I have sometimes been forced to accept that I have made mistakes and have had false views about Others. Through carelessness or oversight, or through misleading evidence, I have fallen into error about what is the case concerning the thoughts, perceptions and feelings of Others. I have found this most commonly when I meet Others from countries other than my own, or Others from a different class than my own, or of a different sex.

Are there any claims about Others which I can regard as certain or certainly true? Of course, there is no problem in my own case. If I have a thought, or see a scene, or feel a sensation, I am certain that I am thinking, perceiving or feeling. But what of the inner states and processes of Others? After all, they are they and I am I. I cannot be present to the referent of their claims (1b) in the way in which they are: the subjective side of the Other's experience is not present for me as it is for him and mine is for me. Here there is an irreducible and definitive limit. What kind of basis or justification is there for drawing a special category of entities of the type (2b)? What do I really know of those entities that I have called Others?

I see my friend N.N. crying out in pain and anxiety. I rush to him, speak to him, console him and so on. He responds positively. He'll be all right. Soon enough we are laughing together about it all. But what do I really know about my friend's state? After all I cannot do his feeling for him, cannot feel his feels.[9] I say I saw my friend crying out in pain and anxiety. But how do I know that it was what I call 'pain' that was making *him* cry out? Can I know that it was the feeling that I call and experience to be 'pain' that *he* felt? And anxiety, that is a very

14

strange state! How can I be certain that what he felt and thought was the same as I have felt and thought when I have been anxious?

Since it is only from my own experience that I know what pain and anxiety are *like*, what evidence do I have that my friend has the same feelings, feels the same feels as I do? This problem can be clarified by considering an analogous case.[10] Suppose N.N. and I each have a box with something in it. We both call what is in the box 'beetle'. I cannot look into my friend's box and my friend cannot look into mine. Here it would be quite possible to imagine that N.N. has something quite different in his box than I do but that, whatever is in there, he uses the same word to refer to it. Indeed, it is even imaginable that what is in his box constantly changes but he does not notice because his memory deceives him.

So perhaps it is not possible for me to know whether he feels precisely the same feelings as I. But, following the analogy further, can't I at least be sure that there is *something* in his box? That is, can't I be sure that there was *something* my friend was feeling when he cried out? But have I any notion of what kind of thing he has in his box except with reference to what *I* have in mine? If it is imaginable that what is in his box constantly changes, isn't it equally conceivable that his box is empty? With what right can I generalise from my own case? How can I say that what I see in his behaviour is *evidence* for something so specific as what I call 'a feeling', if whatever he has (as it were whatever he refers to as his 'beetle') can *never* be an object of my experience? And if I am being presumptuous in saying that his behaviour is evidence for what I call 'a feeling', I can't see how I can even be justified in calling it 'evidence for something inner' at all. It's as if I were to say of N.N. 'He has something. But I don't know whether it is money, or debts, or an empty till.' Anything I say will be presumptuous and arbitrary.[11]

What *did* I treat as evidence in this case? I said I saw an Other, indeed my friend N.N., in pain. I did so because of what he was doing and saying. But just as my claims (1a) can be regarded as a special subset of my claims of type (2), so also what I saw in this case *can* be conceived simply as movements of a body that are fully describable by my claims of type (2a). Liquid was coming out of the things I had always thought of as 'his eyes', and noises were coming out of what I had always thought of as 'his mouth'. With what right can I say that this liquid was the tears of my friend in pain, and this noise, the speech of a man who I had always thought of as someone who means what he says?

These worries might seem like the ravings of a lunatic. But the problem is that if I am asked to justify how I knew my friend was in the inner state I said he was in, I have to concede that I am going beyond and saying much more than what is given in the behavioural, physical, facts that I *really* have *evidence* for.

I am prompted by the following doubt. Can my experiences of the behaviour of a certain body provide a reliable guide to the states of what I want to call 'the soul' of my friend N.N.? The idea that it is a reliable guide seems to be an unproven assumption.[12] And if this is true of my friend, how can I ever be secure in my claims (2b) in general?

How can I be sure that this assumption is correct? Isn't it consistent with all the evidence that all those entities that I call Others are just sophisticated automata, humanoid androids?[13] Isn't it at least conceivable that someone no less cunning and deceiving than powerful has used all his artifice to deceive me?[14]

I have just employed the Cartesian hypothesis of an 'evil genius'. And I realise that I am not the first to have been captured or captivated by a kind of doubt that would normally seem ludicrous and hyperbolical. Strangely, Descartes himself does not consider the doubts about Others that I have been discussing. However, in a famous passage in the *Meditations* he does at least broach the difficulty that arises when one considers the behaviour of those I have called Others. Descartes is looking out of his window at some people passing in the street below him. He notes that he would not normally hesitate to say that he was seeing people out there. However, he considers it to be indisputable that if he restricts himself to what he has sensory evidence for, he has to concede that 'what do I see from this window other than hats and cloaks, which can cover ghosts or dummies who move only by means of springs.'[15]

The point is that whether or not certain entities are Others or automata is not something that can be discovered merely on the basis of what is apparent to the senses, namely the behaviour of bodies, for that is consistent with either state of affairs. This kind of observation is the heart of my problem. How am I to overcome the sceptical hypothesis?

Descartes's conclusion is interesting. He argues that, since his senses cannot decide the case, his belief that they are people (i.e. Others) must have its source in what he calls his faculty of 'judgement' that is in his own mind. It is with this faculty alone that he really *perceives* what something *is*.

This suggestion implies that an investigation into perceptual judgements should, in general, be *split* into two parts.[16] On the one hand, we need an account that explains how an organic body receives sensory information from the world outside it. This, I would suggest, is ultimately a matter for biology and the neurological sciences. On the other hand, however, we need an account which explains how such sensory information is received and processed so that one arrives at a fully conscious perceptual experience of the outside world – that is, so that one arrives at a full-blown perceptual state of a subject. Such a subject is the referent of claims of the type (1b). And while, no doubt, an investigation of its behaviour and operations will have links to biology, an account of its behaviour is fundamentally a matter for logical investigation. We might call it the logical subject. This is not because it is a theoretical concept obtained merely by way of logic. Rather, it is because this is the subject which exercises logical behaviour – specifically, the exercise of concepts – in order to transform the brute sensory information into a full-blown perceptual experience.

Now, if I consider the entities referred to in my claims of type (2b) in the light of this analysis I can see that the assumption that they are Others necessarily goes beyond what is given to me by the senses alone. The facts of brute sense experience cannot ground the assumption that the outward behaviour of certain entities is the behaviour of Others rather than humanoid androids. My concern is this: if the senses cannot provide adequate grounds for this assumption, what right have I to make claims of type (2b) in the way I ordinarily do?

These claims are grounded on the assumption that entities that outwardly behave in certain ways are Others. But when I reflect on this assumption, my ordinary unhesitating willingness to make claims of type (2b) suddenly seems to be highly presumptuous. What a huge jump I am making from a behaving body to the mental operations and personal experience of an Other! Surely, making this kind of assumption stands in need of justification?

Descartes's general route of response to problems of justification or legitimation is to argue that we have the right to judge as we ordinarily do because God 'cannot be a deceiver'.[17] God has not given us a nature such that we will, in general, 'fall into error'.[18] The problem is, however, that Descartes's proofs of God are not convincing even when they are supposedly being intuited, and hence provide no legitimation at all.[19] I'm going to have to do without Descartes.

Where am I to go from here? Let me begin again with my claim to perceive an Other, indeed, my friend N.N. in pain. As I have indicated, I would not ordinarily hesitate to say that what I saw was my friend in pain. If anyone else had disputed it, I think that in this case I would have said: 'I *know* he is in pain.'

The heart of the problem I have identified is that my brute sensory information alone is insufficient to establish whether what I see is really an Other or perhaps only a humanoid android. What is apparent to the senses, namely the behaviour of a body, is consistent with either state of affairs. 'I know that he is in pain – he's wincing.' But how do I know that it is really a 'wince'? After all, it is in principle possible for me to judge what I sense in a way that does not in the least imply the existence or presence of an inner state connected to the movement of the mouth. To say that I know from his wince is already to make a judgement that goes beyond what is given in the sensory information. How on earth can I justify such beliefs? Anything that I judge to be evidence for the presence of an Other may only be the behaviour of an entity that simulates such evidence.

If I cannot justify the judgement 'N.N. is in pain', what can I affirm? In the past, when I have said that he is in pain, this was because I saw a body that behaved in a certain way. But this is not all: the behaviour is basically *the same as mine when I am in pain*. Thus it seems that, although I cannot justify making the judgement 'N.N. is in pain', I am still justified in saying something like 'This entity is behaving as I behave when I am in pain.'

However, I must be clear that this formulation does not amount to the attribution of inner states to this entity. Any attempt to do so still presumes that I can make use of a reliable notion of 'evidence for something inner' in cases other than my own. And, as I have just discovered, that is precisely what I cannot do. Just because there is no difficulty in my own case can only give the appearance of helping in cases other than my own. For example, to say that I am justified in saying something like 'This entity is behaving as I behave when I am in pain' already presumes too much. For, in all rigour, all I am really justified in saying is something like 'This entity is behaving as I behave when *either* I am in pain *or* I am merely simulating being in pain.' And this idea brings me no closer to being able to distinguish between his being in pain or merely appearing to be so. Indeed, it brings me no closer to the idea of *his pain* at all. In the last analysis, it is not merely that 'for all I know Others are androids' but that, in all rigour, I cannot even conceive of an experience that is not, essentially, an experience of mine.

I realise that the only rational conclusion to be drawn is to hold in suspense all attribution of psychological properties to entities other than myself. In future, therefore, I shall refrain from making claims of the type (2b), and I shall mark my judgements in a manner that makes clear that I not claiming knowledge of Others. I shall not say that any entities other than myself think, but only that they 'think'; I shall not say that they feel but only that they 'feel'; I shall not say that they perceive but only that they 'perceive'; I shall not say that they are Others but only that they are 'Others'; etc. In short, I will suspend making judgements which lay something down as true about Others: my judgements about Others will be *hedged*.

The position I have arrived at in this meditation is, in essence, solipsism. The only *sense* I can make of the presence of an 'experience' is with the idea of an experience that is *present to me*. It is no good trying to extend this idea to entities other than myself: that will only give me an idea of me having experiences in another body, not of an *Other* having experiences.[20]

THE SUBJECT OF SCEPTICISM

The form of sceptical arguments

In the last section we saw how a sceptical meditation can motivate the problem of other minds. But how can this problem force itself upon us *without* the loss of other bodies? After all, Descartes's sceptical meditation calls into question one's access to everything 'outside' oneself; one's knowledge of the 'external world' in general. In such a Predicament not even the behaving body can survive to stand mindless. This issue can be clarified by juxtaposing sceptical arguments of the two kinds.

Marie McGinn's summary of the structure of the sceptical argument concerning our knowledge of the 'external world' provides a useful model for this comparison:[21]

> The sceptic is led to construct a conception of the evidence for all his knowledge claims that is, in a crucial sense, purely subjective, that is, its description is allowed to incorporate no assumption that this evidence is revelatory of an objective, independent world. What he is led to, in

19

other words, is the idea that his own immediate experience, conceived purely subjectively, must provide the secure, independent base for all his knowledge of reality. His system of beliefs about the objective world will prove well-grounded, therefore, only if the sceptic is able to show that experience, conceived in this purely subjective manner, can support claims about how things stand in objective reality. The sceptic's former acceptance of the objective judgements that formed an unquestioned framework for confirming and disconfirming beliefs must now be supposed to lie on the previously unexamined assumption that experience, in the sense outlined, provides a reliable guide to the nature of reality.

Suitably reformulated to the problem of other minds this sketch must undergo some significant changes:

> The sceptic is led to construct a conception of the evidence for all his knowledge claims [about Others] that is, in a crucial sense, purely [objective], that is, its description is allowed to incorporate no assumption that this evidence is revelatory of [inner states of Others]. What he is led to, in other words, is the idea that his experience [of the behaving body] must provide the secure, independent base for his knowledge of [Others]. His system of beliefs about [Others] will prove well-grounded, therefore, only if the sceptic is able to show that experience [of behaviour], conceived in this purely [objective] manner, can support claims about [Others]. The sceptic's former acceptance of the judgements that formed the unquestioned framework for confirming and disconfirming [claims about Others] must now be supposed to lie on the previously unexamined assumption that experience [of behavior], in the sense outlined, provides a reliable guide to the [inner states of Others].

Clearly, the conversion of external world scepticism to other minds scepticism can be made quite cleanly. However, for Stanley Cavell the differences here are sufficient to call into question the idea that there is a strictly philosophical or sceptical problem of other minds at all – a problem which might stand in contrast to our pre-reflective or pre-philosophical attitude (see Cavell, 1979, p. 432). According to Cavell there is no 'best case of knowing' in relation to others comparable to the 'best case of knowing' that can motivate philosophical doubts about the external world. The thought here is that, while, say, a tomato *can* at least *seem* to be present, I *cannot* be present to another's experience. For Cavell this is sufficient to suggest that there are no doubts which can be adduced about others that stand in conflict with an everyday alternative. And this would imply that the reformulated argument does not present a strictly or merely sceptical problem – i.e. one which might be removed by philosophical clarification:

there is, Cavell supposes, 'no everyday *alternative* to scepticism concerning other minds' (*ibid.*).

I do not find these claims of Cavell's convincing. The sceptical meditation I have just rehearsed definitely arrives at a conclusion which is in conflict with one's pre-reflective conviction that one can know if and when a friend (surely 'the best case'?) is in pain. The argument clearly leads to hesitations and hedges beyond, and in conflict with, the ordinary. Nevertheless, Cavell is right to draw attention to differences between sceptical doubts in the two cases. First, with respect to the external world the Predicament is that I cannot get out of the circle of my immediate, purely subjective experience in order to compare it with reality. It is this 'gap' or possible distance between what is given to immediate experience and how things really are in the world which allows the sceptical hypothesis to be put forward as an alternative origin to experience. The 'contours of a subjectivity'[22] draw a boundary between reality and my experience of reality which I cannot cross. I must, therefore, 'plead incapacity to prove, through immediate experience, any existence except my own' (Kant, 1933 [1787], B275).

With respect to the problem of other minds, however, the presence of the external and independently behaving body is not in dispute. The Predicament here, therefore, does not seem to be that I cannot escape the circle of immediate experience. Rather, as the major changes to McGinn's summary show, it is the *objectivity* of what I experience which seems to provide the barrier to my access to the other. I can never compare the other's subjective experience with what I can see; the behaving body draws a boundary between the reality of the other's experience and my experience of that reality that I cannot cross.

The common assumption

This way of presenting the two sceptical arguments suggests that there is a basic difference between them. This difference lies in the fact that, while the first argument exploits the *subjectivity* of human consciousness, the second exploits the *objectivity* of the human body. On such a reading it is, as John McDowell argues, 'the objectification of human behaviour [which] leads inexorably to the traditional problem of other minds' (McDowell, 1983, p. 479).

I think that this is misleading, and that the difference pointed out here hides a fundamental continuity between the two sceptical arguments, namely, in their shared conception of what it is to be a human 'subject of experience'. As indicated in the first section of this chapter, this is an objectifying conception in which a person's 'irreducibly subjective character' (Nagel, 1986, p. 28) is determined in terms of his or her self-presence. A human being is, on this view, an entity which is, to itself, 'constantly present-at-hand, both in and for a closed realm'. My claim is that it is this conception of the subject character of a human being which, when imputed to oneself, leads to external world scepticism in the first argument, and which, when imputed to others, leads to the problem of other minds in the second. In the first the problem arises because I suppose that I have *one of these* (a mind) outside of which is supposed to be the world; and in the second the problem arises because I suppose that, if there are Others, there must be *one of these* (a mind) which is not my own but which is *over there* (or, somehow, *in that*). In short, it is the same conception of being a subject which results in a retreat from the position that one holds at the outset with respect to both 'the World' and 'the Other like myself'. My concern is with the sceptical threat to the latter position. And I will argue that, *pace* McDowell, it is not simply the objectification of human behaviour but, first of all, the objectification of the subject character of a living human being which 'leads inexorably to the traditional problem of other minds'.

In the chapters that follow I will defend this reading by showing that any response which adheres to the metaphysics of the subject will always be open to the threat of scepticism. And this holds not only for the sceptic but also his avowed opponent, his refuter. In both cases it is assumed that, if it exists at all, then the other must, like oneself, be conceived in terms of a persisting and self-present subject. On the supposedly anti-sceptical inflection of this metaphysics one will aim to affirm that one can know that such a subject, such an 'other mind', is present 'behind' or 'in' the behaviour of which it is the 'thickening' source.

Reframing scepticism

Who am I? Through a sceptical meditation I become a stranger to myself and my condition:

> I thought I was a man. But what is a man? Shall I say rational animal? No indeed: for it would be necessary next to inquire what is meant by animal, and what by rational, and in this way, from one single question, we would fall unwittingly into an infinite number of others, more difficult and awkward than the first, and I would not wish to waste the little time and leisure remaining to me by using it to unravel subtleties of this kind. But I shall stop to consider here the thoughts that spring up spontaneously in my mind, and which were inspired by my own nature alone, when I applied myself to the consideration of my being. I considered myself, firstly, as having a face, hands, arms, and the whole machine made up of flesh and bones, such as it appears in a corpse . . . I thought furthermore, that I ate, walked, had feelings and thoughts, and I referred all these actions to the soul; but I did not stop to consider what this soul was, or at least, if I did, I imagined it was something extremely rare and subtle, like a wind, flame or vapour, which permeated and spread through my substantial parts. By body I understand all that can be contained in some place and fill a space; that can be perceived, either by touch, sight, hearing, taste or smell; that can be

moved in many ways, not of itself, but by something foreign to it by which it is touched and from which it receives the impulse. For as to having in itself the power to move, to feel, to think, I did not believe in any way that these advantages might be attributed to corporeal nature; on the contrary, I was somewhat astonished to see such faculties were to be found in certain bodies.

(Descartes, 1968, pp. 104–5)

The contours of my subjectivity circumscribe and delimit the spread of my soul. And henceforth my body is a somewhat foreign body: 'such as it appears in a corpse'. Yet this sign of death, astonishingly, shows signs of life. Signs though, not the thing itself – and whispering doubts about such signs gather at once: the lived experience, the subjective side of the other is made known to me only in so far as it is mediately indicated by signs involving a physical side. I am present to myself: the other can only be present to me through outward signs of his presence. But how can I be sure that these outward signs really signify a soul, a soul like my own? . . .

Once the security of one's claims to know others has been called into question, the attempt to establish one's right to judge that the behaviour of a body is reliable evidence of the presence of a (self-present) subjective side can seem to be the only appropriate and rational route of response. Kant states that it is a 'scandal to philosophy that the existence of things outside us must be accepted merely on faith and that we are unable to counter the sceptic with any satisfactory proof' (Kant, 1933 [1787], B xl, fn. *a*). Is not the same true of scepticism about other minds? In fact, very often in writings on the problem of other minds it is simply assumed that the sceptical argument has appropriately motivated the task of providing such a proof or a refutation. We move directly to questions as to the cogency or otherwise of the argument from analogy or from best explanation or from criteria. But what if the very aim to secure one's right to make judgements about others is a symptom of the very confusion which motivates the threat of scepticism in the first place?

On the other hand, if this suspicion is sound, how, then, can we remove the threat? We can do so only if traditional proofs and refutations do not exhaust our options. In the next two chapters, through an examination of the work of J. L. Austin and Martin Heidegger, I aim to make plausible the view that, *pace* Kant, ' "the scandal of philosophy" is not that [a] proof has yet to be given, but that such proofs are expected and attempted again and again' (BT, p. 205). As I have indicated, I will call a response of this sort a reframing of scepticism. A response by reframing does not aim to refute scepticism but to undermine the whole fabric of thinking which sustains it as a threat. It does not aim to show that, and how, we know what the sceptic doubts we know, but to explain why we succumb to the sceptic's threat or feel the need to refute it. In the next chapter, then, I will turn to J. L. Austin's 'ordinary language philosophy' and show how it endeavours to effect a philosophical reframing of scepticism.

2

REFRAMING SCEPTICISM I

J. L. Austin

INTRODUCTION

Why does our thinking about being with others become open so rapidly to the threat of scepticism? According to John McDowell the answer lies with the proneness of both the sceptic and his traditional refuter to treat what is, essentially, the behaviour of a *person* as if it were 'mere behaviour'; as if it were behaviour on a level with 'the behaviour of the planets' (McDowell, 1983, p. 479). For McDowell, then, it is 'the objectification of human behaviour [which] leads inexorably to the traditional problem of other minds' (*ibid.*). I will come back to the details of McDowell's position in the final chapter. Here I want to explore how this route of response is developed in the 'ordinary language philosophy' of J. L. Austin.

It is less widely recognised than it should be that the identification of and implacable opposition to a tendency in philosophy to extend an objectifying mode of conceiving reality to the behaviour of human beings is evident throughout Austin's writings. In 'A Plea for Excuses' (Austin, 1979, pp. 175–204), for example, he criticises the 'vague and comforting idea' that 'in the last analysis, doing an action must come down to the making of physical movements with parts of the body' (p. 178); an idea which invites us 'to think of our behaviour over any time, and life as a whole, as consisting in doing now action A, next action B, then action C, and so on' (p. 179). A similar point is stressed in *How To Do Things With Words* (Austin, 1980), where he notes that 'a great many acts . . . are *not*, as philosophers are prone to assume, simply in the last resort physical movements' (p. 19). By far Austin's most sustained attempt to formulate a conception of behaviour which avoids this proneness is his essay 'Other Minds' (Austin, 1979, pp. 76–116). It is also in this essay that we can most clearly identify in Austin's work what I have called a reframing of scepticism.

In order to appreciate the philosophical significance of the Austinian reframing of scepticism, it is important to see that any such approach is open to a fundamental objection. If the form of one's response to the problem of other minds is not to be a refutation or proof in the traditional sense (namely a demonstration that we do know what the sceptic doubts we know), then it becomes unclear how it can amount to anything other than a dogmatic rejection of the problem. In the first half of this chapter I will present the central lines of Austin's argument with particular reference to this objection. My general aim is to show how an appeal to ordinary linguistic practice can be made without simply and illegitimately assuming to be true what the sceptic supposes to require proof or demonstration. I will argue that Austin's work is not an attempt to refute scepticism by reference to the ordinary use of words, or to *'what we should say when'* (Austin, 1979, p. 181). Rather, it is an attempt to identify and dismantle the whole fabric of thinking which invites us to make hedges or hesitations in judgements about others *beyond the ordinary*.

While I think that it is only through a reframing of scepticism that we can hope to find our way through and beyond the problem of other minds, the line of thinking I have just described does not give the final word on Austin's procedures. As I indicated in the last chapter, I do not think that the diagnostic focus which underlies Austin's response (namely that scepticism results from a distorting objectification of human behaviour) captures the fundamental feature of the tradition he finds so disastrous. Moreover, I think that Austin's own thought is informed by the feature which does (namely the objectifying conception of subjectivity). So, in my view, in reading Austin's work we can see a movement of thought which both puts pressure on traditional ideas and, perhaps unwittingly, repeats its fundamental metaphysical assumptions.

AUSTIN AND THE PROBLEM OF OTHER MINDS

Disengaging from the tradition

The theme of one's relation to traditional ideas, one's inheritance of philosophy, is a more or less constant preoccupation in Austin's writings. His general view is that this inheritance constantly threatens to impose a distorting order on our thought.[1] Specifically, it distorts the understanding of phenomena that we already have, and which is embodied in the ordinary use of language.[2] For this reason Austin argues for 'a positive fresh start' (Austin, 1979, p. 180) in philosophy which can free thinking from the stagnating ruts that our tradition imposes.[3]

Austin's unremitting desire for intellectual liberation from his tradition is plain to see. Indeed, his work seems sometimes to have been written with or out of the desire not to be an heir, or not simply an heir, of philosophy as he found it. However, it is generally assumed that his basic *mode* of such disinheritance, the distinctive style of his criticism of the tradition, is his appeal to ordinary linguistic usage; an appeal which would then serve as the basis for novel 'common sense' solutions to traditional philosophical problems. I think this reading gets Austin wrong. In the case of his response to the problem of other minds in particular, it seems to me that his aims are more adventurous and far-reaching. In what follows I want to show how Austin's argumentation develops a treatment of the traditional problematic which does not so much offer a common sense solution to it as dismantle the thinking which sustains both argument and counter-argument on the topic.

That something other than a common sense refutation is the mode of Austin's response to the problem of other minds can be seen very clearly in 'Other Minds'. Perhaps surprisingly, its basic line of argument aims to defend the idea that there is *no* general justification for believing in other minds (OM, p. 115). Far from being the common sense refutation of scepticism that some have found in Austin, this approach does not even seem to be in conflict with the sceptic's reasoning. So what is Austin doing? What is the Austinian response to the problem of other minds?

The central characteristic of Austin's account in 'Other Minds' is, like so much of his work, the determined attempt to avoid taking a position within the conceptual framework of the traditional inquiry.[4] I will refer to this strategy as his disengagement from the tradition. As we shall see, this strategy is, in a certain way, acknowledged by readings of Austin which treat his work as offering a common sense refutation of scepticism. However, from the perspective of such readings it appears only to foreclose any possibility of providing a satisfactory (that is, non-dogmatic) response to traditional problems. I will explain this.

When Austin's arguments are interpreted on the assumption that the appeal to ordinary usage is an appeal to common sense, his approach appears to find its obvious home alongside that championed by G. E. Moore.[5] Marie McGinn states the case in her reading of Austin:

> To start from the assumption that the assessment of judgements that we make from within the common-sense outlook is correct is implicitly to deny the possibility of the contemplative stance. Without some philosophical motivation for the methodological assumption that the assessment made from within the our practice is correct . . . Austin's position is no less entrenched, and his rebuttal [of the sceptical argument] no less dogmatic, than Moore's.
>
> (McGinn, 1989, p. 64).

The basis of McGinn's criticism rests on the assumption that a non-dogmatic response to scepticism must begin by taking the same reflective or contemplative stance towards the certainties and convictions of ordinary practice which is maintained by the sceptic. That is, such a stance must be taken towards the raft of beliefs about the world and its inhabitants that we ordinarily regard as certain and unassailable.

McGinn calls the special class of judgements which figure in or characterise these beliefs as 'judgements of the frame'. These are the kind of judgements subject to sceptical doubt by Descartes (knowledge claims about facts concerning his hand, desk, dressing gown, people outside his window, simple propositions of

arithmetic, etc.) and positively affirmed by Moore. Crucially, 'they are all propositions which, in a normal context, would either not, without special reason, be
remarked, or, if they were remarked, would not without special reason, be
doubted or questioned' (*ibid.*, p. 103). The significance of such propositions is
that it is upon their basis that our ordinary ('normal context') judgements appear
to rest. As McGinn puts it, 'it concerns a sort of judgement that grounds all our
further judgement' and hence it would seem that 'if they can't be grounded,
then nothing can' (*ibid.*, p. 4).

The task of the philosopher under this conception is to obtain a non-sceptical
understanding of judgements of the frame from a perspective in which our ordinary convictions concerning them are not presupposed or are suspended. The
question then becomes one as to whether 'Austin's procedures [can] offer some
understanding of common sense, or of the workings of ordinary practice, that
might earn us the right to continue to affirm all our ordinary knowledge claims'
(*ibid.*, p. 55).

It should be clear that, from this perspective, Austin's uninhibited affirmation
of 'what we should say when' rules out his achieving such an understanding.
From the standpoint of common sense one simply cannot see, cannot acknowledge, the traditional philosopher's concern with the problem of our right to
judge in the way we ordinarily do. Ultimately, on this interpretation, it is Austin's
refusal to suspend his ordinary convictions which marks what might be taken to
be the decisive character of anything like Austinian disengagement. Attempting
directly to refute the sceptic by appeal to ordinary language, Austin has disen-
gaged from and is thus working in a different region from the traditional
philosopher:

> The sceptic could reasonably object that by confining his enquiry to
> what we should say within ordinary practice, Austin necessarily oper-
> ates in a region where the presumptuous nature of the judgements of
> the frame is never, and could never be, perceived.
>
> (*ibid.*, p. 62)

Can Austin's approach be justified? Or does Austin's disengagement simply
preclude a non-dogmatic response to the problem of other minds?

Hesitations beyond the ordinary

It is of course true that Austin claims that 'we certainly do say sometimes that we
know another man is angry' (OM, p. 103). And he roundly replies to a philosopher who claims that, 'strictly', I do not have knowledge about such things, '*Of
course* I do' (*ibid.*, p. 115). In my view, however, it is wrong to read these affirma-
tions as a Moorean response. As I have indicated, the central argument of
'Other Minds' is that there is *no* general justification for our believing in other
minds; a conclusion that is *prima facie* not in conflict with the sceptic's conclusion.

The task of an interpretation of Austin's views must be to show how the uninhibited affirmation of ordinary practice can be reconciled with this apparently sceptical conclusion.

This task can, I think, readily be achieved once it is realised that the basic target of 'Other Minds' is not simply the sceptic, but rather the perspective or stance which, according to Austin, underpins the sceptical problematic as a whole: the perspective in which it seems that the grounds of our judgements about others *stands in need* of a justification. This orientation can be clarified by considering the following line of thought from 'Other Minds': In ordinary life, Austin notes, we all, occasionally, hesitate to say of another that they are or were in this or that psychological state. This hesitation can take various forms but, in general, it increases the less familiar we are with the person or type of person concerned.[6] The further we depart from the circle of our friends and acquaintances the less secure we become in our attributions. We hedge before the stranger. In philosophy, however, reflection on our concepts leads to *hesitations beyond the ordinary*, beyond 'the feeling of loneliness which affects everybody at times' (OM, p. 112). Why does this happen? Why does the traditional philosopher 'cast himself out from the garden of the world we live in'? (*ibid.*, p. 90).

These question do not motivate an examination of 'what we should say when' in order to refute scepticism. Rather, they aim at the elimination of the assumption that our 'belief in others' stands in need of the kind of justification or grounding which the traditional philosopher has supposed. The sceptic doubts whether such a justification can be supplied, others try to supply or exhibit it (e.g., with arguments from analogy or from best explanation). By contrast, however, by disengaging from the traditional problematic, by restricting his investigation to the 'sort of thing [that] actually happens when ordinary people are asked "How do you know?" ' (*ibid.*, p. 77), Austin aims to show that the *absence* of a justification for our ordinary judgements does not threaten scepticism. This is the Austinian reframing of scepticism. In what follows I will defend this approach to Austin's argument in 'Other Minds'.

Refutation or reframing?

McGinn's interpretation of 'Other Minds' as a refutation of scepticism is built around a review of Austin's discussion of 'the conditions under which certain sorts of objection may be made' to claims to knowledge (*ibid.*, p. 57). In that discussion, Austin observes that there is a kind of cross-examination which is usually, or can naturally be, pursued following the entry of some claim to know something. For example, in actual cases when a claim has been entered, the person who makes the claim is then directly exposed to the question as to whether he or she knows what is claimed or whether he or she merely 'thinks' or 'believes' it. And then, depending on the answer given to this question, new questions, new avenues of examination and objection, requiring a range of explanations and justifications, become pertinent to the claimant's case.

In her reading, McGinn focuses on Austin's examination of the restricting conditions that govern objections of the form 'That's not enough' – a form of objection which can arise when the claimant adduces evidentiary grounds for his or her claim. Two conditions are highlighted by Austin. First, there must be, in the opinion of the objector, a definite lack or insufficiency to the grounds adduced; certain possibilities have not been excluded which need to be excluded if the claim is to be sustained. Second, and in contrast to this insufficiency condition, Austin opposes a sufficiency condition: 'enough is enough' (*ibid.*, p. 84). The point here is that, once the alternative possibilities have been dealt with, the first kind of objection should be dropped.

Appealing to these points, McGinn suggests that it then 'becomes easy [for Austin] to resist the fallacies of the sceptic' since, *in contrast to ordinary claims*, once the claim to know a proposition of the frame has been entered there are simply 'no legitimate objections (i.e. objections meeting the conditions Austin describes) to [it]' (McGinn, 1989, p. 60). Consequently, it would follow that 'a knowledge claim concerning a representative judgement of the frame is capable of being sustained, and that such judgements may therefore quite legitimately ground further claims to know' (*ibid.*).

As I have indicated, the basis of McGinn's objection to this refutation of the sceptic is that it fails to see that claims and doubts about framework judgements are made in a different 'region' than ordinary claims and doubts. It is only because 'we have been imagining [Descartes's claim to know that he is seated by the fire] as a claim made in an ordinary context' (*ibid.*, p. 62) that the accusation that the sceptic flouts the restrictions that govern objections to ordinary claims can be proposed. According to McGinn, Austin's appeal to the ordinary fails to acknowledge the special stance of properly philosophical reflection. Austin's criticism is inappropriate to the region of the contemplative stance, and hence his affirmation of the ordinary is dogmatic and unacceptable.

This 'regional' reading of Austin's approach has not entirely missed the strategy of disengagement. However, it assumes that Austin has, and so misreads it. Against that reading, what needs to be emphasised is that Austin does not put forward his proposed conditions in an attempt to rule out the sceptic's objections to claims to know judgements of the frame, but only to characterise ordinary objections to ordinary claims. McGinn accuses Austin of having illegitimately traversed the boundary between the engaged and contemplative stances, whereas in fact it is McGinn who extends Austin's conditions to the case of claims concerning judgements of the frame ('we have been imagining . . . ').

What, then, is the purpose of Austin's examination of the ordinary? A significantly different interpretation is open to us. What the examination shows is not, as McGinn holds, that knowledge claims concerning judgements of the frame can be sustained because there are no legitimate objections, but rather that being entitled to make ordinary claims does not require that we ground them further than we ordinarily do. That is, the requirement that we ground the grounds (sustain a claim to know a judgement of the frame) makes no sense: having established that a (ordinary) claim is in order with respect to (ordinary) objections the claimant has now done all that 'within reason, and for present intents and purposes' he or she *can* do (OM, p. 84). Now, the sceptic may say: 'Yes, but the belief may still be false, and so he or she does not know what he or she claims to know.' This is quite true, but it would be a mistake to suppose that Austin is denying that, as a matter of logic, one can only know that *p* if *p*. The point is that it does not follow from that that, in fact, we are not often 'right to say we *know* even in cases where we turn out subsequently to be mistaken' (*ibid.*, p. 98). Being entitled to affirm an ordinary claim to know does not require establishing that one cannot be mistaken. Indeed, once we have resituated ourselves with respect to ordinary practice, it becomes clear that, by excluding or wishing to exclude sheer fallibility, we abrogate the very concept which was supposed to be under examination. For making room for fallibility is one of the basic features of the ordinary use of 'I know': 'I thought I knew', 'So you didn't know it then' (*ibid.*, p. 98).

The implications of Austin's reflections on the ordinary use of 'know' for the problem of other minds can be brought out by comparing it to the 'split-level' approach to our judgements about others outlined in the sceptical meditation of the previous chapter. As we have seen, that meditation leads us to view our ordinary judgements about others as going beyond what is given to the senses. According to a split-level theory, one's perception of others consists, in the first instance, of experiences of bodily behaviour construed purely objectively; experiences as of physical movements of parts of a body. But if, as Austin argues, it makes no sense to seek justifying grounds for knowledge beyond the ordinary sort, then the need to found judgement at this 'merely behavioural' level loses its force. We are free to affirm that what we appeal to is not behavioural movements or singular events *simpliciter* but *behaviour in the ordinary sense*; i.e. what, in real situations, a human being says and does. Thus, in the case of the expression of emotions for example, what we 'first see', and so what we appeal to when we justify a claim, are behavioural 'syndromes': characteristic 'displays and manifestations' of the emotion (OM, p. 108). It is, Austin argues, a misunderstanding to suppose that one needs to ground this appeal further by trying to describe what we see 'in non-committal words' (*ibid.*, p. 85). Indeed, according to Austin, one cannot normally describe what is seen in such terms (*ibid.*). Again, what one 'first sees' is not mere movements of a body, as supposed by the split-level theory, but (all or part of) behaviour-in-context; a behavioural 'syndrome' or 'pattern'. And, according to Austin, for someone who is, in this sense, in the know, such patterns carry intrinsic significance.[7] On this view, we do not have to prove against the sceptic that we are 'entitled to trust others' (*ibid.*, p. 82) because judging in the way we do is not founded on the kind of observations of behaviour that both the sceptic and his refuter suppose. 'It is therefore misleading to ask "How do I get from the scowl to the anger" ' (*ibid.*, p. 110).

According to this argument, the hesitations in judgement which scepticism invites are essentially hesitations beyond the ordinary. Such a perspective is, one might say, the perspective of a radical outsider. It is the perspective of someone who, when confronted with a paradigmatic *pattern* of human behaviour, cannot see it as such, cannot see what is, for the insider, simply manifest (e.g., a scowl).

But now, on this line of thought, it is clear that the perspective of the outsider is effectively equivalent to the perspective of the 'contemplative stance'. It is the perspective in which our ordinary grounds of judgement (what someone says and does) are thought to stand in need of further justification. What should now be clear is that this is precisely the perspective from which Austin's work seeks to disengage. And, if we take Austin's argument seriously, it is a perspective one has to avoid if one is to avoid the threat of scepticism.

Habits of *Gleichschaltung*

The question now arises as to why we remain so committed to the objectifying mode of conceiving human behaviour. Why do we adhere so unquestioningly to a perspective which leads to hesitations beyond the ordinary? Austin's most general remarks on this issue appear in the introduction to *Sense and Sensibilia*, where he suggests that a satisfactory account of the phenomenon of perception requires that 'here as elsewhere' we 'abandon old habits of *Gleichschaltung*, the deeply ingrained worship of tidy-looking dichotomies' (Austin, 1962, p. 3). '*Gleichschaltung*', meaning to bring something into line, to make something conform to a certain standard by force, represents, in its most general aspect, the kind of difficulty Austin identifies in the works of philosophy he criticises, and which he sought to overcome.[8] Essentially, what Austin is identifying here is an entrenched and instituted preference for accounts which aim to clarify our thinking through offering *simplifications*, theoretical idealisations, of complex phenomena. In Austin's view, however, in virtue of presenting accounts which are '*too* simple' clarity is effectively foregone (*ibid.*, p. 4). What philosophy's traditional habits of *Gleichschaltung* produce is not a kind of clarity but a kind of coterie; a community in which membership is obtained by becoming 'fully masters of a certain special happy style of blinkering philosophical English' (*ibid.*). The idea is that a thinker's (typically insensible) engagement with time-hallowed ways of formulating and expounding philosophical problems results in the recitation of philosophically familiar line and verse as if its adequacy and salience were obvious to everyone. According to Austin, such habits of *Gleichschaltung* blinker us from the rich understanding of phenomena which we already possess, so that we cannot see that we are in its sway – although, he stresses, we nevertheless 'feel it to be somehow spurious' (*ibid.*, p. 3).

It is, I think, a major shortcoming of Austin's work that he does not really explore *why* we find such distorting routines so compelling. Nevertheless, he is sufficiently impressed by their ubiquity to characterise the 'happy style' as intrinsic to philosophy as such:

> My general opinion about this doctrine [namely, that we never directly perceive material objects] is that it is a typically scholastic view, attributable, first, to an obsession with a few particular words . . . and second, to an obsession with a few (and nearly always the same) half-studied 'facts'. I say 'scholastic', but I might just as well have said 'philosophical'; over-simplification, schematization, and constant obsessive repetition of the same small range of jejune 'examples' are not only peculiar to this case, but far too common to be dismissed as an occasional weakness of philosophers.
>
> (*ibid.*)

The point is made again in the final paragraph of his essay 'Performative Utterances':

> Life and truth and things do tend to be complicated. It's not things, it's philosophers that are simple. You will have heard it said, I expect, that over-simplification is the occupational disease of philosophers, and in one way one might agree with that. But for a sneaking suspicion that it's their occupation.
>
> (Austin, 1979, p. 252)

The philosopher, on this view, is one who is happily at home with a way of going on which cannot but fail to do justice to the phenomena. The effect is a kind of fetishism:[9] certain concepts and conceptual oppositions are privileged to the extent that their pertinence and central position appears to be an unassailable given in properly philosophical investigations. Naturally enough, in the effort to 'dismantle' its procedures and so, as Austin sees it, 'leave us, in a sense, just where we began', things are bound to be complicated (S&S, p. 5).

Austin's identification of, and attempt to dismantle, conceptions which have become fixed in the philosophical imagination can be found throughout his work. In the case of traditional accounts of knowledge, Austin offers the following story:

> The pursuit of the incorrigible is one of the most venerable bugbears in the history of philosophy. It is rampant all over ancient philosophy, most conspicuously in Plato, was powerfully re-animated by Descartes, and bequeathed by him to a long line of successors. No doubt it has many motives and takes many forms . . . But in the case now before us, which descends directly from Descartes . . . there is a general doctrine about knowledge . . . In a nutshell, the doctrine about knowledge, 'empirical' knowledge, is that it has foundation. It is a structure the upper tiers of which are reached by inferences, and the foundations are the data on which these inferences are based.
>
> (*ibid.*, pp. 104–5)

In the foregoing examination of 'Other Minds' we have seen why Austin thinks that this doctrine, 'the real bugbear', is 'radically and in principle misconceived' (*ibid.*, p. 124); there is no justification for our belief in others of the foundational kind the traditional philosopher seeks, and the simplified notion of behaviour with which it works is a distorting idealisation of the facts.

Austin's rejection of the idea that the perceived behaviour of others is, in the first instance, (the incorrigibly knowable data of) 'mere behaviour', is, I think, *on the way* to destroying the picture of being with others which sustains scepticism. However, as I stressed in the previous chapter, my basic claim is that it is not the objectification of human behaviour which leads to the problem of other minds, but the tendency to objectify our 'subject' character. And, in my view, this is a tendency to which Austin's account is not free. In the second half of this chapter I will explain why.

AUSTIN AND THE METAPHYSICAL LEGACY OF FREGE'S PHILOSOPHY

Ordinary behaviour and intentional action

The argument of 'Other Minds' attempts to show why the justification sought for by the traditional philosopher is not required for us to be 'entitled to trust others' (OM, p. 82). The principle result of Austin's approach is to make plausible the idea that the perception of others is not, in the first instance, the observation of 'mere behaviour' but of behaviour which, for those in the know, is intrinsically significant.

We must now ask what it is that, according to Austin, distinguishes 'mere behaviour' from the behaviour that is manifest to such an insider. In my view, it is in his answer to this question that Austin betrays a deep commitment to some very traditional assumptions, assumptions which ruin his attempt to disengage from the traditional problematic.

Briefly stated, Austin rejects the idea of behaviour as the making of physical movements because what the insider sees is, supposedly, behaviour which is 'intimately related to' or 'intimately associated with' or 'related in a unique sort of way' to the presence of subjective, conscious acts or processes.[10] It is behaviour conceived as 'thickened' in this way that Austin identifies as ordinary. And my claim is that Austin cannot explain this without re-introducing the conception of human subjectivity which sustains the threat of scepticism. In what follows, my demonstration of this claim will focus on Austin's treatment of intentional action, and in particular his identification of intentional action with ordinary behaviour. It is important to stress that I do not see this identification as being of itself objectionable. My objection is entirely to the thought that it implies the co-presence in the context of such behaviour of a special, irreducibly subjective side: the self-presence of the intending subject.

Before I proceed to explore this objection against Austin in greater detail, it is worth noting that its first premise (that Austin identifies intentional action with ordinary behaviour) runs counter to the received view of a central principle of Austin's philosophy of action, namely, the principle of 'no modification without aberration' (Austin, 1979, p. 189). This principle, as both Cavell and Searle read it, requires that, unless a situation is unusual or *out of the ordinary* (aberrant) in some way, it makes no sense to characterise the behaviour as intentional, or indeed as *not* intentional (Cavell, 1976, p. 7; Searle, 1966, p. 42). This reading of Austin's principle is quite wrong. Austin's view is not that it makes no sense to say that ordinary behaviour is intentional action. Rather, his claim is that we would not ordinarily say of such behaviour that it is intentional because it is part of what ordinary behaviour *is* that it is done by a person and, therefore, by and large, done intentionally.[11] There is, Austin claims, no special style to intentional action because it just is the style of ordinary behaviour. This is why Austin argues that it is only if something is odd about the occasion that there is any reason to make recourse to an expression modifying the verb. This is simply part of the 'natural economy of language' (Austin, 1979, p. 190). Consequently, 'for the *standard* case covered by any normal verb . . . a verb like "eat" or "kick" or "croquet" – no modifying expression is required or even permissible' (*ibid.*). Again the point is that, for Austin, ordinary behaviour just is, by and large, intentional action. And my claim, to be established in what follows, is that Austin's thinking on this issue leaves his account open to the threat of scepticism.

Performative utterances

In order to clarify Austin's views on ordinary behaviour and intentional action I will concentrate on his work on that most specialised and distinctive mode of human behaviour: the use of language, what Austin calls 'speech-acts'. This work constitutes the text posthumously published as *How To Do Things With Words* (Austin, 1980).

Like his other writings, Austin's argumentation in *How To Do Things With Words* aims to expose and undermine what he considers to be the most fundamental of unquestioned assumptions of traditional philosophy. In this case 'the assumption that the business of a "statement" can only be to "describe" some state of affairs, or to "state some fact", which it must do either truly or falsely' (*ibid.*, p. 1). We must, he states, question 'the age-old assumption in philosophy . . . that to say something, at least in all cases worth considering, i.e. all cases considered, is always and simply to state something. This assumption is no doubt unconscious, no doubt precipitate, but it is wholly natural in philosophy apparently' (*ibid.*, p. 12).

Austin's criticism of this 'descriptive fallacy' is initially developed through the identification and examination of what he calls 'performative utterances'. By essential contrast to (true/false) 'constative utterances', the functioning of the performative is not to be conceived in terms of the communication of a meaning-content that is oriented towards an assessment in terms of truth (*ibid.*). The performative does not describe or represent something that exists outside the speech-act; rather, it is a public performance that *does* something by making use of, by conforming to, a conventional procedure. Consider, for example:

> the utterance 'I do' (take this woman to be my lawful wedded wife), as uttered in the course of a marriage ceremony. Here we should say that in saying these words we are *doing* something – namely, marrying, rather than *reporting* something, namely *that* we are marrying. And the act of marrying, like, say, the act of betting, is at least *preferably* (though still not *accurately*) to be described as *saying certain words*, rather than as performing a different, inward and spiritual, action of which these words are merely the outward and audible sign.
>
> (*ibid.*, pp. 12–13)

So, with the emphasis on what we publicly do with words, has Austin destroyed the idea that verbal behaviour is 'merely the outward and audible sign' of 'inward and spiritual' acts? In what follows I will argue that he has not. Certain fundamental and ineliminable features of Austin's analysis guarantee that the promise of performative communication is not fulfilled.

While Austin's analysis of the performative focuses on what we do with words, he does not think that the performative can be fully or accurately described simply as an act of saying certain words. Part of what Austin is suggesting here is that, in general, 'if the act is to be deemed to have been performed . . . the circumstances, including other actions, must be appropriate' (*ibid.*, p. 9). Crucially, however, public circumstances and acts do not exhaust everything that Austin's analysis requires here. As we shall see, the traditional requirement for 'inward and spiritual' acts of meaning or intending, which offi-cially Austin wishes to avoid, make a silent return. To see this it will prove helpful to examine the way in which Austin's analysis of performative communication inherits the shape of Frege's analysis of the *force* of an utterance.

Frege and the realm of the serious

In Frege's classic essay 'The Thought', the notion of force is introduced in the context of an analysis of the logic and limits of communication. Sentences with force are those which are used to communicate thoughts. Now, because Frege defines a thought as 'something for which the question of truth arises' (Frege, 1967, p. 20), he (basically) restricts the notion of force to sentences in which we 'state something' (*ibid.*, p. 21).[12] This is, of course, precisely the restriction that Austin aims to lift in his analysis of performative communication, and it is almost fortuitous that Frege is willing to admit to the class of sentences with a force anything except indicative sentences. However, the important point is that the concept of force is introduced by Frege not because there are, besides indicative sentences, sentences that express the same thought in another way. Rather, it is introduced in order to distinguish genuine from merely apparent cases of the communication of thoughts, *however* the thought is conveyed. Frege holds that sentential realisation cannot of itself guarantee that an event of speech is a genuine case of a communication of a thought. An indicative sentence-token may lack what he calls 'real assertive force' because, according to Frege, we do not actually have a case of communication unless the thought it expresses is 'actually being put forward as true' (*ibid.*, p. 22). For this reason, Frege has to accept that any sentence-type that can be uttered with real assertive force can also be uttered without it:

> This happens when we do not speak seriously. As stage thunder is only apparent thunder and a stage fight is only an apparent fight, so stage assertion is only apparent assertion. It is only acting, only fancy. In his part the actor asserts nothing, nor does he lie, even if he says something of whose falsehood he is convinced. In poetry we have the case of thoughts being expressed without actually being put forward as true in spite of the form of the indicative sentence. Therefore it must still always be asked, about what is presented in the form of an indicative sentence, whether it really contains an assertion. And this question must be answered in the negative if the requisite seriousness is lacking.
>
> (*ibid.*)

Any sentence-type is, as it were, the standing possibility for tokens that either do or do not possess real assertive force. And whether sentence-tokens do or do not is a matter of whether the circumstances were ones in which the use of words was or was not an expression of a thought being put forward as true.

Returning now to Austin, it is, I believe, of enormous significance that an anonymous objection which he poses to his idea that the performative is 'to be described as *saying certain words*' is clearly Fregean:

> [It is true that] if the act is to be deemed to have been performed . . . the circumstances, including other actions, must be appropriate. But we may, in objecting, have something totally different, and this time quite mistaken, in mind . . . Surely the words must be spoken 'seriously' and so as to be taken 'seriously'?
>
> (Austin, 1980, pp. 8–9)

As I have indicated, Austin's official position is opposed to the idea that performative utterances are merely the outward sign of 'inward and spiritual' actions. However, his response to this 'quite mistaken' objection is complicated:

> Surely the words must be spoken 'seriously' and so as to be taken 'seriously'? This is, though vague, true enough in general – an important

commonplace in discussing the purport of any utterance whatsoever. I must not be joking, for example, nor writing a poem. But we are apt to have a feeling that their being serious consists in their being uttered as merely the outward and visible sign, for convenience or other record or for information, of an inward and spiritual act.

(*ibid.*, p. 9)

Austin's (qualified) endorsement of the Fregean analysis is transparent. Moreover, it is crucial to see that even the qualification cannot be interpreted as a rejection of Frege's account. It is true that, for Frege, if the thought expressed by the indicative sentence *was* laid down as true, then that is so in virtue of the fact that an inward (i.e. publicly impalpable) act of intending to do just that had actually taken place. But this does not mean that the outward utterance is, for Frege, merely 'a description, true or false, of the occurrence of [an] inward performance' (*ibid.*). On the contrary, for Frege, when and if the thought expressed is laid down as true, 'the real assertive force lies . . . in the form of the indicative sentence' (Frege, 1967, p. 22). And my claim will be that, notwithstanding Austin's official position, far from rejecting the Fregean requirement that a private inward act take place in serious speech, Austin's analysis, on all essentials, confirms it.

For Frege, the basic way in which a (genuine) assertion can 'go wrong' is by the thoughts expressed being false. But this kind of occasion still resides within the space of communication because it still concerns an event in which expressed thoughts are being put forward as true. What takes us outside the space of communication for Frege are occasions in which thoughts are merely expressed; i.e., expressed without being put forward as true. That Austin retains the general shape of this Fregean picture can be seen by attending to his methodological programme of isolating the 'happy performative' (Austin, 1980, pp. 12f).

Like Frege, Austin develops his analysis by focusing on ways in which occasions of the use of words 'can be and go wrong' (*ibid.*, p. 14). In the case of performative communication, however, the basic fault cannot be that the utterance is false. But Austin's analysis contains a structural analogue. As Cavell notes, 'Austin "substitutes" for the logically defined concept of truth . . . [the concept of] "felicity" ' (Cavell, 1994, p. 81). And so, as Austin puts it, 'we call the doctrine of the things that can be and go wrong on the occasion of such utterances, the doctrine of the *Infelicities*' (Austin, 1980, p. 14).[13] Such infelicities parallel Frege's treatment of stating falsehoods in that they are included within the space of performative communication. And, for identical reasons: such cases are still events of speech in which, *in a special way*, 'saying certain words' (Frege's 'expressing thoughts') is not all there is to it.

We can begin to clarify what more Austin requires by exploring the passages in which he excludes two possibilities of the use of performative utterances from his current considerations; possibilities which relate to what he conceives of as non-standard or abnormal cases. Such cases are ones in which we would say either that the performance of the act was not 'done' at all (the possibility that the speech-*act* was not performed *freely* – first exclusion) or that the words of the speech-act were uttered in a way which is 'parasitic upon its normal use' (the possibility that the words were used not *seriously* – second exclusion).

The possibility specifically related to speech-acts as utterances (the second exclusion) is our primary concern. Still sticking closely to the Fregean analysis, it involves the possibility for any utterance (performative or otherwise) to be used in stage recitation or fiction. In the case of performatives this involves situations in which the speaker is not putting forward what is said with the intention actually to perform the speech-act whose formula is being uttered. Austin insists that this possibility is a special kind of 'ill' which can befall the utterance:

> As *utterances* our performatives are *also* heir to certain other kinds of ill which infect **all** utterances. And these likewise . . . **we are deliberately at present excluding**. I mean, for example, the following: a performative utterance will, for example, be *in a peculiar way* **hollow or void** if said by an actor on the stage, or if introduced in a poem, or spoken in soliloquy . . . Language in such circumstances is in special ways – intelligibly – used not **seriously**, but in ways *parasitic* upon its normal use . . . **All this we are *excluding* from consideration**. Our performative utterances, felicitous or not, are to be **understood as issued in ordinary circumstances**.
>
> (*ibid.*, pp. 21–2. Austin's italics, my bold.)

Austin aims to exclude from his consideration of performative communication just those occasions in which what he wants to call the 'ordinary circumstances' of speech are not in place. And with this in view it seems undeniable that, for good or ill, Austin's concept of the ordinary is, as Derrida has put it in his reading of Austin, 'marked' by this exclusion (LI, p. 16). For good or ill? That is the question.

Rooting out the ordinary

That Austin's analysis involves an endorsement of Frege's approach is clear. But does this show that this way of going on betrays a 'metaphysical decision', as Derrida has argued (*ibid.*, p. 93)? Has Austin, in accepting the 'important commonplace', really committed himself to 'a strategy fraught with metaphysical presupposition' (*ibid.*, p. 85)? After all, we surely can and do distinguish between 'ordinary' or 'standard' or 'everyday' uses of words and uses of these same words in stage recitation and fiction.

In Austin's defence, both Searle and Cavell have insisted that the moments of exclusion are merely methodological deferrals, not metaphysically motivated attempts to define a context of the 'ordinary circumstances' of communication in a metaphysically problematic way. Thus, Cavell insists that the exclusions in

How To Do Things With Words are simply exclusions *from that work*, and moreover, ones which are taken up directly (if not fully or entirely happily) in the papers published as 'A Plea for Excuses' (Austin, 1979, pp. 175–204) and 'Pretending' (*ibid.*, pp. 253–71): 'what the doctrine of excuses does for cases of extenuation, Austin's work represented in his paper "Pretending" in part does for, and is meant eventually to do more for, cases of etiolation, parasitism, and in general the realm of the "non-serious" ' (Cavell, 1994, p. 91). In short, just as Searle had classed the exclusions as 'a matter of research strategy' (Searle, 1977, p. 205), so Cavell sees them as a matter of 'contingent convenience' (Cavell, 1995, p. 71). By exploring the problems with this reading I will explain why Austin's exclusion of stage recitation and fiction returns us to issues concerning the metaphysics of the subject.

It is clear, I think, that Austin is committed to an ideal of the ordinary speech situation, in the sense that the terms of his analysis (the doctrine of infelicities) are oriented towards a situation or circumstances in which everything goes right. With respect to this ideal Austin acknowledges that, *qua* possibility, the phenomenon of language which he excludes is in fact one of its essential features – for it is a species of infelicity to which *all* speech acts, as such, are *necessarily* heir. But he represents it only as an eventuality, and of a type which strays too far from the ideal circumstances to count as 'ordinary'; *qua* eventuality, this type constitutes a different order of infelicity, 'a sea-change in special circumstances' (Austin, 1980, p. 22). Derrida's objection is that Austin, blinkered by the 'important commonplace', is insufficiently sensitive to the necessity he has acknowledged. Instead of pursuing an investigation of the functional structure of locutionary acts which shows why this 'risk', *qua* possibility, is essential to its *being* such an act, his procedure positions it, *qua* eventuality, as something that transgresses the 'ordinary circumstances' of language use – something that should, therefore, be pared away or excluded from an analysis of the normal use of words in standard cases in ordinary circumstances.

Whether this exclusion is metaphysically problematic or not can be explored by questioning whether this paring away is, even in principle, an ambition which might succeed. Searle and Cavell clearly assume that it can: consideration of 'the realm of the "non-serious" ' can be put off until later. Derrida, on the other hand, is equally convinced that it cannot. Specifically, Derrida's claim is that, because it is internal to the structure of 'the realm of the "serious" ' (the realm which Austin's analysis aims, *here and now*, to consider) that it possesses features held by Austin himself to define the excluded realm, then in this case, and *pace* Searle and Cavell, 'you cannot root-out the "parasite" without rooting-out the "standard" at the same time' (LI, p. 90).

One way of putting Derrida's claim is to say that there is a structural or internal relation between the two realms. Derrida attempts to make this relation perspicuous by describing *non*-citational utterances as being, essentially, 'the modification of a general citationality' (*ibid.*, p. 18). This is not to be taken to imply (absurdly) that non-citational utterances cannot be *contrasted* with, say, events of speech on stage in a theatre. Rather, the point is that this ordinary contrast can arise (can be *constructed*) only within a 'general space of possibility' which can be characterised as citational. This idea will be the focus of close examination in Chapter 7. But the basic point against Austin is simply that the concept of the 'citational' identifies a feature which Austin himself acknowledges as being essential to events which are describable as 'locutionary acts', namely, what Austin calls their 'ritual character', the necessity, as Derrida puts it, of such events 'conforming with an iterable model' (*ibid.*). Thus, to say as a result that the non-citational turns out to be, 'in a certain way', citational is not to deny the ordinary contrast or to affirm that anything goes. Rather, the point is that, as essentially iterable units, non-citational utterances do not 'emerge *in opposition to* citationality'. For the ordinary distinction cannot appear *as such* outside a space of 'a general citationality or iterability' (*ibid.*).

So in Derrida's view the type of event that Austin deems a transgression of the standard is, *qua* possibility, part of the essential structure of every event capable of communicating whatsoever. Again, this does not mean that ordinary language and life is not serious or is really fictional. But it does challenge the idea that the so-called 'realm of the "non-serious" ' is essentially outside of, or para-sitic on, what we call 'ordinary language'. Indeed, for Derrida the former is part of, not apart from, the basic structure of the latter, and so must be acknowledged as such:

> One cannot subordinate or leave in abeyance the analysis of fiction in order to proceed firstly and 'logically' to that of 'non-fiction-standard discourse'. For part of the most originary essence of the latter is to allow fiction, the simulacrum, parasitism, to take place – and in so doing to 'de-essentialize' itself as it were.
>
> (*ibid.*, p. 133)

On this view, as long as one's concern is with the logic of ordinary language, the citational 'realm of the "non-serious" ' cannot even provisionally be excluded.

But what if, with Austin, one supposed otherwise? It should be clear that to do so would require that what will distinguish the realm of the serious (namely, and *ex hypothesi*, the speaker's *vouloir dire*) is something which is capable of specification in terms which are restricted to what, on any occasion, is actually *present* in the circumstances of such speech. In order to see how problematic this assumption is we should remember that the addition or presence of further 'outward' *words* (such as 'I intend this seriously') cannot, even in 'silent speech', be assumed to settle the question; for as far as the Austinian analysis is concerned they, too, can be present without having been used with the requisite seriousness.[14] So, what is specified here will have to be construed as something essentially invisible to others in the circumstances of speech. In short, it will have to be what is classi-cally called a private mental act. Now, given the restrictions on its description, what is specified in this way will perforce stand as something potentially unique:

it would makes sense to say that *it* was present or occurred, without importing into one's description of *it* any *essential* reference to other such events. Thus, what we will specify is something which *could* occur only once; for, given the restrictions imposed by the exclusion, its iteration can be construed *only* as a possible occurrence and not as essential to its being the kind of process we wish to specify. The trouble is that the very idea of attributing meaning to anything specified in this way – that is, independently of the citationality or iterability which characterises it – is *a priori* incoherent. And so, whatever we specify, it cannot be even potentially sufficient to confer the requisite seriousness on the speech-act: anything (and so nothing) will count as 'speaking in accordance' with what, given the restrictions, we manage to specify. Again, the point is that, in this case, 'you cannot root-out the "parasite" without rooting-out the "standard" at the same time'. Such, in any case, is the inevitable consequence of Austin's procedures when it accepts the 'commonplace' distinction – that tidy-looking habit of *Gleichschaltung* – between serious and non-serious utterances.

This argument is merely negative. It does not provide an alternative account of ordinary or non-fiction standard discourse. Nevertheless, it does show that Austin's procedure of excluding the realm of the non-serious is not merely strategic but profoundly oriented towards a quite specific metaphysics of locutionary acts. Indeed, by opposing 'citation or iteration to the non-iteration of an event' (LI, p. 18), Austin's analysis can be seen to repeat an 'age-old assumption' into his account of ordinary speech, namely, that (actually) to *say something*, at least in all cases worth considering, i.e. all cases considered and not excluded, requires the presence-in-the-present of a publicly invisible mental act intimately related to the bodily behaviour, and without which the behaviour would be 'in a peculiar way hollow or void'.

This reading of Austin's account of ordinary language clearly makes problematic Austin's hope to reframe scepticism in 'Other Minds'. If the being 'ordinary' of speech, and *a fortiori* the being 'ordinary' of human behaviour in general, is defined with reference to the presence in the context of private mental acts which that behaviour is said to express or realise, then Austin's claim that there is no general justification for believing in others really does become the sceptical conclusion that he wishes to avoid. For, if the only way one can come by the idea of there being an 'intimate relation' between intentions and behaviour is one's acquaintance with it *in one's own case*, then one's conviction that the behaviour of another really is the behaviour of 'another *like oneself*' is *always* unsatisfactorily hasty and presumptuous. Thus Austin's account leaves wholly unexplained how, with respect to the behaviour of others, one could possibly be 'in the know' and hence leaves us in the dark as to why one is 'entitled' to see the behaviour of the other as other than 'thin'.

It should be stressed that the basic point here is a conceptual one; i.e., as Austin defines it, one cannot come by the idea of what it is that makes behaviour 'ordinary' *except from one's own case*. The epistemological drama then arises from the fact that, from the third person, there is no way of telling whether the other's behaviour is really 'ordinary' or not. This problem also arises for Austin's account of the expression of feelings: that the behavioural 'display' is related 'in a unique sort of way' to a feeling is something one knows only because one is acquainted with it in one's own case (OM, p. 108). As Wittgenstein notes, the question would then arise: 'And how can I generalize the *one* case so irresponsibly?' (PI, §293). Austin has no answer here.

Austin's appeal to the idea of the 'ordinary' promises to escape the snags and lures which 'casts [the philosopher] out of the garden of the world we live in' (Austin, 1979, p. 90). It can now be seen, however, that Austin's account retains the very metaphysics which sustains our exile. In the next chapter I will examine a discussion of being with others which is, in its insistence on the primacy of the everyday and ordinary, quite similar to Austin's but which, in my view, stands a far greater chance of avoiding the problems that beset Austin's account. This is the account of being with others developed by Martin Heidegger in his classic of existential phenomenology *Being and Time*.

3

REFRAMING SCEPTICISM II

Heidegger

INTRODUCTION

In this chapter, I will show that the kind of reframing of the problem of other minds pursued by Austin is also evident in the work of Martin Heidegger. Significantly, however, it will be seen that Heidegger's account is not open to the kind of objection developed in the last chapter against Austin's. Indeed, I will argue that Heidegger's conception of being with others in *Being and Time*, at least as far as being with other human beings is concerned,[1] satisfies the central principle of adequacy outlined in Chapter 1. That is, it preserves the position we hold at the outset; it cannot motivate hesitations beyond the ordinary. Thus, in my view, Derrida is correct to suggest that 'scepticism and everything that is systematic with it' cannot be articulated within the terms of analysis in *Being and Time*.[2]

The reading of Heidegger's philosophy presented in this chapter is an attempt to clarify, not to criticise or defend, its treatment of the traditional problem of other minds. However, even this task of clarification is complicated. Heidegger's text is not structured in a conventional way, nor is it written in conventional terms. We do not find in *Being and Time* a chapter entitled 'The Problem of Other Minds'. Instead we are offered an 'analysis of Dasein' in which Heidegger proposes the thesis that Dasein is, in itself, 'essentially Being-with' (BT, p. 120). In this chapter I will try to explain what Heidegger means by this.

Among the reasons why *Being and Time* is an unconventional treatise is that, like Austin's, Heidegger's thought is characterised by a more or less constant preoccupation with the tradition of philosophy to which his thinking is heir. And, again like Austin's, Heidegger's engagement with this tradition is a kind of disengagement from the currently dominant modes of its inheritance. In the last chapter we saw how Austin both berates what he calls the traditional habits of *Gleichschaltung* and insists that we all feel them to be somehow spurious. As we shall see, Heidegger, too, presents traditional philosophy as being, in Stephen Mulhall's felicitous phrase, 'out of tune with that with which [we are] most fundamentally attuned' (Mulhall, 1996, p. 31). So, for Heidegger, too, the supposedly self-evidently appropriate framework of contemporary philosophy is riven by inherited conceptual distortions (BT, pp. 21–3); and yet we must all, in a certain way, see that it is so (*ibid.*, p. 58).

While there are interesting comparisons to be made between Austin's and Heidegger's thinking on these and other matters, I am not convinced that Heidegger's views can be captured with the thought that we are simply in the grip of a 'happy style of blinkering philosophical language' in the way Austin suggests (S&S, p. 5). For Heidegger, being out of tune, being misaligned with ourselves, is a definite characteristic of the kind of entity that we are, not simply an intellectual error which can be more or less readily overcome. Indeed, the Heideggerian suggestion seems to be that the of kind of entity which we are 'is' in such a way that it will *constantly* tend to draw its self-understanding in distorting terms. This, as I read his work, is what Heidegger conceives as the strange fatality of the entity which can take up the contemplative stance.

As we shall see, Heidegger's investigation of this entity develops as a radical and compelling critique of modern philosophy since Descartes. To put this into polemical form, the charge will be that modern philosophy operates with an objectifying conception of what it is to be human. This is the conception of the 'subject' character of a living human being which I have called the metaphysics of the subject. This chapter will, therefore, provide an opportunity to outline and examine this metaphysics in some detail.

HEIDEGGER AND THE TRADITION

Dislodging the background

In *Being and Time*, Heidegger presents the epistemological problematic and sceptical questions which characterise modern philosophical inquiry as sustained by an inadequate and distorting background conception of what it is to be a human being. In Heidegger's terms, modern philosophical inquiry is sustained by a misunderstanding of the kind of Being which belongs to the entity which can take up such an inquiry. For this reason a basic task of philosophy is, for Heidegger, the clarification of this kind of Being.[3]

It belongs to this orientation that it does not offer solutions to traditional epistemological problems. Rather, it aims to dislodge the background conception which makes such problems pressing. This relation to traditional routes of response is clearly invoked in Heidegger's infamous re-writing of Kant's famous remark about the 'scandal of philosophy':

> The 'scandal of philosophy' is not that [a proof of the 'existence of things outside me'] has yet to be given, but that such proofs are expected and attempted again and again. Such expectations, aims and demands arise from an ontologically inadequate way of starting with

something of such a character that independently *of it* and 'outside' *of it* a 'world' is to be proved as present-at-hand. It is not that the proofs are inadequate, but that the kind of Being of the entity which does the proving and makes requests for proofs has not been made definite enough . . . Our task is not to prove that an 'external world' is present-at-hand or to show how it is present-at-hand, but to point out why Dasein, as Being-in-the-world, has the tendency to bury the 'external world' in nullity 'epistemologically' before going on to prove it.

(BT, p. 205)

The accusation of ontological inadequacy is not intended to imply that the starting 'something' is taken to be unknown to the inquiring entity. On the contrary, the latter 'always says "*I am* this entity"' (*ibid.*, p. 115). But, and for just this reason, further interrogation seems unnecessary: for 'what is more indubitable than the givenness of the "I"?' (*ibid.*). The accusation of inadequacy is directed against precisely this assurance that what is 'given' here is sufficient to determine the kind of Being of the entity which does the proving. According to Heidegger, what makes it look sufficient, the real 'given' here, is the background conception.

In the opening chapter of *Being and Time*, Heidegger broaches a thematisation of this background conception with the suggestion that 'what stands in the way of the basic question of Dasein's Being (or leads it off the track) is an orientation thoroughly coloured by the anthropology of Christianity [the conception of man as made in God's image] and the ancient [Greek] world [the conception of man as the *zoon logon echon* (*animal rationale*)]' (*ibid.*, p. 48). This identification of the sources of the background conception is sharpened in the later essay published as 'The Letter on Humanism', where traditional anthropology is traced as a fundamental humanism.

In both *Being and Time* and 'The Letter on Humanism', Heidegger characterises humanist anthropology as that tradition in which what is called 'man' is defined by setting it off as one kind of entity present among others. Of course, human beings are not then simply equated with mere things or even with other living creatures. On the contrary, 'man' is accorded a specific and special difference: 'man' is the animal endowed with the power of reason or language; or is the *ens finitum* which is made in God's image. According to Heidegger, modern philosophy has inherited the essential features of this classical anthropology. That is, modern philosophy, too, conceives the human being primarily as a kind of entity present in the world alongside others and only then supplies it with a distinctive trait. It rejects the baldly naturalistic[4] assumption that 'the essence of man consists in being an animal organism', but proposes that 'this insufficient definition of man's essence [can] be overcome or offset by outfitting man with an immortal soul' or by 'adjoining a soul to the human body, a mind to the soul . . . and then louder than before singing the praises of the mind.' (LH, pp. 228–9). Thus, with respect to the issue of the background conception, Heidegger's thesis

45

is that in modern philosophy, where consciousness is the point of departure, humanism remains the background conception: 'In principle we are still thinking of *homo animalis* – even when *anima* is posited as *animus sive mens*, and this is later posited as subject, person or spirit' (*ibid.*, p. 227).[5] According to Heidegger, then, construing what is distinctive about human existence in this quasi-naturalistic way has opened us up to a determination of ourselves which invites and sustains scepticism: the possibility of the human organism having 'access to the world' can be conceived only in terms of a (more or less mysterious) extra property of this entity, and one whose mechanism and success is intrinsically problematic and uncertain.

Heidegger's alternative *begins* with the complete rejection of the idea that something like 'access to the world' is merely a fortunate, secondary supplement, a supplementary benefit, to our existence: for the entity that we are, 'being in a world is something that belongs *essentially*' (BT, p. 13). To emphasise that this is a basic state of Being, Heidegger coins the compound expression 'Being-in-the-world' to describe it, stressing thereby that the 'in the world' aspect of our existence is not an added extra but an essential and irreducible feature of it. Existence, for human beings at least, *is* this 'unitary phenomenon' (*ibid.*, p. 53). With this in view it is clear that, for Heidegger, the fundamental and recurrent feature of modern philosophy informed by the humanist background conception is that it '*splits the phenomenon*' which, in our Being, we *are* (*ibid.*, p. 132).

Reframing scepticism

Heidegger's claim, then, is that the humanist background conception of 'man' has given rise to a pervasive *subject/object dualism* in philosophy. Such a dualism shows itself in analyses which take their point of departure from the assumption that the task of philosophy is to clarify or explain the 'relations' that can hold between an individual human 'subject' on the one hand, and 'the world' or 'other such subjects' on the other.

With such subject/object dualism, philosophy takes on a characteristically epistemological orientation. Henceforth the fundamental problem of philosophy is the problem of the *transcendence* of the human 'subject': 'how can a proximally isolated and worldless subject reach beyond itself into realms which are "other and external"' (*ibid.*, p. 60)? As I have indicated, according to Heidegger, once we have determined our existence in terms of such a subject, the threat of scepticism is unavoidable: we have split the unitary phenomenon of Being-in-the-world and any retrospective attempt to '"cement"' it back together again always arrives '"too late"' (*ibid.*, p. 206). Clearly, if this is the case, then one must treat the vocabulary which has articulated the phenomenon-splitting conception of our Being with great caution. Thus, Heidegger urges that terms such as 'subject', 'I', 'reason', 'spirit' and 'person' must, at least provisionally, be *avoided* (*ibid.*, p. 46).

Heidegger's view is that a resolution of the problem of transcendence requires that we break free from the conception of our Being which sustains it. The task is not to refute the sceptic – provide the 'cement' – but to establish why 'the entity which is essentially constituted by Being-in-the-world' has the tendency to '"bury" its Being-in-the-world in nullity "epistemologically" before going on to prove it.' (*ibid.*, p. 206). This entity Heidegger calls by the traditional German term for existence in general: 'Dasein'. 'Dasein' is not *simply* another name for 'man' or for 'human being' or 'person', but re-inscribes within an onto-logically appropriate setting what is named by, but misconceived in, the discourses with those other names. That is, 'Dasein' is defined as that entity for which its own Being is 'not a matter of indifference' to it (*ibid.*, p. 42) – and whose characteristic tendency is to *misinterpret* its own Being in the ways described.

This ontological re-inscription of the entity 'man' positions Heidegger's anal-ysis at a distance from, but also in an internal, critical, relation to, traditional philosophical anthropology and its modern epistemological problematic. It also indicates why, in essence, his analysis of Dasein as Being-in-the-world is not an (oppositional) refutation of scepticism but its reframing. For Heidegger, liberating thinking from the problem of transcendence does not mean developing a new and more powerfully anti-sceptical 'theory of knowledge'. Rather, it is a question of a clarification of Dasein's Being. This is the Heideggerian reframing of scepticism.

Existential and categorial characters of being

For Heidegger, the fundamental task of philosophy is not to answer the episte-mological question 'How can a subject gain access to what is other and external to it?' but to resituate ourselves with respect to the ontological question concerning the understanding of entities *as* entities; the understanding of the *Being* of entities. For Heidegger, then, the basic question of philosophy is what is understood in such an understanding: i.e., the question of 'the meaning of Being' (BT, p. 1). Now Dasein clearly has a special privilege within such an inquiry since it, uniquely, 'is' such that an 'understanding of Being is itself a defi-nite character of [its] Being' (*ibid.*, p. 12). It is for this reason that the ontological inquiry takes its point of departure from an analysis of Dasein.[6]

As I have indicated, this orientation does not simply pass by or by-pass the modern epistemological problematic of the transcendence of the subject. Indeed, it immediately puts pressure on the humanist background. For, in virtue of conceiving 'man himself' (*ibid.*, p. 11) as that entity which 'is' only in an understanding of Being, affirming that 'man' *qua* 'Dasein' 'is' can no longer denote simply that some (no doubt special) type of entity is, as it were, objec-tively present in the world. On the contrary, it is to affirm that 'there is' 'an understanding of something like a "world"'; a 'within which', that is, within which entities can be manifest *as such* (*ibid.*, p. 13).

The attempt to theorise or render conceptually transparent what occurs when 'there is' Dasein is what is undertaken in *Being and Time*. Of course, since we already are, in each case, Dasein, the structures of its existence cannot be wholly foreign to us. The basic misalignment problem is, however, that the unitary phenomenon which specifies Dasein's basic state of Being also constantly invites Dasein to conceive itself wrongly and in inappropriate terms. It is at this point that we see how the analysis of Dasein engages most directly with the traditional problematic:

> For the most part this phenomenon [Being-in-the-world] has been explained in a way which is basically wrong, or interpreted in an onto-logically inadequate manner. On the other hand, this . . . is itself based upon nothing else but this very state of Dasein's Being, which is such that Dasein itself . . . gets its ontological understanding of itself in the first instance from those entities which it itself is *not* but which it encounters 'within' its world, and from the Being which they possess.
>
> (*ibid.*, p. 58)

The contrast drawn here between entities which do and entities which do not have the kind of Being that belongs to Dasein plays a key role in the analysis of *Being and Time*, underpinning the terms of the analysis of Dasein and the account of Dasein's misalignment.[7] Thus Heidegger states that any attempt to provide an analysis of Dasein must do so in terms of two basic possibilities for characterising the Being of any entity (*ibid.*, p. 45): either one can think of it in terms of '*existentialia*' (ways for a '*who*' to be) or '*categories*' ('*what*' it is). The former are appropriate to entities which have the kind of Being of Dasein and the latter are appropriate to entities which do not.[8] Heidegger's suggestion is that concep-tions of 'man' of the humanist type are, essentially, the result of an inappropriate, but explicable, categorial determination of what it is to be human:

> The kind of Being which belongs to Dasein is . . . such that, in under-standing its own Being, it has a tendency to do so in terms of that entity towards which it comports itself proximally and in a way which is essen-tially constant – in terms of the 'world'.
>
> (*ibid.*, p. 115)

From the categorial perspective, Dasein can only be interpreted as having, first of all, the kind of Being of a thing; something present in the world which is, in the first instance, isolated and worldless. As a consequence all 'relations' to what is 'outside' 'it' are fundamentally problematic and insecure. Now, Heidegger's response to this interpretation is not simply to oppose it but to reframe it: from an existential perspective what is decisive is that this interpretation is *itself* a way of Dasein's Being-in-the-world, and must be understood on that basis.

So, in summary, 'man' *qua* 'Dasein' is, essentially, 'an entity which, in its very Being, comports itself understandingly towards that Being' (*ibid.*, p. 53). But

Heidegger's diagnostic point is that when an entity with this kind of Being attempts to make that understanding explicit (and it is the only entity which can attempt such a thing) its virtually unavoidable tendency is to *mis*understand its own Being by interpreting itself, as humanism has, categorially. Nevertheless, and this is what I want to move on to in the second part of this chapter, an interpretation of Dasein which avoids such misunderstanding is *a priori* possible. We are able to reject categorial interpretations, not because we can 'disprove' them, or 'refute' them, but

> because this phenomenon [Being-in-the-world] itself always gets 'seen' in a certain way in every Dasein. And it thus gets 'seen' because it makes up a basic state of Dasein, and in every case is already disclosed for Dasein's understanding of Being, and disclosed along with that Being itself.
>
> (*ibid.*, p. 58)

The force of this account does not accrue from the rigour of its proofs and demonstrations, but, rather, from something like the authenticity of its testimony or of its attestation (*ibid.*, p. 267).[9] Dasein must attest to its Being-in-the-world. And it must be able to do so because, *as* Dasein, it is, in every case, *already* disclosed as such.

The charge of dogmatism

With this starting point, Heidegger necessarily lays his approach open to the charge of dogmatism raised by McGinn in her reading of Austin. That is, Heidegger's account, by *beginning* with the 'assumption' that Dasein has Being-in-the-world as its basic state of Being, has not refuted scepticism, but dogmatically foreclosed its threat from the outset.

Heidegger is aware of this kind of objection, and his initial response to it demonstrates the sense in which his analysis must, like Austin's, appear unjustifiably dogmatic to the traditional philosopher. In response to the suggestion that scepticism has simply been defined away, Heidegger asks: 'What higher court is to decide whether and in what sense there is to be any problem of knowledge other than the phenomenon of knowing as such and the kind of Being which belongs to the knower?' (*ibid.*, p. 61). The last clause here is crucial. As noted, in Heidegger's view the kind of Being belonging to Dasein has been interpreted, quite dogmatically, in terms of the Being of entities which do *not* have Dasein's kind of Being, i.e., categorially. And the problem of knowledge only seems pressing against the background of such an interpretation. Consequently, the task cannot be to 'solve the problem' but to clarify 'the kind of Being that belongs to the knower'. Again, the point is that, for Heidegger, the aim is not to refute the sceptic but to provide an attestation of our Being-in-the-world which reframes it. And in such a context the charge of dogmatism cannot get a grip.

HEIDEGGER'S ANALYSIS OF DASEIN

Dasein's everydayness

The following problem now arises for Heidegger. If the most powerful and influential interpretations of human existence have been drawn in terms appropriate to entities which do *not* have the kind of Being that belongs to Dasein, then the appropriate point of departure in an analysis of Dasein's Being is 'far from self-evident' (*ibid.*, p. 43). In order to avoid the blind alley of categorial interpretations, Heidegger orients his analysis towards the clarification of that way of Being-in-the-world (i.e., one of Dasein's existentialia) with which we are already familiar *prior* to taking up the contemplative stance; that way of Being-in-the-world which is '*closest* to Dasein' (*ibid.*, p. 66), to which Dasein can thus most readily attest, and yet which is 'again and again *passed over* in explicating Dasein' (*ibid.*, p. 43): 'Dasein's everydayness' (*ibid.*).

Everydayness characterises that (unspecific) 'way of existing' 'which [Dasein] has proximally and for the most part' (*ibid.*, p. 43). It thus orients the inquiry towards achieving an understanding of what occurs when 'there is' Dasein. Now, as I have already indicated, to say that 'there is' Dasein, or that Dasein 'exists', does not simply denote the objective presence of some entity within the world, but, rather, that 'there is' an understanding of something like a 'world' within which entities can be manifest *as such*. Note, however, that this formulation leaves it open whether, when, in Dasein's everydayness, entities are 'manifest as such', *they* are manifest as objective presences either. In fact, in Heidegger's view, they are not. To understand this we need to introduce the contrast he draws between two modes in which entities are typically encountered in Dasein's everyday world, namely, in their readiness-to-hand [*Zuhandenheit*] or in their presence-at-hand [*Vorhandenheit*]. The contrast here relates to two modes of Dasein's everyday Being-in-the-world; modes which can be provisionally denoted as, respectively, active (or practical) and contemplative (or theoretical), i.e., something like the difference between purposefully using or manipulating something and just looking at it.

It would, I think, be quite natural to assume that the encounter with entities in their presence-at-hand (i.e., encountered as objectively there) has an obvious priority. After all, if an entity is not actually present-at-hand, one cannot encounter it in any way. However, as will become clear in what follows, Heidegger resists the thought that encountering entities in their readiness-to-hand is *founded* on Dasein's having discovered it beforehand as something present-at-hand.[10] Indeed, as I hope to show, for Heidegger the opposite is true: when an entity is manifest within the everyday world it is always something which is manifest, in the first instance, in its readiness-to-hand.

Encountering the ready-to-hand

Heidegger introduces the idea of encounters with entities in their readiness-to-hand with the famous example of someone using a hammer:

> In dealings . . . our concern subordinates itself to the 'in-order-to' which is constitutive for the equipment we are employing at the time; the less we just stare at the hammer-Thing and the more we seize hold of it and use it, the more primordial does our relationship to it become, and the more unveiledly is it encountered as that which it is – as equipment. The hammering itself uncovers the specific 'manipulability' ['Handlichkeit'] of the hammer. The kind of Being which equipment possesses in which it is manifest in its own right we call '*readiness-to-hand*' [*Zuhandenheit*].
>
> (*ibid.*, p. 69)

In such circumstances the hammer is encountered in its readiness-to-hand. At issue, therefore, is the 'being there' of an entity with a quintessentially 'relational' identity: it is an entity manifest *in its relation* to Dasein's manipulation and use of it. Paradoxically, however, Heidegger presents this in terms which at once tend to erase that relation: it is an entity manifest 'as that which it is' and 'in its own right'. This is not a quirk of phrasing in this passage, nor is it confined to man-made instruments like hammers. On the contrary, Heidegger is quite explicit that, in general, '*readiness-to-hand is the way in which entities as they are "in themselves" are defined ontologico-categorially*' (*ibid.*, p. 71, italics in original). In order to understand Heidegger's claim that readiness-to-hand is not founded on presence-at-hand, we first need to clarify this important idea.

Even with respect to things like hammers, Heidegger's formulation is fairly obscure. When we actually use a hammer we do not ask 'What does it serve to do?' or 'For whom is it equipment?', indeed we do not thematically investigate it at all. To use a metaphor of Wittgenstein's, we employ it 'blindly' (PI, §219). And yet, according to Heidegger, it is precisely at such times that the entity is most primordially disclosed or unveiledly encountered as that which 'in itself' it *is*. Thus Heidegger is suggesting that it is when the hammer is encountered most relationally and least thematically that it is encountered in a way that, in classical terms, would be called most objectively.

The puzzle here can be made even more vivid by juxtaposing two ways in which Mulhall, quite correctly, formulates Heidegger's views:

1 'Heidegger . . . claim[s] that Dasein's capacity to encounter objects as ready-to-hand involves grasping them in relation to its own possibilities-for-Being.' (Mulhall, 1996, p. 78)
2 'There is no disclosure without Dasein; but what is disclosed are entities as they are in themselves.' (*ibid.*, p. 104)

The tension (if there is one) would be between affirming an essentially 'relational' conception of what is disclosed in Dasein's everyday world and affirming the idea that *that same disclosure* affords Dasein with access to entities as they are 'in themselves'. I think there is no doubt that Heidegger wants to affirm both. And as the quotation on the ontologico-categorial definition of readiness-to-hand indicates, this is not intended to apply only to entities which are produced to be used. However, as I say, the position is *prima facie* problematic, if not straightforwardly contradictory. How can (1) and (2) be jointly affirmed?

In order to see how they can, we need to recall the anti-anthropological stance of the Heideggerian analysis of Dasein. As we have seen, implicit in Heidegger's characterisation of *Dasein's* openness to entities is a contrast with approaches in which 'man' is conceived, in the first instance, as an organic, animal presence in the world (*homo animalis*). As we shall see in detail in the next chapter, according to Heidegger animals in general (what he conceives of as, essentially, mere biological organisms), apes for example, have some access to entities within the world. But such access is, he argues, always circumscribed by the Being of the animal such that it has no access to them 'as such'; no access to entities in their Being. The (ontological) difference of 'man' is then expressed with the thought that, in virtue of being such that it 'is' only in an understanding of Being, 'the essence of man consists in his being more than merely human' (LH, p. 245). So Heidegger draws a fundamental contrast between 'man' *qua* Dasein and 'living creatures' in general. For the latter 'are as they are without standing outside their Being as such and within the truth of Being' (*ibid.*, p. 229), adding that the existence of 'man' (this 'standing outside its Being') is *not* a standing outside its essence. On the contrary, '[man] preserves in such standing the essential nature of its Being' (*ibid.*). In short, since 'man' 'is' only in an understanding of Being, to be more than merely human is of the essence of the human. On this conception, 'mere animals', apes for example, have, as it were, a wholly instrumental, or a merely relational 'openness' to the world (what Heidegger calls being 'lodged' in an environment). By contrast, even while, as Wittgenstein puts it (and I think there is no doubt that Heidegger would accept this), 'concepts . . . are the expression of our interest' (PI, §570), the openness characteristic of 'we' human beings *qua* Dasein is openness to entities within the world *in their Being*. That is, as they are 'in themselves'.

Returning this analysis to the two sentences from Mulhall's reading, we can see that they would be contradictory (or at least wholly dogmatic) if one insisted on an overly 'pragmatic' or 'anthropological' reading of Heidegger. But what we should see is that Dasein is essentially more than merely the human animal. Because 'understanding of Being is itself a definite characteristic of Dasein's Being' when entities are disclosed in relation to *Dasein's* own possibilities-for-Being, 'what' is thus disclosed just are entities as they are in themselves.

For my own part I find this conception magical, in both a positive and a negative sense. I cannot but admire, for example, a formulation like this:

Man – one being among others – 'pursues science'. In this 'pursuit' nothing less transpires than the irruption by one being called 'man' into the whole of beings, indeed in such a way that through this irruption beings break open and show what they are and how they are. The irruption that breaks open, *in its way*, helps beings above all *to themselves*.

(Heidegger, 1977, p. 95, my emphasis)

On the other hand, however, I cannot resist posing questions to the 'humanism' of this picture; to the special, essentially privileged, position it ascribes to human existence.

The question of Heideggerian humanism will be the theme of the next chapter, and I will not pursue these worries further at this point. Suffice it to say in summary that, in Heidegger's view, 'the kind of dealing which is closest to us is . . . not a bare perceptual cognition, but rather that kind of concern which manipulates things and puts them to use' (BT, p. 67); and that this everyday encounter with entities in the world gives us access to entities 'as such and in their Being'.

The world of the ready-to-hand

For Heidegger, the non-thematic, 'blind' manipulation or putting to use in which equipment is most 'primordially manifest' in its Being is not to be thought of as a mysterious or non-conscious dealing. Practical behaviour, Heidegger claims, 'has *its own* kind of sight' (*ibid.*, p. 69). But, and here we see why everydayness is constantly passed over by traditional philosophy, such sight does not denote a cognitive grasp, or, in general, the 'consciousness of an object present-at-hand'. In this section I want to explain why Heidegger rejects the idea that it is predicated upon or *founded* on such a consciousness of presence either.

If we begin with a subject/object dualism we will have to conceive practical dealings as secondary to the discovery (sensing) of entities present-at-hand, entities with such-and-such perceived properties. In Heidegger's view, this dualist conception simply cannot explain the phenomenological facts: 'No matter how sharply we just look at the "outward appearance" of Things in whatever form this takes, we cannot discover anything ready-to-hand' (*ibid.*). The basic reason for this has already been indicated, namely, that it is only within a context of involvements determined by Dasein's concern with the 'in-order-to' that an entity is manifest in its own specific character. The hammer, for example, can be manifest as what it is only in virtue of its place in a structure of internal relationships or 'involvements' which are simply not explicable in terms of spatial or temporal relations which are or could be present-at-hand.

In the work required for the making of a shoe, for example, there is a chain of interconnected spatio-temporal relations: to animals from which comes the shoe's leather; to the wood and steel which compose the hammers and tools; to the foundry where the steel was forged; to the various stages of production and design and the totality of equipment required to complete it; to the other Dasein for whom the shoe is made; and so on. But none of these relations are, as it were, 'given' with the spatial and temporal arrangement of the entities mentioned, conceived in their pure presence-at-hand. The structure of involvements is not, to use Austin's expression, something which could be manifest to 'just anyone you please', and, specifically, not something that is or could be manifest to bare perceptual cognition of an entity present-at-hand. On the contrary, according to Heidegger, the involvements which determine the Being of what is encountered within Dasein's everyday world always come back to Dasein as Being-in-the-world:

> In a workshop, for example, the totality of involvements which is constitutive for the ready-to-hand in its readiness-to-hand, is 'earlier' than any single item of equipment; so, too, for the farmstead with its utensils and outlying lands. But the totality of involvements goes back ultimately to a 'towards-which' in which there is no further involvement: this 'towards-which' is not an entity with the kind of being that belongs to what is ready-to-hand within a world; it is rather an entity whose Being is defined as Being-in-the-world, and to whose state of Being, worldhood itself belongs.
>
> (*ibid.*, p. 84)

Dasein's disclosedness

On this account, only because Dasein 'has already got itself into definite possibilities' of its own Being (*ibid.*, p. 143) can it have access to entities in their Being. It is this 'being on its way' (*ibid.*, p. 79) of Dasein which discloses or unveils or 'illuminates' entities in their Being. More precisely, the disclosure of entities within the world presupposes and is coordinate with Dasein's understanding of possibilities of its own Being-in-the-world that are 'transparent to itself' in different possible ways and degrees' (*ibid.*, p. 144). For, to the extent to which Dasein 'comports itself understandingly' towards some possibility of its own Being-in-the-world, that is, to the extent that Dasein, *as Being-in-the-world*, has 'competence' over its own 'potentiality-for-Being'[11] (*ibid.*, p. 143), entities within a world will, *at once*, be disclosed, and disclosed with coordinate intelligibility. *This is what occurs when Dasein 'is'.* Thus an entity can be manifest *as such* only in so far as it is embedded in a context of interconnected involvements 'shaped' by Dasein's 'primordial familiarity' with its own Being (*ibid.*, p. 86). Such an entity is, therefore, always and essentially, discovered *first* in its readiness-to-hand.[12]

We are now in a position to have a far clearer view of Heidegger's claim that when Dasein 'is' 'there is' always also 'an understanding of something like a "world"'. As we have seen, describing an entity in its readiness-to-hand requires that we include in its description the structure of involvements which are constitutive for it. Encountering such an entity thus presupposes a familiarity with that structure. It can, that is, only be encountered *in view* of that structure. But what is 'in view' here is not a further entity. It is, rather, that 'wherein concern always dwells' (*ibid.*, p. 72); something 'constantly sighted' when Dasein is getting something done, but not thematically, and never as an object. Indeed, perhaps the most distinctive aspect of Heidegger's analysis of Dasein's everyday world is that the 'within which' within which entities are manifest as such is not itself an entity.[13] This is the phenomenon of the 'world'.

I think the best way to summarise this conception of the 'world' is with the idea of an horizon of intelligibility or significance – 'significance' being the name that Heidegger gives to the totality of involvements which, as he puts it, 'makes up the structure of the world' (*ibid.*, p. 87). Thus Heidegger states that Dasein's *familiarity with significance* is 'constitutive for Dasein' and 'makes up' its 'understanding of Being' (*ibid.*, p. 86). Again the point is that what occurs when Dasein 'is' is 'an understanding of something like a "world"'. On this account, '"world" is not a way of characterizing those entities which Dasein essentially is not; it is rather a characteristic of Dasein itself' (*ibid.*, p. 64). In summary, Dasein is not 'an entity with the kind of being that belongs to what is ready-to-hand within a world', rather:

> it *is* in such a way as to be its 'there'. To say that it is 'illuminated' means that *as* Being-in-the-world it is cleared in itself, not through any other entity, but in such a way that it *is* itself the clearing ... *Dasein is its disclosedness.*
>
> (*ibid.*, p. 133).

The idea here is not that Dasein is always and constantly 'conscious of the world'. On the contrary, the language of 'clearing' and 'disclosedness' is intended to afford a conception of openness to the world which does not conceive that as a subject's consciousness of an entity at all. Indeed, on Heidegger's alternative to the categorial interpretation, the world cannot be conceived as an entity. Rather, as that with which Dasein is primordially familiar, it is the horizon of significance within which entities can be encountered in their Being.

On this view, the fundamental characteristic of Dasein's 'relation' to the everyday *world* (its familiarity with significance) is such that it does not *stand out* in Dasein's dealings: 'The ready-to-hand is always understood in terms of a totality of involvements ... [Such] an understanding does not stand out from the background. And this is the very mode in which it is the essential foundation for everyday circumspective interpretation' (*ibid.*, p. 150).

It should now be clear why classical humanism cannot achieve a resolution to the problem of transcendence. For 'access to the world' is not, according to Heidegger's analysis of Dasein, an epistemic, propositional or even 'conscious' (or un-conscious) 'relation' of a subject to transcendent objects at all. Thus, if Heidegger is right, the problem of transcendence is not only compelling for every Dasein, it is also essentially irresolvable. This is why the contemplative stance of traditional philosophy can never escape the sceptical threat. On the contrary, according to Heidegger, as an interminably tempting categorial objectification of Being-in-the-world, it both produces and sustains it.

SPLITTING THE PHENOMENON OF BEING-WITH

The 'who' of Dasein

As we have seen, Heidegger's view is that the traditional epistemological problematic presupposes an inappropriate categorial interpretation of Dasein's Being. It will bear stressing that this is, fundamentally, an interpretation of it as something which has the kind of Being of an entity present-at-hand. Of course, there is no suggestion that what it is to be human is then reduced to being a type of object. On the contrary, the type of entity 'man', it will be said, is distinguished by being, in each case, not simply present but present to itself: self-present.

Perhaps it will be readily acknowledged that this sort of conception is apparent in Descartes's philosophy. But Heidegger insists, and I think rightly insists, that it is not confined to Cartesian thought alone. For the first and most insistent consequence of the categorial interpretation of Dasein is not a Cartesian metaphysics of 'mental substance', but an objectifying conception of the Being of Dasein as something which is 'in each case already constantly present-at-hand, both in an for a closed realm' (*ibid.*, p. 114):

> Even if one rejects the 'soul substance' and the Thinghood of consciousness, or denies that a person is an object, one is still positing something whose Being retains the meaning of present-at-hand, whether it does explicitly or not. . . . Yet presence-at-hand is the kind of Being which belongs to entities whose character is not that of Dasein.
>
> (*ibid.*)

On such a conception, whether classically Cartesian or not, it always makes sense to ask how the entity that we are can secure and maintain a relation to what must now be described as 'outside' it. Notions such as the 'external world' presuppose an ontological understanding of our basic state of Being as constant presence-at-hand 'inside' (i.e., constant self-presence).[14] On such a conception, whether the problematic is or has been made explicit or not, our access to anything like a 'world' of entities, even entities present-at-hand, requires the transcendence of the 'subject'; somehow this 'subject' must 'come out of its inner "sphere" into one which is "other and external"' (*ibid.*, p. 60).

As we saw in Chapter 1, the problem of other minds appears, on this kind of view, to be a special case of a more general concern with the question of our knowledge of the external world; it concerns our access to a special kind of entity. Now, in an interesting movement of thought, Heidegger's analysis of Dasein also treats questions concerning the encounter with entities with the kind of Being of Dasein as secondary. More fundamental, according to Heidegger, is that we recognise that the illuminating 'who' of Dasein's everydayness simply cannot be adequately conceived in terms which presuppose the individuation of a self. That is, just as he rejects the idea of a *worldless* subject, so, too, he rejects the idea of 'an *isolated* "I" without Others' (*ibid.*, p. 116). It is with this proposal that we reach the heart of Heidegger's reframing of the problem of other minds.

As we have seen, Heidegger's view is that, by beginning with a proximally worldless subject, one's analysis necessarily forgoes achieving a phenomenologically adequate conception of the everyday world. The categorial interpretation of our Being irretrievably 'splits the phenomenon' of 'Being-in' that Dasein *is* (*ibid.*, p. 132). Heidegger's fundamental target here is our tendency to conceive Being-in-the-world in terms of the 'relation' between two entities, a 'subject' and the 'world'. What is clear is that such an approach not only relies on the idea of 'a bare subject without a world' but also on 'an isolated "I" without others'. As we shall see, it is this assumption which is the target of his elaboration of Being-in-the-world in terms of Being-with Others.

Again, this target must not be hastily identified with Cartesian thought alone. However much one insists that a person is not an object, as long as one retains the idea of a 'persisting subject' – something which 'maintains itself as something identical throughout changes in its Experiences and ways of behaviour' (*ibid.*, p. 114) – one remains within the metaphysics which 'splits the phenomenon': 'Ontologically we understand it [the subject] as something which is in each case constantly present-at-hand, both in and for a closed realm' (*ibid.*). According to Heidegger, however, if we are to achieve an adequate understanding of Being-in-the-world, 'what persists' has to be interpreted existentially, i.e. in terms of a basic 'way' of Dasein's Being-in-the-world. What, we must ask, persists through the changes in Dasein's Being-in-the-world? Against accounts which posit the constant self-presence of an isolated 'subject'-Thing, Heidegger proposes the following thesis: 'what persists pertains not to the enduring Being-present-at-hand of something [i.e., an abiding 'subject'], but rather to Dasein's kind of Being as *Being-with* [*Mitsein*]' (*ibid.*, p. 128).

This is a difficult notion to explain succinctly. The claim here is not that the disclosure of the world is a social or *inter*subjective achievement – an assumption which still presupposes subjects, only now as a related plurality. Rather, what Heidegger is insisting on is that the intelligibility of Dasein's closest everydayness is, in each case, characterised by a *constant anonymous publicness*. In the next section I will clarify this thought in order to show that Heidegger's analysis of Dasein opens the way for a fundamentally non-sceptical conception of being with others.

Being-with

One of the central features of Heidegger's reframing of the problem of other minds lies in its questioning whether being with others is a 'relation' which is, primarily, epistemological in character. That is, his analysis of the 'who' of everyday Dasein calls into question the assumption that being with others stands in need of an epistemic foundation. Such a foundation is typically sought for because it is supposed that one's claims about others are otherwise hasty and presumptuous, resting on the unproved assumption that one's experience of the behaviour of a body is a reliable guide to its mental states. Traditionally, then, it has been thought that the task of philosophy is to show how we can bridge the apparent gap between a body's 'outward' behaviour and its 'inner' goings-on. As Heidegger puts it, such a bridge would take us from one subject, which is given as present to itself, to another subject, which is otherwise 'quite closed off' (*ibid.*, p. 124). We then quickly pass to a consideration of putative bridges: arguments by analogy, or best explanation, or satisfied criteria.

Heidegger's analysis of Being-with suggests why, far from escaping the threat of scepticism, responses of this type necessarily operate in a framework which sustains it. The reason for this is that they remain committed to the same 'baleful interpretation' of human existence that motivates the threat of scepticism in the first place. Specifically, they presuppose as coherent the idea that 'others' are entities which a proximally isolated 'subject' first apprehends as behaving bodies and then somehow and subsequently discovers to be 'other subjects like oneself'. As with his response to the Kantian response to scepticism in general, Heidegger's central claim is that any attempt to recover a basis for being with others from such a point of departure comes 'too late'. Once one has defined others as being 'like oneself' in being, in each case, 'constantly present-at-hand both in and for a closed realm' they will always remain 'quite closed off'. According to Heidegger, however, this categorial interpretation is wholly inadequate and distorting; being a 'subject' is not to be conceived in terms of the 'internal' presence to itself of an isolated ego-thing. Rather:

> the 'subject' character of one's own Dasein and that of Others is to be defined existentially – that is, in terms of certain ways in which one may be. In that with which we concern ourselves environmentally the Others are encountered *as* what they *are*; they *are* what they do.
>
> (*ibid.*, p. 126)

Heidegger is here completely rejecting the traditional assumption that being a 'subject' is a matter of being an entity which possesses attributes capable of being directly manifest only 'from the inside' or in a distinctively first-personal way – in short, as a matter of its self-presence. Against this, Heidegger's suggestion is that the 'being inside' that defines our 'subject' character should be conceived in terms of our competence over 'ways in which one may be'; i.e., roughly, in terms of being an insider to ways of acting that are always 'outside' in the world and wholly manifest to others like oneself, in other words manifest to other such insiders; other entities whose basic state of Being is 'Being-outside-alongside'. On such a conception we are no longer compelled, as Austin was, to conceive 'being with *another* like oneself' in terms of the presence-at-hand of an entity which one 'believes to possess consciousness like oneself'. Rather, it is an (existential) Being-with 'those among whom one is too' (*ibid.*, p. 118).

This is a powerful response to the traditional problematic. Against accounts which begin with an isolated 'subject', Heidegger's analysis proposes that Dasein is 'in-itself, essentially Being-with' (*ibid.*, p. 120). That is, in having the kind of Being of Dasein the possibility of being with others (the possibility of determining something like a 'we') is already in place. The intention here is not to contradict the fact that 'one must always use a personal pronoun when one addresses [Dasein]' (*ibid.*, p. 42). Nor does it seek to establish that 'I' am, in fact, never alone (*ibid.*, p. 120). Rather, it aims to show why any such phenomenal Being-oneself or Being-alone presumes that the intelligibility of the 'there' of Dasein's disclosedness is constantly such that, in each case, the possibility of a 'being there too' of Others is already *necessarily* implicated in its structure:

> The 'who' [of everyday Dasein] is not this one, not that one, not oneself, not some people, and not the sum of them all. The 'who' is the neuter, the 'they' [*das Man*]. . . . *The 'they' is an existentiale; and as a primordial phenomenon, it belongs to Dasein's positive constitution.* . . . The 'they' itself prescribes that way of interpreting the world and Being-in-the-world which lies closest. Dasein is for the sake of the 'they' in an everyday manner, and the 'they' itself articulates the referential context of significance. When entities are encountered, Dasein's world frees them for a totality of involvements with which the 'they' is familiar. . . . Proximally Dasein is 'they', and for the most part remains so.
>
> (*ibid.*, pp. 126–9)

This 'who' of everyday Dasein explains the constant anonymous publicness alluded to above.[15] Dasein is such that its world is, from the start and as such, a 'with-world' [*Mitwelt*] (BT, p. 118). Again, the point is not that Dasein is 'an essentially social entity' (although we might entertain something like an 'originary sociality' to summarise the position being outlined) but that the everyday world is such that, within the world, an encounter with 'another like oneself' is, in each case, necessarily possible for Dasein. This is what Heidegger means by saying that 'Being-in is *Being-with* Others'.

As I have indicated, this analysis does not attempt to provide answers to sceptical questions. However, it does allow us to see how it can be respectable to ignore them by relieving us of the conception of our 'subject' character which sustains the problem. As Heidegger puts it, 'by "Others" we do not mean everyone else but me – those over against whom the "I" stands out. Rather, they are those from whom, for the most part, one does not distinguish oneself – those among whom one is too' (*ibid.*). Thus, on Heidegger's alternative conception, as far as being with Others (being with those who have Dasein as their kind of Being) is concerned, the threat of scepticism simply cannot arise. For Dasein to take up some possibility of its own Being is, *eo ipso*, to disclose a world whose intelligibility is such that the possibility of Others being 'there too and there with it' is part of its essential structure (*ibid.*).

CONCLUSION

In the previous chapter, the work of J. L. Austin was examined with the aim of showing how his linguistic phenomenology attempts to reframe the problem of other minds. The examination focused on his pursuit of the question as to what leads us to hesitations beyond the ordinary. Austin's account highlights how certain 'habits of *Gleichschaltung*' distort the understanding that we already have which is embodied in ordinary language. It was then shown how Austin's own approach itself succumbs to these distortions. In this chapter, through an examination of Heidegger's approach, it has been suggested that the real 'bugbear' underlying the problem of other minds is not, as Austin argues, the institutional prejudice that knowledge requires incorrigible foundations, but the conception of our 'subject' character, the metaphysics of the subject, which calls for such foundations in the first place.

So, with this diagnosis, has Heidegger done it? Is being with others now secure from the threat of scepticism? In a certain sense the answer has to be 'yes'. However, while I think that Derrida is thus right to suggest that 'scepticism and everything that is systematic with it' cannot be articulated within the terms of analysis in *Being and Time*, I do not think that this precludes the possibility that a related problem of a different order lurks in its pages. In the next chapter I will pursue this thought as we allow on stage the entity which, so far, has been, for the most part, hibernating in the footnotes: the animal.

4

THE HUMAN ANIMAL

INTRODUCTION

In the previous chapter, Heidegger's analysis of Dasein was contrasted with what, following Heidegger, I have called 'humanist' conceptions of 'man'. As we saw, according to Heidegger, humanism conceives 'man' primarily as a kind of entity present in the world alongside others and only then supplies it with a distinctive trait. Humanism thus rejects the baldly naturalistic assumption that 'the essence of man consists in being an animal organism' but proposes that 'this insufficient definition of man's essence [can] be overcome or offset by outfitting man with an immortal soul' or by 'adjoining a soul to the human body, a mind to the soul'. Heidegger's thesis is that, in modern philosophy, where consciousness is the point of departure, humanism remains the background conception.

The kind of relationship between modern philosophy and humanism which interests Heidegger is clearly exemplified by Sartre in his popular (and, it should be mentioned, later disowned) lecture published as *Existentialism and Humanism*: 'At the point of departure [in philosophy] there cannot be any other truth than this, *I think, therefore I am*, which is the absolute truth of consciousness as it attains to itself ... This theory alone is compatible with the dignity of man' (Sartre, 1948, p. 44). By the 'dignity of man' Sartre means that in virtue of which 'man' is 'greater' than all other entities. Unlike human beings, other kinds of entity merely are. They are present but they do not 'attain' to themselves; they are not given to themselves as something present. Moreover, for Sartre, it is only on the basis of the presence-to-itself of human existence that other entities can be present at all. That is, in so far as entities are present, the 'consciousness of man' is what is constantly there, present and present-to-itself throughout all changes. It is this conception of human existence which underlies Sartre's anthropocentric conclusion that 'there is no other universe except the human universe, the universe of human subjectivity' (*ibid.*, p. 55; see also p. 33).

It is important to note that the exclusive character of this conclusion depends upon the cogency of drawing a *fundamental* or *absolute* contrast between 'man' as the possessor of a subjective life, and every other kind of entity. Sartre lists stones, tables, moss, fungus and cauliflowers (*ibid.*, p. 28). It is perhaps surprising that he does not mention animals here. While he conceives man as one (special) kind of entity in contrast to others, he does not ask whether snakes, lions or even apes possess a subjective life. Heidegger's thesis on humanism and modern philosophy suggests that this fact does not so much as hide a problem as highlight a matter-of-course orientation. In common with the traditions of thinking about the 'dignity of man' that he wants to criticise (specifically, the Christian and naturalist traditions), Sartre's conception is marked by an unexamined humanism; its commitment to an interpretation of 'man' as that kind of entity which is essentially more than a mere living thing. Indeed, when human existence is conceived from subjectivity, the special 'dignity of man' is awesome: as the centre and origin of the presence of entities, man is elevated to being, as Heidegger puts it, 'the lord of entities' (LH, p. 245).

As we saw in the previous chapter, Heidegger's thesis founds a rich and powerful critique of the sceptical consequences of the modern metaphysics of the subject. However, in this chapter I hope to show that his own position remains stubbornly and problematically humanist. There is what Derrida calls a 'magnetic attraction' between Heidegger's analysis of Dasein and the humanism of the traditional metaphysics (Derrida, 1982, p. 124). The claim here is not that Heidegger, too, 'thinks of man on the basis of *animalitas*'. Rather, it is that Heidegger shares the classical humanist's dogmatic and idealising tendency to conceive humanity by way of essential contrast to animality. In short, the claim is that Heidegger does not pursue the critique of humanism *far enough*: the humanist background to be dislodged remains largely in place.

This claim will be explored by investigating the limits of Heidegger's analysis and delimitation of Being-with [*Mitsein*]. I will argue that his analysis, while relieving us of the traditional problem of other minds, still retains certain essential and essentially idealising traits of classical conceptions of the human subject. I will explain how this retention is a function of a humanist account of human existence, an account which separates the essence of humanity from animal nature. I conclude by suggesting how a satisfactory conception of human and animal existence can be developed in a more smoothly naturalistic way.

THE BEING OF ANIMALS

The limits of Heidegger's reframing

In the last chapter we saw that Heidegger's analysis of Dasein does not attempt to provide answers to sceptical questions. However, it does allow us to see how it can be respectable to ignore them by relieving us of the conception of our 'subject' character which sustains the problem. As Heidegger puts it, 'by "Others" we do not mean everyone else but me – those over against whom the "I" stands out. Rather, they are those from whom, for the most part, one does not distinguish oneself – those among whom one is too' (BT, p. 118). Thus, on

Heidegger's alternative conception, *as far as being with other Dasein is concerned*, the threat of scepticism simply cannot arise.

As I have indicated, this conclusion explains why Derrida's assertion about the anti-sceptical character of Heidegger's thought, quoted in the previous chapter, is broadly correct. However, we are now also in a position to see why, taken in isolation, it overstates Heidegger's distance from the tradition against which he recoils. The issue to be focused on can be identified through the restriction or limit I highlighted in summarising Heidegger's relieving alternative; the idea that the threat of scepticism cannot arise 'as far as being with other Dasein is concerned'.

The claim is that this restriction evidences a general and stubbornly unrevisable feature of Heidegger's thought, namely, its retention of the basic traits of classical humanism. In this section I will prepare the ground for a demonstration of this claim through a clarification of the relationship between Heidegger's conception of Dasein and traditional conceptions of the human subject.

Heidegger's criticism of the traditional (broadly Cartesian or Cartesian-inspired) conception of what it is to be human can be summarised in terms of the way in which it challenges two of its central assumptions. First, it challenges the assumption that 'the world' is something blankly external to human subjectivity; and second, it challenges the assumption that the behaviour of a living human being is merely the outward effect of its inward or mental goings-on. One of the most compelling features of Heidegger's work is that it tackles these twin assumptions with a single line of thought, namely, with the thought that the kind of Being-in-the-world that we *are* is world-disclosing. With this thought secured, we can say both that 'Being outside alongside' objects in the world is our basic state, and that 'we are what we do'.

This thought may be compelling, but how are we to secure it from the distortions and confusions which beset traditional interpretations of our existence? Heidegger's strategy is to orient his inquiry towards that way of Being-in-the-world with which we are already familiar; that way of being-in-the-world which, as he puts it, is 'closest to Dasein' (BT, p. 66): 'Dasein's everydayness' (*ibid.*, p. 43). Now, as we have see, everydayness is precisely not a context in which an isolated subject has an intentional consciousness of some object present-at-hand. Rather, it is that way of everyday Being-in-the-world which is open to a world of objects in the mode that he calls readiness-to-hand. And Heidegger's suggestion is that because we, *qua* Dasein, are in a fundamental sense already at home in the world of the ready-to-hand, everydayness is something to which we can, in principle, attest without prejudice or distortion.

The significant feature of Heidegger's analysis of the world of the ready-to-hand lies in its contrast to approaches in which human existence is conceived in terms of constant self-presence. Thus, rather than begin with a self-present 'subject' related in some way to undiscriminated 'objects', Heidegger emphasises that, in Dasein's everydayness, entities are typically disclosed *as* the very things that, in their Being, they are. Heidegger presents this point in the following way:

> In dealing with what is environmentally ready-to-hand . . . we 'see' it *as* a table, a door, a carriage, or a bridge. . . . Any mere pre-predicative seeing of the ready-to-hand is, in itself, something which already understands. . . . When we merely stare at something, our just-having-it-before-us lies before us as *a failure to understand it anymore*. This grasping which is free of the 'as', is a privation of the kind of seeing in which one merely understands. It is not more primordial than that kind of seeing, but is derived from it.
>
> (*ibid.*, p. 149)

In everydayness we have immediate access to entities in the world *as such*. Or again, what is first disclosed in everydayness is already saturated with significance. Indeed, even the most 'alien world' is, in so far as it is a world at all, an 'in which' in which Dasein 'knows its way about' (*ibid.*, p. 356). And, as the passage just quoted indicates, only a being which is capable of such access to a world can be deprived of it: non-seeing-as, seeing-without-understanding 'is not more primordial than that kind of seeing, but is derived from it'.

In its opposition to views which posit a level of pre-conceptual experience or a non-conceptual experiential 'given', this observation is, surely, phenomenologically acute. However, there is a feature of Heidegger's account which is troubling, and that is its commitment to the view that what can be said of human beings in this regard *cannot* be said of other animals. That is, on Heidegger's account, only an entity that has Dasein as its kind of Being, and thus 'as far as our experience shows' only human beings, have access to 'the world *as* world' (LH, p. 228).[1]

It is important to note that Heidegger does not support his claim about the uniqueness of human beings with reference to empirico-biological facts, or even to his own studies of animal behaviour. As we shall see, for Heidegger, as for Sartre, there is an implicit and *a priori* assumption that non-human animals, along with stones and plants, are, in some way, *absolutely* deprived of the kind of 'sight', and hence also of the kind of 'world', that belongs to Dasein.

The problems with Sartre's anthropocentric conclusion can be identified with his adherence to a traditional and broadly Cartesian conception of subjectivity. And I have accepted that these problems cannot arise for the Heideggerian analysis of Dasein. It is equally true, however, that Heidegger's overcoming of that conception involves a kind of appropriation or internalisation of 'the world' into Dasein which is itself problematic. For Heidegger, 'the world' as such is not blankly external to Dasein. Indeed, there is no world *as such* outside of Dasein. This position outlines what might be called a quasi-transcendental idealism: it is not a question of identifying the contents of the walled garden of an individual or collective subjectivity as 'the world' – man as the 'lord of entities' – but the world-disclosing ecstatic existence ('ek-sistence') of Dasein – man as the 'shepherd of Being' (LH, p. 245).

Heidegger does not attempt to cover over this relationship to idealism.

Indeed, he explicitly affirms that 'idealism is the only correct possibility for a philosophical problematic' *in so far as* idealism amounts to the view that 'Reality is possible only in the understanding of Being' (BT, pp. 207–8). Of course, this 'in so far as' must not be ignored. There is no doubt that the Heideggerian re-evaluation of man as that which 'occurs essentially in such a way that he is . . . the clearing of Being' (LH, p. 229) is utterly opposed to any attempt to say that reality is 'in consciousness' or is 'ultimately subjective'.[2] Moreover, Heidegger explicitly denies that the being as it is of 'the Real' (in contrast to 'Reality') is dependent on entities with Dasein's kind of Being (BT, p. 212). So Heidegger's position must not be equated to classical idealism or subjectivism; Dasein is not the human subject of traditional philosophy. Nevertheless, his characterisation of Dasein's essential trait – 'standing freely in the clearing of Being which alone is "world"' (LH, p. 230) – still represents the 'world' as pertaining essentially to the Being of Dasein. For Heidegger it is only because Dasein has already got itself into definite possibilities of its *own* Being that it can 'have a world' at all (BT, p. 84 and p. 143). That is, as we have seen, '"world" is not a way of character-izing those entities which Dasein essentially is not; it is rather a characteristic of Dasein itself' (*ibid.*, p. 64). Or, as he puts it elsewhere, 'even in this "being-outside" alongside the object, Dasein is still "inside"' (*ibid.*, p. 62). Thus, as Heidegger in fact later acknowledges, Dasein is determined *in a certain way* as the '*solus ipse*' (*ibid.*, p. 188). For these reasons it seems right to suppose, as Derrida suggests, that 'Dasein comes to occupy . . . the place of the "subject", the *cogito* or the classical "Ich denke". From these it retains certain essential traits' (Derrida, 1991, p. 98).

Heidegger calls his conception 'existential "solipsism"' (BT, p. 188). But he stresses that, since it concerns Dasein as Being-in-the-world, 'in an extreme sense what it does is precisely to bring Dasein face to face with its world *as* world' (*ibid.*). That is, like the 'solipsism' of Wittgenstein's *Tractatus*, it is intended to 'coincide with pure realism' (TLP, 5.64). The crucial question is whether this is really the result. Does not the fact that Dasein is at least formally equivalent to a transcendental subject threaten to install an idealised representation of humanity within an account which aims to eschew metaphysics? For, while Heidegger's conception aims to arrest the movement towards idealisation by bringing 'Dasein face to face with its world *as* world', it is not clear that this is actually effected without relying on gestures that are dogmatic and distorting. I think that this suspicion is well founded, and in the next section I will explain why.

The question of animality

In this section I hope to explain why the founding concepts of *Being and Time* articulate a conception of humanity which cannot but prevent his account from 'co-inciding with pure realism'. What we need to see is that Heidegger's recoil from classical humanism merely proposes an alteration of detail within the clas-sical humanist's framework. Within that framework it is not a matter of according humanity *some* differences to animals but of marking an absolute oppositional limit. The claim is that Heidegger's existential 'solipsism' remains within this framework because it continues to think 'the essence of man' through its *absolute* distinction from merely animal life. I should stress that my primary concern here is not merely that Heidegger's analysis fails to do justice to the existence of other animals, or even of our relation to other animals, but rather that, like the classical humanism against which it recoils, it presents an idealised determination of a living human being.

Heidegger does not engage with the question of animality in *Being and Time*. However, an interpretation of animality is advanced in a lecture course given in the winter semester of 1929–30 in Freiburg, entitled *The Fundamental Concepts of Metaphysics*. The lectures divide into two major parts. The first explores boredom [*Langeweile*] as a founding mood of Dasein; the second takes up the path which, in *Being and Time*, leads to the issue of a radically individualising anticipation of death: the path towards an analysis of the world of Dasein in its connection with finitude and individuation (FCM, p. 169).

But what is the 'world' of Dasein? While this is the ostensible topic of the second part, Heidegger's discussion is largely oriented towards a reply to the question of the essence of life in general.[3] Employing a method which is also central to the procedure of *Being and Time*, the analysis is pursued through a 'comparative examination' of the sense of 'having a world' in relation to three 'realms' or kinds of beings: the stone (material object), the animal, and man (*ibid.*, p. 177).[4]

Heidegger's analysis is, in crucial respects, continuous with the critique of humanist anthropology which begins in *Being and Time*. Just as the latter text had subjected anthropology, as an ontical science, to the ontological clarification of Dasein's Being, so, in the 1929–30 lectures, Heidegger argues that the biological and zoological sciences presuppose, but do not exhibit, an ontological determination of 'life' (*ibid.*, p. 188). The question remains, however, whether Heidegger's 'statements of essence' (*ibid.*, p. 186) actually escape the ambit of the humanism he opposes. In what follows I will explore Heidegger's 'comparative analysis' solely with a view to clarifying this issue.

The first example entity, the stone, is described as '*weltlos*' or 'without world' (*ibid.*, p. 177). This is the pure and simple absence of any access to entities: the stone has no experience, no world. One cannot even say of a stone that it is indifferent to Being without being anthropomorphic. As Heidegger puts it in *Being and Time*, it is 'neither indifferent nor not indifferent to Being' (BT, p. 42). The being-without-world of the stone is absolute.

Turning briefly to the third example, human beings, Heidegger's analysis offers a diametrically opposed account. The human being is characterised as '*weltbildend*' (FCM, p. 177), a term that can be translated either as 'world-forming' or 'world-picturing' and has aspects of both. This term indicates that the human being not only has access to entities and thus 'has' a world but that it has access to entities as such and in their Being. Such access is the openness characteristic of Dasein outlined in the previous chapter and sketched again in the previous section: *we* 'see' the objects that we encounter *as* the things that, in their Being, they are; *as* a table, a door, a carriage, or a bridge, and so on. They are disclosed with the '*as such*' of an intrinsic and non-inferential intelligibility.

Before passing on, it is important to note that, for Heidegger, this capacity of a human being to grasp something *as* something is not due to its possession of a language such that it can name things as this or that. Rather the reverse: that the phenomenon of language is possible for human beings is explained because the kind of Being-in-the-world that it *is* is open to entities in the mode of something *as* something. Thus, Heidegger insists that when this *Weltverstehen* or world-understanding is made explicit in a language, 'we do not, so to speak, throw a "signification" over some naked thing which is present-at-hand', rather, 'when something within-the-world is encountered *as such* the thing in question already has an involvement which is disclosed in our understanding of the world' (BT, p. 150).

For Heidegger it is the *absolute* absence of the possibility of an encounter with an entity in this manner that marks the peculiar 'privation' which characterises animal existence. That, according to Heidegger, 'they lack language' (LH, p. 230) does not *explain* why animals are thus deprived; but it is still taken to be decisive (as it were criterially) in demarcating the distinction between humanity and animality. In the 1929–30 lectures Heidegger registers this (ontological) distinction by describing the second example, the animal, as being '*weltarm*' or 'poor in world' (FCM, p. 177).

As Derrida notes in his reading of Heidegger's lecture, this determination of the second example is 'median in character': it is 'the animal *between* the thing and the human' (OS, p. 57). That is, 'the animal' is defined by double contrast to 'the stone' and 'human beings', the latter pair themselves being defined as polar opposites. In contrast to the stone, the animal is not absolutely without access to entities, and in this sense it can be said to have a world. However, in comparison to human beings the animal is impoverished: its mode of *having a world* is in the form of *not having a world as such*. This determination of animality is not a simple contradiction. The animal 'has' a world to be deprived of which the stone does not, it has access to entities, but it does not have the kind of *Weltverstehen* which characterises the Being-in-the-world that belongs to human beings. Consequently the privation at issue in the case of the animal cannot be equated to the 'privation of the kind of seeing in which one merely understands' that we are capable of: it is not that the animal has a non-conceptual or merely sensory access to entities, it has an altogether *other* relationship.

In the 1929–30 lectures Heidegger explains this peculiar relationship in terms of the way in which the 'circle' of biological drives which supposedly characterise an animal organism is 'disinhibited' by external factors (FCM, p. 255).[5] This idea is glossed in 'The Letter on Humanism', where the openness characteristic of the animal is conceived, as I indicated in the previous chapter, as a matter of being 'lodged' in an environment (LH, p. 230). As such, animals 'are as they are without standing outside their Being as such and within the Truth of Being' (*ibid.*). And Heidegger is insistent that this means they are 'separated from our ek-sistent essence by an abyss' (*ibid.*). In short, for Heidegger,

> the animal can have a world because it has access to entities, but it is deprived of a world because it does not have access to entities *as such* and in their Being. . . . The lizard on the rock in the sun does not relate to the rock and the sun as such . . . And yet, however little we can identify with the lizard, we know that it has a relationship with the sun – and with the stone, which itself has none, neither with the sun nor with the lizard.
>
> (OS, pp. 51–2)

Derrida advances three related objections to this account. First, that it massively underestimates the innumerable structural differences that in fact separate one species of animal from another. That is, it assumes that 'animality' is 'one thing', that there is 'one homogeneous type of entity, which is called animality in general' (*ibid.*, p. 57). In my view, the importance of this objection is that it highlights the extent to which Heidegger's analysis passes over the possibility that different animals can be, in different respects, 'another like myself'. But having enclosed animality in general within the sphere of organico-biological drives, Heidegger forecloses an investigation of such resemblances beyond a cursory and grudging acknowledgement of our 'abysmal bodily kinship with the beast' (LH, p. 230).

This line of criticism is developed in Derrida's second objection, namely, that a distinctive 'original *Mitsein*' between a human being and non-human animals 'is not seriously envisaged' by Heidegger (OS, p. 57). Indeed, as Derrida continues, 'one cannot think it or talk of it in terms of . . . the concepts which structure the existential analytic of *Being and Time*' (*ibid.*). I will return to this objection in a moment.

These two objections feed a third objection to Heidegger's account of animal existence, namely, that the vocabulary of privation which informs it 'cannot avoid a certain anthropocentric or even humanist teleology' (*ibid.*, p. 55). The claim here is that, 'whether one wishes to avoid this or not, the words "poverty" and "privation" imply hierarchy and evaluation' (*ibid.*, p. 56).

As I hope to show, it is this feature of Heidegger's approach which destroys his claim to provide an analysis of human existence that avoids the distortions of the more traditional metaphysics of the subject. Against such a reading, however, it might be suggested that the unsatisfactory aspects of Heidegger's account of animality can be dismissed as a marginal problem to be rectified by a more 'enlightened' Heideggerian. For example, Theodore Schatzki claims that Heidegger has simply imported 'the biology of his day' into his account of animality, and 'a more contemporary view' that explicitly acknowledges certain analogies and resemblances between human beings and other animals can replace it without affecting the basic structure of the existential analytic (Schatzki, 1992, p. 83).

As Derrida's second objection indicates, however, the problem of 'the animal' actually arises from the conceptuality that informs the 'basic structure' of Heidegger's account. Derrida glosses this with the claim that the animal must receive the *a priori* determination of being *weltarm* because Heidegger has left 'no category of original existence for it' (OS, p. 57). This way of making the second objection is not helpful. As we saw in the previous chapter, it is true that the text of *Being and Time* only specifies a distinction between existential and categorial 'characters of Being', the latter being a blanket term for the 'characteristics of Being for entities whose character is *not* that of Dasein' (BT, p. 44). And Derrida is obviously right to insist that, for Heidegger, the animal 'is evidently not a *Dasein*, nor is it *Vorhandensein* or *Zuhandensein*' (OS, p. 57). But the problem with Heidegger's account would not be removed by adding an additional category. For the crucial point is not that the existential/categorial distinction fails to make space for the Being of animals. The problem is not that Heidegger's distinction is exhaustive; rather, the problem is that he requires us to make it so 'sharply' (BT, p. 44). For, by delimiting Dasein through such a sharp distinction from any 'entity whose character is not that of Dasein', one is already conferring on the unique exemplar, human beings, a special status; one which is essentially, indeed ontologically, something more than a living thing. In short, it is not the absence of a place for the animal that is so problematic about Heidegger's basic concepts but the unexamined privilege conferred on human beings that they entail. In particular, they re-impose the humanist dogma that, despite our 'bodily kinship', we are separated from other animals 'by an abyss'.

It is at this point that we reach what I have called the stubbornly unrevisable feature of Heidegger's analysis. Heidegger treats his distinction between Dasein and (any) entities whose character of Being is not that of Dasein as marking a distinction of absolute rigour. And the result is that animality and humanity are excluded *a priori* from anything like a *Mitsein*. The residual notion of 'bodily kinship' cannot rescue the account either. For, given the restriction or limit of *Mitsein* to human Dasein, an animal *cannot* be included in a circle of a 'we', cannot be included, even in a distinctive way, with those 'among whom one is too'. In short, and *pace* Schatzki, the difficulties Heidegger faces in his treatment of animality cannot be revised without recasting the existential analytic as a whole.

It can now be seen that Heidegger's conception of Dasein, while avoiding the sceptical threat of the traditional metaphysics of the subject, does not fully displace that metaphysics. On the contrary, in the guise of an account which claims to surpass the humanism of this tradition, the conceptuality of *Being and Time* transpires to re-impose it. Thus, as Derrida rightly notes, while it would be wrong 'to imprison all of Heidegger's text in a closure that this text has delimited better than any other' [i.e. classical humanism] the basic conceptual machinery of *Being and Time* remains 'a kind of reevaluation or revalorization of the essence of the dignity of man' (Derrida, 1982, p. 123 and p. 128). Indeed, Heidegger's recoil from classical humanism is a stance which criticises the traditional metaphysics of the subject not because it sets man *too high* but, in Heidegger's words, because it fails to 'set the *humanitas* of man high enough' (LH, pp. 233–4). For Heidegger, that is to say, 'man' as the *animal rationale*, as *homo animalis*, still remains *too much* of an animal.

On Heidegger's account, then, the world *as* world, the world *as such*, is essentially the world of humanity, a world which must be absolutely distinguished from the world of animality. The idea of something which is manifest *as* something but which is not manifest to Dasein is, for Heidegger, inconceivable; the dumb animal is 'separated from our ek-sistent essence by an abyss', and thus, access to the incomparable 'as such' belongs contingently but essentially to human beings alone.

As I have indicated, my view is that this means that Heidegger's existential analytic distorts the very facts it aims to describe without prejudice. Such an approach is distorting not just because it fails to do justice to the existence of animals but, first of all, because it presents as descriptive a determination of a living human being that is compromised by a humanism that is, I will argue, idealising in its inception. 'Man', for Heidegger, remains the entity that is absolutely privileged: the centre of the 'being there' of the world *as* world.

On this reading, the Heideggerian conception of everydayness remains, in a certain way, a repetition of the classical idealist and subjectivist idea of the *lumen naturale*. The sight of man remains a privileged and completely closed horizon of intelligibility. Thus, even while Heidegger bitterly opposes Sartre's classical conception of subjectivity, he agrees in principle with the Sartrean thesis that 'there is no other universe except the human universe, the universe of human subjectivity'. To the question 'Why is there something present and not darkness, nothing?', Heidegger answers, with the tradition he also wants to criticise: Because our distinctive way of Being-in-the-world, uniquely, illuminates entities as such and in their Being.

Is there an alternative to this picture? In what follows, I want to make a start in this regard by considering what at first sight appears to be an analogous position to Heidegger's defended in the later work of Wittgenstein.

THE SPIRIT OF THE LION

Wittgenstein's lion

Various features of the later work of Wittgenstein suggest that he supposes that something like a 'humanist teleology' is actually internal to the logic of conceptuality itself.[6] In Wittgenstein's view, conceptual forms are grounded in 'forms of life' which must be 'accepted' as a kind of 'given' (PI, p. 226). Add to this the thought that the forms of life that belong to other animals are incommensurable with our own, and it becomes clear that, for Wittgenstein, the conceptual intelligibility that characterises human openness presents just the kind of 'closed horizon' I have identified in Heidegger's analytic of Dasein. The 'spirit of a lion', for example, is absolutely opaque to us: 'If a lion could talk we could not understand him' (*ibid.*, p. 223).

On the other hand, however, given Wittgenstein's insistence on 'family resemblances', there is no reason to assume that what it is, on his view, to be 'another like myself' must be defined with regard to only one feature or only one respect. Indeed, it is characteristic of Wittgenstein's later work that it often exploits such resemblances; appealing to the perspicuous patterns of animal life in order to shed light on the inconspicuous 'depth grammar' of human language-games. In short, for the later Wittgenstein, humanity and animality are not absolutely distinguished from each other: the human being is itself a living thing, not something essentially different from other living things as the humanist insists.

Nevertheless, while Wittgenstein resists the assumption that animals form an homogeneous set which must be absolutely distinguished from human beings, he does accept that a human being's understanding of the lives of non-human living things is distinctively limited. Indeed, he stresses a difference of *order* in the 'opacity of the other' that a human being can encounter in its respective relations with other human beings and other animals:

One human being can be a complete enigma to another. We learn this when we come into a strange country with entirely strange traditions; and what is more, even given a mastery of the country's language. We *do not* understand the people. (And not because of not knowing what they are saying to themselves.) We cannot find our feet with them.

If a lion could talk, we *could not* understand him.

(*ibid.*, my emphasis)

The life of a lion, it seems, is just *too different* from a human life for there to be the kind of 'transparency' (*ibid.*) that one human being can present to another human being.

Again, however, this conception is not humanist in character. This can be seen by comparing Wittgenstein's later views with the extreme and extremely traditional humanism of his youth. In contrast even to Heidegger's conception of animality as so radically 'other' that all but 'bodily kinship' is ruled out, according to the early Wittgenstein the spirit of the lion is really one's own spirit: 'Only remember that the spirit of the lion is your spirit. For it is only from yourself that you are acquainted with spirit at all' (NB, p. 85). I have already noted a connection between Heidegger's 'existential "solipsism"' and Wittgenstein's early realism. In both cases these positions are fundamentally connected to an insistent humanism.[7] In fundamental contrast to his early humanism, however, it seems to me that one of the outstanding features of Wittgenstein's later 'naturalism' is its willingness to acknowledge a *non-appropriating* openness to 'the spirit' of many

71

other living things. This acknowledgement does not contradict the intuitive thought that the spirit of the lion is *not* one's own spirit. On the contrary, the intuitive thought presupposes such acknowledgement. That is, it is only because 'the spirit of the lion' is *already* manifest *as such* (i.e. as a radically other spirit) that 'the spirit of the human' can attest to the fact that 'if a lion could talk I could not understand it'.[8] At issue here is not, of course, the *Mitsein* of human Dasein envisaged by Heidegger. But it does perhaps allow for a variety of cases of an 'original *Mitsein*' of the human and non-human; something simply unenvisagable in the analytic of Dasein. (Opening parentheses, it is worth mentioning here that John McDowell – whose conception of animals is (in virtue of its debt to Gadamer) strongly Heideggerian – is happy to acknowledge that 'in some respects' human and animal lives 'simply match' (McDowell, 1994b, p. 183). McDowell does not give any examples, but I imagine that what is in question here will circulate around the sort of thing that Heidegger refers to as our 'bodily kinship' with the beast. Perhaps surprisingly, I feel somewhat uncomfortable accepting the idea of 'simply matching'. I am inclined to think that no animal expression is just like that 'the same' as a human one. There is a kind of 'near/far' dimension to this which the concept of 'match' does not capture. In my view, or at least, in my experience, it is precisely when animals are *most* like humans that they are most *uncanny*. And they are so in virtue of not *simply* and not *quite* matching; that is, in virtue of *so closely* resembling humans while *remaining* cats or apes or whatever, and so, in another way, still being *very distant* indeed. What I want to say is: The human is open here to an other which it simply cannot fully appropriate into 'the same'. And I also want to say: In their own ways many other animals are, in their relations with humans, 'the same too', uncannily.)

The phenomenon of language

What, however, of the enigmatic 'as such' with which the lion's alterity is manifest? Is this not still, essentially, something manifest in the world informed by human conceptuality, and hence, essentially, by 'our spirit'?

It is, I think, very hard to get things right here. Even if we accept that the concept of others is, in the way I have suggested, a vague one, such an affirmation need not prevent an idealised picture of human conceptuality from imposing itself that slides one's account into humanist confusion. The following response to the more tolerant position might still seem deeply plausible: 'But surely there is at least one aspect of human life which is peculiar to us alone: the capacity or power to use a language. Are we not absolutely distinguished from mere animals through our possession of the *logos*? And doesn't this distinctive difference mark the special dignity of man? For what is the world without man?' (Cp. 'Though the ether is filled with vibrations the world is dark. But one day man opens his seeing eye, and there is light' (PI, p. 184).)

In a remark from the early paragraphs of the *Investigations* Wittgenstein calls into question this certainty at the heart of humanist metaphysics:

> It is sometimes said that animals do not talk because they lack the mental capacity. And this means: 'they do not think, and that is why they do not talk.' But – they simply do not talk. Or to put it better: they do not use language – if we except the most primitive forms of language. – Commanding, questioning, recounting, chatting, are as much a part of our natural history as walking, eating, drinking, playing.
>
> (*ibid.*, §25)

The supplementary qualification to the 'better' formulation should be stressed. *If we are to maintain anything like the traditional humanist assumption that 'only man is endowed with the "logos"'* (mental capacity, understanding, rationality, access to the 'as such', etc.) which makes language possible, then we will have to *exclude* the primitive forms of language and of communication which are *in fact* exhibited in the lives of other animals. And where is the rigour in that exclusion? The implication of Wittgenstein's remark is that language is not essentially or uniquely human (or is so only if we except . . .). Hence even the fact of human language cannot be appealed to in order to establish a sharp break or pure cut between humanity and animality – and only such a cut could support the idea of a privileged and closed horizon of intelligibility.

In the interview published as 'Eating Well', having just risked the provocative suggestion that 'it is perhaps more "dignified" of humanity to maintain a certain inhumanity', Derrida makes a remarkably similar point:

> The idea according to which man is the only speaking being, in its traditional form or in its Heideggerian form, seems to me at once unplaceable [i.e. has no determinate historical origin] and highly problematic. Of course, if one defines language in such a way that it is reserved for what we call man, what is there to say? . . . But I would contest [the view] that [the conditions of possibility of a language] give rise to a single linear, indivisible, oppositional limit, to a binary opposition between the human and the non-human.
>
> (Derrida, 1991, pp. 116–17)

In my view, this line of thought opens the way for a fundamental reassessment of the humanist desire to completely appropriate and contain 'the world as such', including the 'spirit' of other animals in that world, within an horizon of significance or intelligibility which is contingently but *essentially* human. Indeed, it suggests that this desire is destroyed by the very phenomenon which invites it: our language. As Derrida puts it: 'Human language, as original as it might be, does not allow us to "cut" once and for all where we would in general like to cut' (*ibid.*, p. 117).

Such an approach does not deny the specificity or distinctive 'originality' to the forms of life that belong to different living things. But I think Derrida is right to insist that these distinctive differences are misconceived if they are construed, as Heidegger does, such that it is 'always a matter of marking an absolute limit' between human beings and other animals (Derrida, 1987a, p. 54).

And now the Heideggerian restriction or limit to *Mitsein* identified in the last chapter looks unacceptably and unnecessarily dogmatic. We need to question the ancient assumption that accounting for what is distinctive in human life must lead us away from our natural, animal history, as if our '*humanitas*' places us with one foot or even both feet outside nature. Not only are there respects in which the lives of human beings have uncanny (if not 'matching') parallels in the lives of other animals, but even the existence of human language cannot be adduced to support the idea of a radical gulf or 'abyss' between humanity and animality. And hence, the attempt to position humanity as the centre of an absolutely privileged and closed horizon of intelligibility cannot be sustained. Humanism, one might say, has lost itself in its first utterances, being already defeated by the phenomenon of human language.

What, then, of Heidegger's recoil from classical humanism? It should be clear that that recoil is characterised by a claim which, when taken *au pied de la lettre*, exactly contradicts the position I want to defend, namely, his claim that the classical humanist is *insufficiently* anti-naturalistic, that the 'rational animal' remains *too much* an animal. Heidegger's basis for this claim is his view that a human body is quite other than an 'organic thing' which occurs in the world and which turns out to be (in a more or less mysterious way) the point of occupancy for a subjectivity or personality. It will bear stressing that I think that Heidegger's argument against classical humanism on this point is profoundly correct and important. What seems quite wrong to me, however, is that we should see it as posing a challenge to our thinking about human beings alone. We have to rethink what it is to be an animal. And rethink this, not 'as well', but, and now including human beings, *simpliciter*.

What, I submit, is essential is to re-evaluate the baldly naturalistic assumption, rejected by both classical and Heideggerian humanism, that 'the essence of man consists in being an animal organism'. Such a re-evaluation would have to target the idea that the sub-personal (or, say, sub-canine) accounts offered by the sciences in this area exhaust what can sensibly be said of the life of an *animal*; as if *everything* that we say about animals and the behaviour of animals must 'ultimately' have a naturalistic explanation; as if, for example, all attribution of psychological states to the behaviour of living things is just a ('folk') way of talking and not a response to the facts.[9] For it is precisely when we do conceive an animal organism, and animality in general, in a baldly naturalistic way that, especially when it comes to considerations about human beings and the use of language, the humanist's supplement, whether in its classical or Heideggerian form, seems almost unavoidable, and in its distinctively 'subject'-centred form makes the problem of other minds irresistible. But, freed from this narrow conception of animality, we will not find it problematic to reject the humanist assumption that human life is separated from animal nature by an 'abyss'. As before, we will reject conceptions of human behaviour which reduce it to the complex workings of an anatomical apparatus. But this will no longer force us to conceive even our most distinctive form of behaviour, our use of language, as separate from (or as separating us from) the life of an animal. For we are no longer forced to conceive all *non-human* animal behaviour as reducible to the complex workings of an anatomical apparatus either. Thus, on this view, human life can be comfortably acknowledged as being itself a manifestation of animal nature; relatively distinctive no doubt, but not absolutely so.

This conception does not ignore the differences between human beings and other animals. And it certainly does not wish to give an inch to the scientism of bald naturalism. But it is smoothly naturalistic.[10] And, if, for this reason, it allows us to lift the Heideggerian restriction of *Mitsein* to entities with Dasein's character of being, then it may also make it possible to affirm quite generally that, as Wittgenstein puts it, 'to see the behaviour of a living thing is to see its soul' (PI, §357). This is, of course, precisely what I hope to affirm in this book. What can now be seen, therefore, is that what stands in the way of a fully satisfactory account of being with others is not simply the metaphysics of the subject but, more generally, humanism. In the next chapter I will begin to formulate a conception of human language which resists both bald naturalism and humanist idealisation, a conception which will thus take us a step further towards the Wittgensteinian affirmation.

5

PHILOSOPHY AND THE IDEAL
OF EXACTNESS

INTRODUCTION

In the previous chapter I argued that humanism, whether in its classical or Heideggerian form, rejects naturalism because it presumes that the fact of human language marks the distinction between the human and non-human with an absolute 'cut' or pure break. In virtue of its possession of a word-language, the *zoon logon echon*,[1] or rational animal or thinking thing or Dasein, is credited with a uniquely distinctive capacity or mode of existence which situates it at the centre of a privileged and closed horizon of intelligibility; the space of the world *as such*. My claim against this conception is not that the traits which are usually reserved for human beings alone (thought, self-consciousness, openness, etc.) are, in any developed way, actually possessed by other animals. It is rather that accounts of these distinctive traits which begin with or posit a radical break between humanity and animality cannot be other than idealised and distorted. In the chapters that follow I aim to defend this view by showing that, while we cannot conceive even our most distinctive form of behaviour, our use of language, as separate from (or as separating us from) the life of an animal, this does not require that it be reducible to the behaviour of a biological organism. In doing so I hope to show how something manifest in the behaviour of the human animal, something 'immanent to the behaviour as such' can, yet, be 'transcendent in relation to the anatomical apparatus' (PP, p. 189).[2]

I have suggested that, in one way or another, humanism is motivated by or inspired by the phenomenon of human language. More specifically, it is motivated by the assumption that the possession of language marks humanity's radical break with every other ('mere' or 'baldly natural') animal existence. In what follows I will argue that, at least within the framework of classical humanism, this assumption rests on an interpretation (one might call it 'an experience') of the fact that the words of language, in order to be what they are, must 'have a meaning', an interpretation which is both terrifically inviting and irredeemably distorted.[3] To put it in its most informal form, this is an interpretation according to which 'having a meaning' implies that *there is* something (as it were, some *thing* present-at-hand) that is the meaning of a word; that *there is* something (as it were, some *specific* thing) that one *means* when one speaks or writes, or that one grasps when one understands speech or writing. To put this more formally: the assumption is that language is the realisation or expression of quasi-objective and determinate senses or meanings; senses or meanings which 'man' alone is capable of grasping. On this conception the meaning of words or the sense of expressions of human language – for example, the words 'human' and 'language' – *should* be clear and identifiable; an *irreducible* polysemia internal to conceptuality as such, internal to the 'as such' as such, is inconceivable. In short, the idea is that univocity or the reducibility of polysemia is the essence or *telos* of language and meaning; that only thoughts with a determinate content are properly *thoughts* (as such). I will call this foundational assumption of classical humanism the thesis of ideal conceptual exactness. In this chapter I will explore it, not as the thesis of this or that philosopher, but as the basic target of the writing of both Jacques Derrida and Ludwig Wittgenstein.

DERRIDA AND THE AFFIRMATION OF DISSEMINATION

Deconstruction

In the previous chapter I outlined Derrida's reading of, and objections, to Heidegger's delimitation of Dasein. Despite these criticisms, however, there is no doubt that Heidegger's work enjoys a very special place in Derrida's thinking. Indeed, the very term 'deconstruction' so commonly linked to the critical practice of Derrida's readings of traditional philosophy is a translation of two words from Heidegger: *Destruktion* and *Abbau* (see Derrida, 1985, p. 86). Neither word is to be taken in a negative sense. *Destruktion* is not destruction (destroying) but destructuring (dismantling of structural layers). Similarly *Abbau* is not demolition, but a 'taking apart' which seeks the constitution of a thing. Of course, such gestures are classical ones.[4] What distinguishes 'deconstruction' is that what it 'analyses' are not simply 'the problems of philosophy' but, in a certain way, the history of its inscription, 'the history of (the only) metaphysics' (Derrida, 1976, p. 3).[5] Thus, while Derrida's reading of Heidegger does not 'stop with mere confirmation' (Derrida, 1993, p. 14), his relation to Heidegger is akin to a critical follower rather than a straightforward critic. Indeed, for Derrida, the deconstruction of the Heideggerian conception of the 'as such' of the intelligibility of Dasein's 'there' is a procedure or 'experience one has to go through' (Derrida, 1991, p. 107) in order to achieve clarity concerning the limits of conceptual clarity. And clarity on this issue is, as I hope to show, a feature of all of Derrida's work in philosophy (see, e.g., LI, p. 119).

In my view, what needs to be foregrounded in Derrida's work is the way in which it explores and develops the consequences of the logical impossibility of rigorously delimiting conceptual identities. In what follows I will briefly outline, in an introductory fashion, what I understand to be Derrida's central claims and lines of thought on this issue. This will be achieved by taking my point of departure from what I consider to be his basic target.

Derrida's basic target

Running throughout Derrida's work is a sustained effort to liberate thinking from a particular conception of the essence of human language. This conception is characterised by the thesis that *what is meant* by an utterance, its *meaning*, must be, at least for the speaking subject, 'specific, univocal, and rigorously controllable' (*ibid.*, p. 1). The first point to note is that the immediate consequence of this conception of language is a general thesis about communication. For, in an interesting doubling-up of the account, the 'unified meaning' of the word 'communication' must now be determined as the transport or transmission from one subject to another of thoughts (beliefs, desires, etc.) with a 'determinate content' or 'unified meaning' (*ibid.*). Thus, on this conception of language, even if what is meant leaves this or that open, the meaning (or what I mean) must always be *sharp*; i.e., in principle it must be capable of complete disambiguation. As Wittgenstein puts it, what 'one would like to say' is 'an indefinite sense – that would not really be a sense *at all*' (PI, §99).

According to Derrida, the idea that 'what is meant by an utterance' should, ideally, be exact or definite in this way is not one prejudicial inclination among others in philosophy. Rather, it is *the* philosophical prejudice, *the* philosophical injustice. In the following passage Derrida identifies it in Aristotle:

> A noun is proper when it has but a single sense. Better, it is only in this case that it is properly a noun. Univocity is the essence, or better, the *telos* of language. No philosophy, as such, has ever renounced this Aristotelian ideal. *This ideal is philosophy.* Aristotle recognizes that a word may have several meanings. This is a fact. But this fact has right of entry into language only in the extent to which the polysemia is finite, the different significations are limited in number, and above all are sufficiently distinct, each remaining one and identifiable. Language is what it is, language, only in so far as it can then master and analyze polysemia. With no remainder. A nonmasterable dissemination is not even a polysemia, it belongs to what is outside language. 'And it makes no difference even if one were to say a word has several meanings, if only they are limited in number; for to each formula [*logos*] there might be assigned a different word. For instance, we might say that "man" has not one meaning but several, one of which would be defined as "two-footed animal", while there might be also several other formulae if only they were limited in number; for a particular name might be assigned to each of the formulae. If, however, they were not limited but one were to say that the word has an infinite number of meanings, obviously

reasoning [definition, discourse, *logos*] would be impossible; for not to have one meaning is to have no meaning, and if words have no meaning, reasoning with other people, and indeed with oneself, has been annihilated; for it is impossible to think anything if we do not think one thing; but if this is possible, one name might be assigned to this thing. Let it be assumed then, as was said at the beginning, that the name has a meaning, and has one meaning' (*Metaphysics*, 4, 1006a34-b13). Each time that polysemia is irreducible, when no unity of meaning is even promised to it, one is outside language. And consequently outside humanity.

(Derrida, 1982, pp. 247–8)

This philosophical conception of the essence of human language, and its relation to a conception of the essence of humanity (as the *zoon logon echon* or rational animal), is the basic target of Derrida's criticism. It is a central aim of his work to demonstrate that the desire to limit polysemia, what I will call the desire for ideal conceptual exactness, must involve the dogmatic or non-logical exclusion of possibilities of the phenomenon of language, an exclusion practised in the hope of 'isolating' a supposedly *essential* (and thus indefinitely repeatable-as-the-same) identity or content (cp. PI, §90).[6] This identity is the *essence* of what is meant and which, ideally, can be fully captured or isolated in a definition or formula.

A key feature of Derrida's readings from the *de*constructive point of view is to identify *within* the very text which aims to *construct* such an ideal identity by exclusion, that exclusion's transgression – and to show that such construction *depends* on such transgression. As we saw in Chapter 2 in Derrida's reading of Austin's exclusion of stage recitation and fiction, the excluded 'outside' can always be found to inhabit, *in a certain way*, the 'inside'. In this way Derrida aims to show that the distinctions which have been so carefully constructed lose their analytic pertinence. And then the field is opened up for an account of the structure and functioning of language which is no longer dominated by the ideal of exactness.

In this regard it is crucial to see that Derrida's claim is not simply that the actual use of a language does not *in fact* exhibit the univocity or conceptual purity ascribed to it by what, in the passage just quoted, Derrida calls 'philosophy'. Derrida's approach is not a novel form of empiricism but an attempt to account for the necessary or *structural possibilities* of the functioning of any language (LI, p. 57; cp. PI §92). In its most clearly critical aspect, this approach aims to show that the condition of possibility for conceptual identity is at the same time the condition of *im*possibility of the rigorous unity required by the ideal of conceptual exactness. Thus Derrida opposes 'philosophy' as 'speech dreaming its plenitude' (Derrida, 1976, p. 71; cp. PI §358 and p. 216) – as speech which dreams of attaining the ideal of a determinate semantic horizon present to speaking, reasoning subjects – with the attempt to think about the conditions of possibility for conceptuality in terms which are no longer dominated by the ideal of exactness. As we shall see, according to

Derrida, conceptual identities are not characterised by ideal purity but by impurity, by *play*.

Conceptual play

The concept of play is deployed by Derrida in the course of an examination of 'the *limits* of decidability, of calculability or of formalizable completeness' in the structure and functioning of any system of signs (LI, p. 114). When Derrida's arguments are explored in detail in Chapter 7 I will show how this examination is part of a sustained attempt to avoid 'splitting the phenomenon' of language; to account for or 'think' '*at once* both the rule and the event, concept and singularity' (*ibid.* p. 119). In the present chapter, and by way of introduction, I shall simply provide a clarification of the often misunderstood Derridean concept of 'play'.

The term 'play' is used in Derrida's work in a way which draws upon both its ludic and its operational senses. These senses can be illustrated with the following slogan: Within the '*game*' of language there is always a certain '*give*'. Or again: In sign-games the functioning of signs is 'not everywhere circumscribed by rules' (PI, §68). In its operational sense 'play' refers to 'the spacing between the pieces of an apparatus [which] allows for movement and articulation' (Derrida, 1992, p. 64; cp. PI, §194). As we shall see in Chapter 7, according to Derrida the condition of possibility for the functioning of any language necessarily introduces into the identity of its concepts, into what we call 'the *same* sense', an analogous 'play' or 'give'.

In its most clearly positive aspect, Derrida's analysis aims to show that such 'play' is not of itself bad, a fault or deterioration in the functioning of a language, even if it may on occasion give rise to failures. On the contrary, according to Derrida, if we deprive the functioning of a language of the possibility of such 'play' we deprive ourselves of the possibility of it functioning *normally* (Derrida, 1992, p. 64). Provisionally, we might say that this position identifies and describes a necessary or *structural ambiguity* in the workings of any language. And Derrida's claim is that 'philosophy' *is* the insistent desire to eradicate or reduce ambiguity in order to secure a determinate semantic horizon.

The idea of structural ambiguity must be carefully treated. The claim is not that our use of language is congenitally riven by misunderstandings like that which arises when someone thinks that 'Mary had a little lamb' refers to Mary's repast. Structural ambiguity certainly makes such an eventuality possible; but it *also* makes it possible for someone to understand that 'Mary had a little lamb' refers to a case of possession of a young sheep.[7] Structural ambiguity does not mean that nothing is ever achieved through the use of language, nor does it mean that there are a great number of (countable) 'correct' or 'proper' meanings or understandings of expressions. Rather, as Geoffrey Bennington felicitously puts it, it is the idea that any text has, necessarily, '*not one*' reading that delivers, in each case of its inscription, *the* proper understanding (Bennington, 1989, p. 207).[8]

From this perspective the requirement that conceptuality attain the ideal of exactness is the work of a non-logical desire to 'restrict play' (Derrida, 1976, p. 59). However, Derrida stresses that this 'longing' for a language which can secure the rigorous purity and unity of a word's meaning cannot just like that be removed (see, e.g., LI, pp. 115f). On the contrary, the promise of a unity of meaning appears to be absolutely necessary for the possibility of thinking or communicating anything at all and as such. As noted already, Wittgenstein voices this desire, as a desire, very clearly in the *Investigations*: 'The sense of a sentence – *one would like to say* – of course, leave this or that open, but the sentence must nevertheless have *a* definite sense. An indefinite sense – that would really not be a sense at all' (PI, §99). Or, again, as his younger self uncritically assumed, 'what we MEAN must always be "*sharp*"' (NB, p. 68).

Thus, while language itself constantly invites or incites us to conceive 'meaning' in this way, the necessity of 'play' ensures that any putative 'unity of meaning' is *a priori* 'dispersed' in advance. In his writing, 'dissemination' is the concept through which this dispersal of the 'seme' (unit of meaning) is affirmed. The concept of dissemination is thus opposed to the classical concept of polysemia (LI, p. 2) in an affirmation of the 'play' which, according to Derrida, necessarily marks *all* conceptual identities.

The play of the world

In summary, Derrida's claim is that 'play' or 'structural ambiguity' is not an exceptional condition of the use of signs but a necessary and universal condition of the possibility of any language. Indeed, in Derrida's view, 'play' is a universal feature of all 'experience' in so far as it is inseparable from the field of signs (*ibid.*, p. 10). Put another way, any perception which has the structure of 'something *as* something' – i.e., what Heidegger calls our everyday openness – necessarily exhibits the same structural ambiguity which belongs to the conceptuality that informs it. In the final analysis this implies that the analogy with the operational sense of 'play' outlined above is insufficiently rigorous. In the case of the play of the plug in the socket, the socket sets a determining and independently identifiable external 'container' or limit to play. If, however, openness is riven by the play which characterises conceptuality in general, then 'this play . . . is not a play *in* the world'. That is, we cannot independently identify a determinate 'something' which might be set up as an 'in which' that determines and contains the play of concepts. Thus, Derridean play implies, ultimately, 'the play *of* the world' (Derrida, 1976, p. 50) and as such 'it is no longer determined and contained by something' (Derrida, 1985, p. 69). This does not mean that '*any* amount of "play" is permissible'; but it does mean that we cannot determine, once and for all, an absolute limit or pure cut beyond which the 'as such' of openness has no chance. For Derrida there is 'nothing outside the text', no 'outside text' (LI, p. 136), that is, no meta-language of 'super-concepts' (PI, §97) uncontaminated by 'play', which might be appealed to in order to set limits to 'play'. Indeed, any concept through which we wished to establish such a limit is, *a priori*, subject to the very play it is supposed to limit (cp. PI, §208).

It is worth noting at this point how these thoughts relate to that aspect of the Heideggerian conception of Dasein's everyday 'world' which we have already identified as most problematic. For 'an absolute limit or pure cut beyond which the "as such" of openness has no chance' is, of course, precisely what is presupposed and required by Heidegger's limitation to human Dasein of a 'world *as* world'. The 'play of the world', in so far as it is recognised at all by Heidegger,[9] remains 'within' the privileged and absolutely closed contour of an 'inside' (Dasein as constituted by familiarity with significance); an 'inside' which is 'sharply distinguished' from its 'outside' (namely, access absolutely free of the 'as') and which is thus also 'uncontaminated' in its Being by the Being of this 'outside' (namely, animality). The upshot is, as Franck notes, a conception of our Being which is 'profoundly disincarnated': 'the ecstatic determination of man's essence implies the total exclusion of his live animality' (Franck, 1991, p. 146). Hence Heidegger's charge that the 'rational animal' remains too much an animal. As will become clear, it seems to me that Derrida's work, by contrast, points towards just the kind of re-evaluation which I have been urging of the naturalistic assumption rejected by both the Heideggerian and classical humanist. I have already noted that Derrida explicitly denies that the conditions of possibility for language (for the 'as such') 'give rise to a single linear, indivisible, oppositional limit, to a binary opposition between the human and the non-human' (Derrida, 1991, p. 117). The general point will be that, for Derrida, our possession and use of language should not be conceived in absolute opposition to, and so as absolutely 'uncontaminated' by, our animality. I will return to this.

Thus far I have merely sketched in some of the lines of thought that characterise Derrida's work. Nevertheless, it should already be clear that his approach seeks fundamentally to breach the restrictive interpretation of conceptuality required by the ideal of exactness. In Derrida's view, what necessarily prevents the meaning of a word from being a unity that is identical to itself is the standard, ordinary, normal, or generally, the actual structure and functioning of any language (see, e.g., LI, pp. 89–90; and Derrida, 1992, p. 65). If the concept of necessary non-self-identity is troublesome, we can say that dissemination implies that conceptual identity is irreducibly or structurally 'impure', or 'rough'. In terms of the Aristotelian version of the ideal of exactness with which we began, 'this can be expressed like this: I use a name without a *fixed* meaning' (PI, §79).

Throughout this section I have drawn upon and referred to remarks from Wittgenstein's later writings as comparisons and supplements. In my view this coordination of the central theme in Derrida's work with ideas from the work of the later Wittgenstein is highly suggestive and interesting. But how far does the parallel extend? In the next section, through a re-appraisal of the basic target of Wittgenstein's *Investigations*, I aim to show that the parallels are both deep and reciprocally clarifying.

WITTGENSTEIN AND THE AUGUSTINIAN PICTURE OF LANGUAGE

Clarity about the essence

Wittgenstein's *Investigations* opens with a passage from Augustine's *Confessions* in which it is implied that the noun is the fundamental grammatical category of language. The privilege accorded the noun form is also a central feature of the passage from Aristotle quoted by Derrida. In what follows, taking this parallel as my clue, I will show that the basic target of Wittgenstein's later philosophy is precisely the ideal of conceptual exactness that Derrida identifies with philosophy itself.

The extract from the *Confessions* contains Augustine's account of how he learned his language as a child. Following the extract, Wittgenstein makes the following comment:

> These words, it seems to me, give us a particular picture of *the essence of human language*. It is this: the individual words in language name objects – sentences are combinations of such names. – In this picture of language we find the roots of the following idea: Every word has a meaning. This meaning is correlated with the word. It is the object for which the word stands.
>
> (PI, §1)

I have stressed Wittgenstein's identification in Augustine's words of a picture of the essence of human language. In my view, if we are to read the *Investigations* with any rigour whatsoever, this cannot be stressed highly enough. Early or late, Wittgenstein always conceives the task of his work in philosophy to be the achievement of clarity about the essence of human language (see PI, §92). To understand Wittgenstein's work we must understand this overriding concern.

Despite what will be seen to be a dramatic change in his approach, Wittgenstein's reasons for this concern remain remarkably continuous throughout his writings. This can be brought out by exploring the way in which Wittgenstein's investigations of language, both early and late, circulate around the idea that 'philosophy, if it were to say anything, would have to describe *the essence of the world*' (PR, §54).

In my view, it is characteristic of Wittgenstein's work in philosophy that he passionately shares the spirit of this traditional endeavour.[10] Implicitly referring to the 'fundamental principle' of his early writings, the later Wittgenstein acknowledges that 'it was true to say that our considerations could not be scientific ones' (PI, §109; cp. TLP, 5.551, 4.111). Philosophy aims at a distinctively conceptual understanding. It strives for complete clarity, and Wittgenstein's basic concern, early and late, is with whatever prevents such clarity. As we shall see,

Wittgenstein's view in the later philosophy is that what prevents clarity is precisely a confused conception *of* conceptual clarity.

Although Wittgenstein shares the spirit of traditional philosophy's quest for clarity about 'the essence of everything empirical' (PI, §89; TLP, 5.4711), it is equally true that, early or late, he holds the view that the attempt to give propositional expression to the essence of the world *cannot* be successful. Stances which are committed to the opposite view he calls 'metaphysical': 'From the very outset "Realism", "Idealism", etc. are names which belong to metaphysics. That is, they indicate that their adherents believe they can *say* something specific about the essence of the world' (PR, §55). It is at this point that Wittgenstein's concern with language comes to the fore. In both his early and later work Wittgenstein's objections to 'metaphysics' are based on the view that any such attempts to 'say the essence' demonstrate a basic failure 'to understand the logic of our language' (TLP 4.003; PI, §38, §93, §111, §345). That is, metaphysics, as the attempt to describe the essence of the world, rests on a crucially distorting preconception of the *essence of human language*. Consequently, this issue is the central focus of Wittgenstein's thought.[11] Early or late, clarity about the essence of language is the 'fixed point of our real need' (PI, §108).

These continuities in Wittgenstein's thought are important. But they must not make us overlook the extent to which his conception of the impossibility of 'saying the essence' changed between the early and late writings. While the early Wittgenstein claims that the essence of the world cannot be *said* because it could only be *shown* (TLP, 4.121–4.1212), the later Wittgenstein completely and radically discards the idea that 'the world' has the kind of *unitary essence* that might be said *or* shown at all. As will become clear in the chapters that follow, this change cannot be understood except against the background of Wittgenstein's break with his early humanism.

Closing philosophy

There are many fascinating continuities between Wittgenstein's early and late philosophies.[12] However, in my view Wittgenstein's later approach involves a special kind of break from both his early work and 'metaphysics' in general. It is on the nature of this break that we can see a clear and deep correspondence between the thought of the later Wittgenstein and Derrida.

The most salient contrast to previous philosophy lies in their common refusal to accept that their work marks the 'apocalyptic' *end* of philosophy in the sense of a final completion or 'once and for all' achievement of a state of complete clarity that stands in need of no further (essential) supplementation (PI, §§91–2, §§132–3; Z, §447; cp. TLP, p. 4; Derrida, 1993, pp. 144–6). Moreover, both name the attempt to achieve such complete clarity 'philosophy'. Of course, it is not in the least peculiar to either Wittgenstein or Derrida to write of, and hence in some sense to write beyond, a tradition they are willing to call simply 'philosophy'. Indeed, no philosophy can really do otherwise. However, it is a recurrent feature of the history of philosophy that 'new' modes of thought (new 'signatures': Aristotelian, Cartesian, Humean, Kantian, Hegelian, Fregean, etc.) have always positioned themselves in some way in a relation of final mastery over those discourses they claim to supersede.[13] With each new stage in the history of philosophy a new claim is made to have found a way of achieving complete clarity which brings philosophy to an end.

It is precisely in this respect that the kind of approach pursued by both Wittgenstein and Derrida constitutes a new 'kink' in the history of philosophy which separates their writing from previous Western thought.[14] In contrast to the classical 'discourses of the end', the writings of Derrida and Wittgenstein effect what might be called a 'closure' of a tradition. Closure does not aim to bring a tradition or 'historical totality' to an end by fulfilling its aims. Indeed, it resists the assumption that it can ever 'end' in that sense. Rather, it aims to identify the basic structural figure which characterises the tradition as such.[15] In the sketch of Derrida's reading of the 'history of (the only) metaphysics' outlined above, this figure was identified with the ideal of exactness. In what follows I aim to show that Wittgenstein's later work has precisely the same basic target in view. It is this ideal which sustains the assumption that 'the world' has a unitary essence about which we might become completely clear, and hence sustains 'philosophy' as a discourse of the end.

Opening philosophy

The *Confessions* extract enables Wittgenstein to announce the central concern of his book: the question of the essence of human language. The extract itself, however, is not a philosophical text in any conventional sense. Nevertheless, within it Wittgenstein identifies an idea of meaning which could not be more philosophical. How is this possible?

There are, no doubt, many reasons why Wittgenstein opens his book with the Augustinian text.[16] However, one of the most profound effects of its placement is graphically to illustrate a point which is central to the later Wittgenstein's conception of philosophical problems. Specifically, it establishes from the outset that the 'haze' or 'fog' (PI, §5) of unclarity which characterises philosophical difficulties is, in an important sense, unplaceable: it is neither peculiar to the texts of a history that bears its name, nor are these texts its determinate origin. So Wittgenstein does not see any essential need to cite actual texts from the history of philosophy in order to 'close' it. The unclarity that opens philosophy is unplaceable because, as Norman Malcolm puts it, 'non-philosophers become *immersed* in philosophy at the drop of a hat'.[17]

As I read it, a central claim of the *Investigations* is that a certain seductive conception of conceptual clarity *is* the mental mist of unclarity that structures the Western tradition of philosophy as discourses of the end. Perhaps paradoxically, this conception of clarity is derived from the ordinary conception.[18] That is, according to Wittgenstein, traditional philosophy operates with a conception of clarity which is modelled on the way in which 'we eliminate misunderstandings' in ordinary linguistic exchanges, namely, 'by making our expressions more exact' (PI, §91). In Wittgenstein's view, philosophy is characterised by an urge to sublime or idealise the logic of this procedure. 'All at once it strikes us' (*ibid.*, §88), at the drop of a hat, that *when every possible ambiguity has been removed the sense of an expression will be completely clear*. The precise identity of a thought or an idea or a concept will be precisely captured with a linguistic formula. The 'discursive intelligibility', the 'as such', or *logos* of the phenomenon that is *meant* will then be *perfectly delimited*.[19] The sharp boundary delimits what is 'inside' or 'outside' our conception of a thing, and thus tells us what, *in essence*, it *is*. The desire for 'complete clarity' in this sense is, of course, the desire for ideal conceptual exactness (cp. TLP, 4.112).

The ideal of exactness then defines the task of *philosophical* investigations as one of making the *logos* of 'the world' as such 'completely clear'. In my view, the ideal of clarity in play here (and along with it the conception of philosophy it engenders) is the basic target of Wittgenstein's later philosophy. That is, for the later Wittgenstein, it is our attachment to this conception of clarity which prevents clarity in philosophy: for the traditional '*urge to understand*' the essence of the world in this way (PI, §89) is, *at once*, an '*urge to misunderstand*' the actual structure and functioning of language (PI, §109).

The sprawling *Urbild*

This interpretation conflicts, in certain respects, with the influential readings of Wittgenstein developed by G. P. Baker and P. M. S. Hacker in their *Analytic Commentaries* and elsewhere. On their approach, the basic target of Wittgenstein's criticism is identified not with the ideal of conceptual exactness but what they call the 'Augustinian picture'. In my view, this interpretation lacks a certain sensitivity to the specificity of Wittgenstein's target. In this section and the next I will further develop my approach to the *Investigations* by following their reading.

Baker and Hacker introduce their conception of the Augustinian picture of language with the minimal idea of a conception of language which claims that 'the individual words of a language are names of objects and sentences are combinations of names' (AC, p. 33). However, the limits of this picture are rapidly extended until it comes to represent a sprawling '*Urbild*' which is held 'to inform vast ranges of philosophical thought in a multitude of different and frequently unrecognized ways' (*ibid.*, p. 60). This '*Urbild*' is characterised as a 'paradigm towards which [philosophical] theories gravitate' that 'has no owner or author'. It is 'a pernicious and widespread weed' and the *Investigations* 'constitutes an elaborate campaign to eradicate it' (*ibid.*, pp. 45–6). Clearly, for Baker and Hacker, the Augustinian picture is Wittgenstein's basic target. While I have tried to acknowledge a crucial place to what might be called the Augustinian picture, my interpretation is significantly different to theirs.

The basic difference turns on the broad way in which Baker and Hacker define the Augustinian picture. On their reading, the 'fundamental aspects' of the picture can be identified by their being either 'natural, smooth extensions of the primitive picture' or 'directly related to arguments in Wittgenstein's writings' (*ibid.*, p. 36). Ultimately, therefore, 'there is no unequivocal boundary separating what falls within it from what falls without' (*ibid.*, p. 34). I am not, of course, unsympathetic to this refusal rigidly to fix conceptual limits. Furthermore, there is little doubt that on this reading we will be able to include the ideal of conceptual exactness somewhere within it (see *ibid.*, p. 314). However, it is not certain that this ideal (or indeed any other) will have any special privilege in a critique of traditional philosophy carried out on its basis. When philosophy is conceived as 'a family of accounts' (*ibid.*, p. 36) that can grow out of this sprawling '*Urbild*', we will certainly not wish to say of any particular ideal of traditional philosophy, as Derrida does, 'this ideal is philosophy'.

The ideal

The central difficulty with Baker and Hacker's identification of Wittgenstein's basic target is that the so called 'Chapter on Philosophy' (PI, §§89–133) which follows Wittgenstein's discussion of vagueness and family resemblance *does* appear to focus on and identify an ideal of some sort at the heart of thinking which he calls 'philosophical'. For example (at PI, §103): 'The ideal, as we think of it, is unshakable. You can never get outside it; you must always turn back. There is no outside; outside you cannot breathe.' By drawing the boundaries of Wittgenstein's basic target so vaguely Baker and Hacker's determination loses sight of the significance of remarks such as this one. I will explain this.

An obvious alternative to the very wide determination of the Augustinian picture favoured by Baker and Hacker is to limit it to what Wittgenstein actually describes as its content. This is what Baker and Hacker call the 'primitive form' of the picture: 'every word is a name and every sentence a combination of names' (*ibid.*, p. 34). As Baker and Hacker note, this characterisation 'says nothing about what words or sentences mean, what it is to understand an expression, or what it is to explain meaning. At best, the picture suggests answers to these questions' (*ibid.*). I think that this narrow definition of the Augustinian picture is the correct one. This can be seen from the fact that, in Wittgenstein's view, the Augustinian picture is not necessarily misleading. Indeed, he holds that it can be used to *lift* the mental mist of unclarity.[20] In what follows I will show that Wittgenstein's basic target is not Augustine's picture *per se* but the specific 'idea of meaning' that has its roots in such pictures.

I have suggested that at least one reason why Wittgenstein begins the *Investigations* with a non-philosophical text is that it helps us to see that the 'first' opening of the kind of philosophy that he aims to 'close' does not have its origin in abstruse metaphysical theorising. The Augustinian picture is the kind of picture of language that comes naturally to almost anyone. And Wittgenstein's claim is that, even if it does not have to be misleading, it *invites* idealisation into the philosophical idea of meaning. This idea of meaning is not the thesis that all words are names but the thesis that words in general and especially general terms have or signify a 'meaning', where this is conceived as a quasi-objective identity that is present-at-hand, along with but distinct from the word – an idea which strongly suggests that all words are basically names: 'You say: the point isn't the word, but its meaning, and you think of the meaning as a thing of the same kind as the word, though also different from the word. Here the word, there the meaning' (PI, §120). The word, as it were, stands next to and names its 'meaning'.

It is this tendency to idealise or objectify the 'meaning' of words which Wittgenstein calls 'a tendency to sublime the logic of our language' (PI, §38). It is this tendency to posit a quasi-objective identity, an ideal identity which is 'grasped' by speakers of the language, that prevents clarity by suggesting the possibility of providing 'a *single* completely resolved form of every expression' (PI, §91). As Baker and Hacker also suggest in their treatment of the Augustinian picture, it would be wrong to think that this tendency is to be blamed on the work of high-minded but wrong-headed intellectuals who call themselves 'philosophers'. On the contrary, the idea of a unified and indefinitely repeatable '*meaning*' is not entirely alien to any speaker of a language. Indeed, 'language seems to repeat it to us inexorably' (PI, §115) – same, same, same, same, same . . .

Wittgenstein's later philosophy abandons the assumption that the lack of clarity which characterises the opening of philosophy is a lack of definitional sharpness. Why, then, can we become immersed in philosophy at all, let alone at the drop of a hat? Against the idea of a lack of definitional sharpness, Wittgenstein proposes the idea that we can become captivated by the ideal of exactness because 'the real foundations of enquiry' are 'hidden because of their simplicity and familiarity' (PI, §129); they are, that is to say, normally inconspic-uous.[21] In normal contexts, and for practical purposes, we do not need to be able to give an account of our language's structure and functioning and hence we are not prepared for such a task (RPP1, §554). Hence, as Derrida also suggests, the logic of language 'often passes unseen' (LI, p. 18). It is this inconspicuousness of the actual logic of language which allows the inviting philosophical ideal to sustain its grip. Of course, according to Wittgenstein, what we discover if we actually look at the facts of language usage is that our concepts do not exhibit the clear and closed borders which we are inclined to expect: 'We expect a smooth regular contour and get to see a ragged one. . . . Rules occur to us, no doubt, but the reality shows nothing but exceptions' (RPP1, §§554–7). Thus, the tendency to idealise the Augustinian picture is not simply 'widespread', as Baker and Hacker suggest: it is normal. As Henry Staten puts it, 'normality is the necessary background against which it would be possible to think the essence' (Staten, 1985, p. 79). This normality condition, the 'automatism' of our normal use of language (*ibid.*), thus connects us all – 'philosophers' or not – to the dream of our language that is the desire for ideal conceptual exactness.[22]

In summary, the principle focus of Wittgenstein's treatment of the philosophical idea of meaning is not the *nomen-nominatum* model as such but the assumption that the *nominatum* is a determinate, quasi-objective identity which is indefinitely repeatable as self-identically 'the same'. This is the fundamental characteristic of the 'philosophical concept of meaning' (PI, §2), the 'general notion of the meaning of a word' (PI, §5) informally introduced in the first remarks of the *Investigations* and subsequently refined and developed in the remarks which follow and which conclude at the end of the 'Chapter on Philosophy' (at PI, §133).

The divergence of this reading of the *Investigations* from that provided by Baker and Hacker can be made perspicuous in the following way. Baker and Hacker read the remarks that conclude at the end of the 'Chapter on Philosophy' (*ibid.*) in terms of a progressive working out of the consequences of an original confusion: the development of the Augustinian picture. In my view, by contrast, starting from an exemplification of the 'first' opening of philosophy in the Augustinian picture, these remarks work towards the uncovering and specification of the basic prejudice of philosophy that will 'close' it: the 'unshakeable' ideal of conceptual exactness. In my view, therefore, Derrida's identification of the ideal of exactness as the *archon* of philosophy is precisely shared by Wittgenstein:

> A noun is proper when it has but a single sense. Better, it is only in this case that it is properly a noun. Univocity is the essence, or better, the *telos* of language. No philosophy, as such, has ever renounced this Aristotelian ideal. This ideal is philosophy.
>
> (Derrida, 1982, p. 247)

> A picture is conjured up which seems to fix the sense *unambiguously*. The actual use, compared with that suggested by the picture, seems like something muddied. . . . In the actual use of expressions we make detours, we go by side-roads. We see the straight highway before us, but of course we cannot use it, because it is permanently closed.
>
> (PI, §426)

> The ideal, as we think of it, is unshakable. You can never get outside it; you must always turn back. There is no outside; outside you cannot breathe.
>
> (PI, §103)

The intact kernel

Readings of Wittgenstein cannot but acknowledge that he is critical of the idea of setting clear boundaries to conceptual identities. However, as Norman Malcolm has noted, the idea of family resemblances has not seemed to demand any significant retreat from the practice of 'conceptual analysis' that seeks 'the universal, the essential' (Malcolm, 1993, p. 48). John Searle provides a quite typical response to the question of conceptual 'looseness' that is explored in Wittgenstein's *Investigations*:

> One of the most important insights of recent work in the philosophy of language is that most non-technical concepts in ordinary language lack absolutely strict rules. . . . But this insight into the looseness of our concepts, and its attendant jargon of 'family resemblance' should not lead us into a rejection of the very enterprise of philosophical analysis; rather the conclusion to be drawn is that certain forms of analysis, especially analysis into necessary and sufficient conditions, are likely to involve (in varying degrees) *idealization* of the concept analyzed. In the present case our analysis will be directed at *the centre of the concept* of promising. I am ignoring *marginal, fringe*, and partially defective promises.
>
> (Searle, 1969, p. 55, my emphasis)

What is clear from this extract is that, according to Searle, the kind of 'looseness' that belongs to 'non-technical concepts' is *ideally* or in principle reducible. Looseness is something extrinsic, essentially accidental; an empirical eventuality that befalls a structure in which ideally there is no 'fringe'. This account of the fact that the terms of 'ordinary language lack absolutely strict rules' is fundamentally unsatisfactory. It is, of course, true, and of great importance, that very often 'we are in no doubt what to say in this or that case' (PI, §142). Indeed, as I have suggested, the absence of doubt in the employment of words is *normal*. Normally one does not or even is unable to doubt that this is what one should say in this case. However, as I will show in the next chapter, the mistake is to picture such cases as ones in which one recognises the recurrence of an identity which is *unambiguously* 'the same again'; a case in which the boundary between being or not being a certain thing is absolutely unambiguous and clear cut. By contrast, just such a construal is defended by Searle with his appeal to a distinction between the 'centre' and 'margin' of concepts, a distinction which aims to ensure that a conceptual kernel remains intact. That is, the centre/margin distinction is assumed to be capable of setting a limit to looseness by restricting it to the marginal and defective, like cutting off the lace trim of a doily. At the centre there is clarity, determinacy, a residue that is ideally 'the same' in every 'normal' case.

But what if this centre/margin distinction is itself contaminated by the looseness that it is supposed to limit? Is the boundary between being or not being at the centre absolutely unambiguous and clear cut? And, if the concept of the 'centre' also has a 'margin' of looseness, will we need to apply a further distinction which ensures that we are at the centre of the centre? And so on.

In the interest of an *ideal* of exactness, Searle's analysis is forced into *exclusions of possibilities of the phenomenon of language* – what he calls 'marginal cases' – which are neither rigorous nor logical. What is not considered by Searle is the possibility that 'looseness' is a structural or essential feature of conceptuality as such. That is, Searle does not seriously examine the consequences of the idea that the *possibility* of what we call 'marginal cases' is part of the structure of concepts as such. Instead, the rigorous purity of the centre/margin opposition is dogmatically assumed in order to satisfy the non-logical desire to restrict 'looseness' – to restrict play.

Two remarks in *Zettel* summarise Wittgenstein's reading of the ideal of exactness and the desire to restrict play:

> How should we have to imagine a complete list of rules for the employment of a word? – What do we mean by a complete list of rules for the employment of a piece in chess? Couldn't we *always* construct doubtful cases, in which the normal list of rules does not decide? Think e.g. of such a question as: how to determine who moved last, if a doubt is raised about the reliability of the players' memories?
>
> (Z, §440, my emphasis)

> Consider also the following proposition: 'The rules of a game may well allow a certain freedom, but all the same they must be quite definite rules.' That is as if one were to say: 'You may indeed leave a person enclosed by four walls a certain liberty of movement, but the walls must be perfectly rigid' – and that is not true. – 'Well, the walls may be elastic all right, but in that case they have a perfectly determinate degree of elasticity.' – But what does this say? It seems that it must be possible to state the elasticity, but that again is not true. 'The wall always has some determinate degree of elasticity – whether I know it or not.': that is really the avowal of adherence to a form of expression. *The one that makes use of the form of an ideal of accuracy.* As it were like the form of a parameter of representation.
>
> (*ibid.*, §441, my emphasis)

What is not tolerated by thinking dominated by this ideal of accuracy or exactness is indefiniteness *internal* to human conceptuality as such – internal to the conceptual 'as such' as such. In Searle's work the purity of rules is acknowledged to be an ideal, but, as his exclusion of the marginal indicates, for Searle this is an ideal which is still approached or approximated in normal cases. This is precisely *not* what Wittgenstein is suggesting with the notion of family resemblances (see PI, §81).

Of course, as I have noted, the promise of a unity of meaning appears to be absolutely necessary for the possibility of thinking or communicating anything at all and as such:

> The sense of a sentence – one would like to say – may, of course, leave this or that open, but the sentence must nevertheless have *a* definite sense. An indefinite sense – that would really not be a sense at all.
>
> (PI, §99)

However, as I have tried to show, Wittgenstein, like Derrida, conceives what 'one would like to say' here as motivated by the non-logical desire to restrict 'play'. In reality there is no determinate 'wall' or contour within which human conceptuality has some leeway: it is not that the 'as such' of our concepts is contained within a closed space with 'some determinate degree of elasticity'. Again, the point is that any concept through which we wished to establish such a 'wall' is, *a priori*, subject to the very looseness or play it is supposed to limit (see PI, §208).

On this conception, the idea of a perfectly smooth contour of conceptual intelligibility (or closed horizon of significance) presumes an idealisation of the structure and functioning of our language which is, *a priori*, unrealisable. But, as I have suggested, this means that the 'urge to understand' the essence of the world is, at once, 'an urge to misunderstand' the structure and functioning of our language (PI, §89 and §109). In short, the idea of achieving complete clarity about the world 'as such', the idea of containing or limiting 'the world' within a horizon of intelligibility or significance which escapes 'looseness', simply cannot be achieved.

The desire to restrict 'play', the ideal of exactness, is at the heart of every humanism – including, one must say, the Heideggerian form. But it is destroyed by the very phenomenon which seems to invite it: '*Human language*, as original as it might be, does not allow us to "cut" once and for all where we would in general like to cut' (Derrida, 1991, pp. 116–17). As I suggested in Chapter 4, humanism has lost itself in its first utterances, being already defeated by the phenomenon of human language.

But where does this lead or leave us? At bottom, do we know what human language is if it is *not* the means or medium for the communication of thoughts with a determinate sense? And is it not simply a fact that the possibility of such communication lies at the heart of our being with others? In the next two chapters I will outline an approach to the logic of language and of communication which forgoes the humanist ideal.

6

RULES AND EVENTS OF LANGUAGE

INTRODUCTION

In the previous chapter it was argued that the tendency to idealise the notion of 'meaning' is not something that it is possible simply or finally to bring to an end, as we might, say, a recurrent logical fallacy. The 'prejudices' with which we are concerned here are not errors that are 'vestigial or accidental', 'rather [they are] a kind of structural lure' (Derrida, 1981, p. 33).[1] The claim was that, while the ideal of exactness does not actually play a role in the functioning of language, our language ceaselessly enjoins the ordinary speaker to presume its necessity. The philosophical urge to isolate ideal identities signified by words is, therefore, 'indestructible' (LI, p. 116): and yet it 'carries within it the destiny of its non-fulfilment' (Derrida, 1976, p. 206). In this chapter I will pursue a critique of the ideal of exactness through an examination of the way in which it informs philosophical investigations of the phenomenon of language and of communication. As I noted at the start of the previous chapter, one of the basic features of thinking dominated by the ideal is a conception of communication as the transport or transmission from one subject to another of thoughts with a unified meaning capable of complete disambiguation. As should be clear, this general thesis about communication entails a distinction between determinate identities of sense which are, ideally, *indefinitely repeatable as the same* (concepts), and behavioural events of speech or writing, etc., that are, in themselves, *unique and dateable* (singular applications, uses).

Such an approach clearly 'splits the phenomenon' of language between something 'intellectual', 'spiritual', 'mental' or 'inorganic' on the one hand, and something, as it were, 'material', 'physical', 'merely behavioural' or 'organic' on the other. Now, while I have been urging for a conception of the human animal which avoids such a split, it is difficult to see what alternative there might be to this kind of picture. If concepts are riven by 'play', what sense can we give to the idea of using a word 'in accordance' with its meaning? Or, again, what content can we give to the idea of using a word 'in the *same* way' if the 'meaning' is not an indefinitely repeatable identity? In short, if we affirm dissemination, 'what meaning is the expression "the rule by which he proceeds" supposed to have left to it' (PI,

§82)? In this chapter, through a reconsideration of Wittgenstein's remarks on rules and rule following, an account of the normative nature of meaning will be presented that forgoes the phenomenon-splitting ideal of exactness.

THE PHENOMENON OF LANGUAGE

Splitting the phenomenon

As I have noted, it is very difficult to see where the affirmation of dissemination leads or leaves us with respect to the possibility of *communication*. Heidegger's approach to the 'Being-in' that Dasein *is* enabled a first step beyond the sceptical threat posed by the metaphysics of the subject. We can make cautious use of a Heideggerian point of departure on the topic of communication, too.

In *Being and Time*, Heidegger provides the following suggestive, if negative, determination: 'Communication [*Mitteilung*] is never anything like a conveying of experiences, such as opinions or wishes, from the interior of one subject into the interior of another' (BT, p. 162). Now, as we have seen, Heidegger argues that the threat of scepticism is sustained by a quite specific conception of the 'subject' character of Dasein. His negative determination of communication is targeted at the same conception. That is, it is targeted against approaches which assume that communication presumes a relation between subjects who are, in their own case, 'constantly present-at-hand, both in and for a closed realm' (*ibid.*, p. 114). If followed through to its logical end, such a conception drives us towards a picture of communication which splits the phenomenon between inner, 'private' contents of consciousness and outer, 'public' words.

This tendency to 'privatize content' is a familiar target in writings which have been influenced by Wittgenstein.[2] However, it is important to see that the drive to privacy is only an inflected version of a more general picture of communication, a picture which does not exclude Fregean-type theories which aim to establish the *objectivity* of the sense of thoughts. What needs to be stressed is that, while Frege abandons the psychologistic conception of 'inner ideas' communicated by 'outward signs', he maintains a picture of communication which is its formal double: 'One communicates a thought. How does this happen? One brings about changes in the common outside world which, perceived by another person, are supposed to induce him to apprehend a thought and take it to be true' (Frege, 1967, p. 38). If we are to construe the Heideggerian negative claim in a manner which determines its target as broadly as possible, it must be read as a criticism of a general model of the scene of communication and not a narrowly psychologistic or empiricist inflection of it.[3] Derrida summarises this general model in the following way:

> Communication presupposes subjects (whose identity and presence are
> constituted before the signifying operation) and objects (signified

concepts, a thought-meaning that the passage of communication will have neither to constitute, nor, by all rights, to transform). *A* communicates *B* to *C*. Through the sign the emitter communicates something to a receptor.

(Derrida, 1981, pp. 23–4)

The subjectivist empiricist and the objectivist Fregean accounts can, I think, both be captured by this schema.

Having made use of Heidegger's graphic summary of the traditional model of communication, we should note the problems which would necessarily arise if we attempted to defend a purely Heideggerian approach. Following the critical reading of Heidegger's humanism pursued in the previous chapters, we can see that a Heideggerian approach would only overcome the more classical 'inner/outer' picture of communication at the cost of reproducing a dogmatic restriction of communication to human 'insiders'; the 'Being-with' of Dasein. This suggests that the fundamental problem with traditional approaches to communication is not the idea of conveying a content from 'the interior of one subject into the interior of another'. Rather, following the argument of the previous two chapters, we can broach the possibility that what is decisive is a specific idea of humanity as having access to the 'as such' of determinate senses or meanings.

In my view it is this picture of human understanding which first splits the phenomenon of language and of communication. That is, the decisive split here is not, in the first instance, an 'inner/outer' dualism, but, inspired by the ideal of exactness, a split between pure conceptual intelligibility (meaning) and singular events (use).[4] We are, of course, some way from clarifying what it means to say, against the phenomenon-splitting interpretation, that conceptuality is inherently riven by play. However, one thing is clear, namely, that if what we call 'communication' does not have a determinate sense that is indefinitely repeatable as the same, then the affirmation of possibilities of communication beyond the limits of two adult human beings who have 'shared command of a language' is at least left open to us.[5] As before, the point of affirming dissemination is not to attack a theory because it fails to do justice to possibilities of phenomena other than the normal or ordinary. Rather, the claim is that such a theory fails to do justice to such possibilities because it presents as descriptive a determination of the 'normal' or the 'ordinary' which is axiological and idealising in its inception (cp. PI, §§130–1; and, LI, p. 16, p. 18).

Drawing boundaries

As we have seen, thinking committed to the ideal of exactness, and hence to the phenomenon-splitting approach to language and communication, is profoundly oriented towards the idea of formulae or definitions which perfectly delimit the identity of concepts. Grasping the meaning of a word, for example the words 'language' and 'communication', is to grasp the essential formula or '*logos*' of the phenomenon. On such a conception, concepts are, essentially, 'rules' that dictate or govern the correct application of concept-words in particular cases.[6] Anyone who understands the formula (grasps the rule) thereby knows what is and what is not an application 'in accordance' with the formula (following the rule).

Everything that I have said about the claims of Wittgenstein and Derrida thus far can be summarised with the idea that accounting for the normative nature of meaning cannot require recourse to such formulae or definite rules. But what does this mean? As I have indicated, this question can also be posed like this: if the use of words is *not* governed by definite rules, 'what meaning is the expression "the rule by which he proceeds" supposed to have left here?' (PI, §82, slightly altered).

In response to this problem, we are inclined to say that, even if definitions or rules do not confer absolute regularity on the use of a word, for example on the use of the words 'language' and 'communication', there must be some limit to the *irregularity* allowable for conceptual distinction, and hence for language, to be possible. There must be *some* boundary of distinction between concepts or there is no language at all. Let us consider this point.

We want to be able to say: 'At *this* point there is not enough regularity for a language to be possible'. Here, we think, we have found the 'wall', the limits of play for the rules of concept-words. Maybe now we can form a scientific or rigorous concept of the limit of language.

There is no question of denying that, in the absolute absence of regularity, 'the distinction and limits of concepts would have no chance' (LI, p. 117). However, this is not to affirm the necessity or possibility of drawing an absolutely rigorous boundary. Before we are serenely led to assume that we can now finally state the limits of play, Wittgenstein reminds us that 'regularity' is itself just an ordinary word; it is part of, not apart from, the set it is being positioned to limit:

> Then am I defining 'order' and 'rule' by means of 'regularity'? – How do I explain the meaning of 'regular', 'uniform', 'same' to anyone? – I shall explain these words to someone who, say, only speaks French by means of the corresponding French words. But if a person has not yet got the *concepts*, I shall teach him to use the words by means of *examples* and by *practice*. – And when I do this I do not communicate less to him than I know myself.
>
> (PI, §208)

There is no precise dividing line to be drawn in general between what is and what is not 'regular', and hence none for what we call a 'rule'. Meaning or understanding something by these words, like any others, does not presuppose the grasp of a concept capable of 'complete clarification' – a concept whose explanation by examples 'communicates less to him than I know myself'.

Two options seem to be available to the philosopher seeking clarity about the essence of language. On the one hand, one can decide to practise a 'logic of exclusion' which ignores the so-called 'marginal cases'. The idea here is to isolate the supposed 'central kernel of the concept', thus aiming at constructing a theoretical idealisation of the rules governing concept-words.[7] Or, on the other hand, one can seek to render an account of the phenomenon of language which shows why no such ideals, no such rules actually exist. The second option is that followed (risked) by Wittgenstein and Derrida. The arguments of Wittgenstein and Derrida that I am focusing on aim to show why ordinary concepts are in general not as clear cut and final as we are tempted to expect. No boundary will ever entirely coincide with the actual usage, 'as this usage has no sharp boundary' (BB, p. 19).

It must be stressed that abandoning recourse to the ideal of exactness is not to replace a logic of purity with a logic of indistinction or approximation. For example, neither Wittgenstein nor Derrida seek to 'bargain away' the rigour of the law of the excluded middle.[8] However, in their view, the use of conceptual distinctions and oppositions 'irresistibly drags us on' (*ibid.*, p. 108) to the idea of determinate identities of sense which are, ideally, capable of isolation and complete clarification (see LI, pp. 116f), as if concepts anticipate and determine the possibilities unmistakably, unambiguously, in every context. This is what is denied by Wittgenstein and Derrida. The claim here is not that the use of antithetical distinctions has no practical value in particular cases (BB, p. 87). For example, as we shall see, the antithetical distinction between 'mechanical' and 'conscious' cases of 'deciding which is the right step to take at any particular stage' has a use. What is denied is that the absence of doubt in the application of concepts should be explained in terms of a speaker's grasp of a rule which tells him or her, at least for a vast range of central cases, what is and what is not 'the same again': 'Now we know what is in question – we think. And that is precisely what it does not tell him' (PI, §352).

Fully explaining meaning

These ideas can be clarified by considering their relation to Wittgenstein's middle-period slogan: 'The meaning of a word is what is explained by the explanation of the meaning' (PG, p. 69; cited at PI, §560). This slogan does not rule out the claim that we have at our disposal rules which satisfy the ideal of exactness. But it does direct us towards an examination of what we *actually* call 'explanations of meaning'. And here, I would suggest, we do not find definite rules but, for the most part, explanations by examples of the use of words in particular cases. Now, as we have already noted, Wittgenstein claims that explanations of meaning of this sort do not 'communicate less than I know myself'. Another way of putting this point would be to say that, in certain cases, this just is what we call '*fully* explaining the meaning'. Clearly, if this is correct, then it is wrong to say that such explanations fall short of or are striving after 'a formal unity' of meaning, an ideal identity which is essentially the same in every case.

But now, if explaining by means of examples of *use* can *be* 'fully explaining *meaning*', then we need no longer invoke the idea of an absolute split between determinate conceptual forms or definite rules and singular behavioural events or uses of language.

What gives rise to the impression that explanations by examples of use fall short of, and hence do not *really* fully explain the meaning of an expression? One clear source is that, when we cite example cases in giving explanations of the meaning of an expression, we are not normally limiting the use of the expression to just this set of cases. It can then come to seem that there *must* be some kind of 'gulf' between the limited number of examples cited in explanation and an indefinitely repeatable 'meaning' which we must grasp: 'If I am to know how to continue correctly beyond this limited set, what I grasp must be something which *cannot* be *fully* presented in an explanation by examples. Only when every possible misapplication (misunderstanding) has been averted will the sense be *completely* clear. And for this we need not examples but an essential definition, a rule.' But is that true?

Wittgenstein accepts that we *can* draw 'rigid limits' to a concept (PI, §68). If this is possible, doesn't this show that explanation by examples of use is not a full explanation of meaning? Further, doesn't this show that play or looseness is just a 'pragmatic' feature of our concepts? If, by this, one wants to say that most of our concepts are 'empirically useful, provisionally convenient, constructed without great rigour', then I will agree to this (LI, p. 128; cp. PI, §71a). However, if it is taken to imply that 'play' is an accidental or extrinsic feature of concepts (even if, in fact, it occurs frequently and nearly everywhere) the essence of which is to attain purity, then this objection misses the point. The classical assumption that the (teleological) essence of the sense of words of a language is to have a well-defined identity is not called for out of a militant prejudice in favour of purity.[9] Rather, it is thought that such an identity is absolutely necessary for me to mean or understand something at all ('what I mean MUST be *sharp*'). As I have indicated, the crucial assumption is the idea that 'what I mean' must be capable of complete clarification, complete disambiguation, and hence is *fully* understood by another only when *every* possibility of misunderstanding has been settled.

According to the readings of Wittgenstein and Derrida presented in the previous chapter, it is on this issue that we find the fundamental point of divergence between Wittgenstein and Derrida and the classical tradition. For on their view no actual expression, no use of words, no text, does or could have a sense or meaning which is 'exact' in that sense. Any definition, any explanation of meaning, however tightly drawn, can be misunderstood or misapplied. We can, that is, '*always* construct doubtful cases, in which the normal list of rules does not decide' (Z, §440). This claim introduces a massive complication into the account of the phenomenon of language and of communication. If *every* explanation of meaning is, when compared to the ideal, 'rough', how is it to be decided what is the *right* use to make of an expression in *any* particular case? In short, how are we to account for the normative nature of meaning once we have given up the idea that a word is the external mark of an ideal sense which, once grasped, comprehends and determines its whole use in advance? Again: 'What meaning is the expression "the rule by which he proceeds" supposed to have left to it here?' (PI, §82). Does the affirmation of dissemination destroy the possibility of the very phenomenon that it was intended to clarify? In the next part of this chapter I will propose an account of the rule-governed nature of language which can answer these questions.

THE LIMITS OF CALCULABILITY

A calculus of rules

How is it possible to say and mean anything at all if conceptuality is inherently riven by 'play'? The accounts of both Wittgenstein and Derrida on this question are, in my view, best understood through their shared response to the classical idea that 'if anyone utters a sentence and *means* or *understands* it he is operating a calculus according to definite rules' (*ibid.*, §81).

Clearly, when the meaning of a word is explained, the explanation will contain further words with meanings which, in their turn, can be explained.[10] On the classical conception, this process will come to an end, ideally, with a complete specification of the meaning, a specification which *unambiguously* leaves just one course of action, one correct continuation, one correct understanding, open to us. As we have seen, this account is fundamentally flawed. There is and can be no 'ideal' which could 'stop up all the cracks' of possible doubt. There is and can be no such thing as a 'complete list of rules for the employment of a word' such that they 'never let a doubt creep in'. This observation can readily make the problem of the gulf look insuperable: '"How does an explanation help me to understand, if after all it is not the final one? In that case the explanation is never completed; so I still don't understand what he means and never shall"' (*ibid.*, §87). The 'rules' as they are given (e.g., the limited number of examples of use cited in an actual explanation) are theoretically undecidable with respect to a particular understanding (continuation). Wittgenstein affirms this but does not draw the sceptical conclusion which the defender of the traditional conception finds insurmountable. That we can always imagine a doubt is sufficient to ruin the ideal of exactness – there is no such thing as 'knowing the meaning of a word' in the sense required by the classical conception. 'But', Wittgenstein stresses, 'that is not to say that we are in doubt' (*ibid.*, §84):

> I can easily imagine someone always doubting before he opened his front door whether an abyss did not yawn behind it, and making sure about it before he went through the door (and he might on some occasion prove to be right) – but that does not make me doubt in the same case.
>
> (*ibid.*)

How is our ordinary, non-doubting behaviour to be reconciled with the *possibility* of such radical doubt? Wittgenstein's claim is that the problem of the gulf cannot be overcome by recourse to a speaker's knowledge of definite rules. However, by endorsing the reasoning that undermines this conception he is not endorsing his interlocutor's view that to do so undermines the idea of the normative nature of meaning altogether. Rather, Wittgenstein draws the conclusion that the impossibility of the traditional view shows that there must be a way of grasping a rule which is not a theoretical or cognitive achievement (see, e.g., *ibid.*, §201 and §679).[11]

Wittgenstein does not approach the problem of the gulf by positing definite rules but by looking at 'what we call "obeying the rule" and "going against it" in actual cases' (*ibid.*, §201). And, again, his claim is that, if we do so, we will not find a rule for the expression 'obeying the rule' but examples of its use; examples here of practical activity. This approach, according to Wittgenstein's argument, '*fully explains*' the ordinary concept of 'obeying a rule'. There is no 'deeper explanation' (*ibid.*, §209).[12]

These are relatively familiar lines of thought in Wittgenstein's later writings, but their significance is disputed. In what follows I want to address Wittgenstein's views by focusing on a claim he makes which is, as we shall see, also central to Derrida's approach to the structure and functioning of language. This is the claim, made in response to the drama of the possible yawning abyss, that in the use of language something like 'a new decision' (*ibid.*, §186; cp. LI, p. 116) is always called for on each occasion of the employment of a concept-word.

As I have indicated, in my view Wittgenstein shares his classical interlocutor's concern with the apparent gulf between explanations of meaning and subsequent uses 'in accordance' with that meaning. However, their responses to it differ. On the classical conception the gulf is interpreted in terms of a necessary shortfall of ordinary explanations of meaning. The gulf is then removed by suggesting that someone who understands the meaning of a concept-word must grasp a definite rule or 'instant talisman' which can anticipate an indefinite number of applications.[13] Wittgenstein, on the other hand, rejects the idea that ordinary explanations of meaning are in some way 'less than full'. Consequently, in *that* sense there is no gulf to bridge. However, there is still the problem that the explanation *cannot* 'stop up all the cracks'.

According to Wittgenstein there is no magic trick: nothing can force us to go on in a particular way beyond the initial instruction and explanation. We are left to take the plunge alone:

> How can he know how he is to continue a pattern by himself – whatever instruction you give him? – Well, how do I know? – If that means 'Have I reasons?' the answer is: my reasons will soon give out. And then I shall act, without reasons.
>
> (PI, §211).

The very idea of correctness, of rule-governed behaviour, seems to be crumbling here. If my action is not finally or fully grounded in reasons or knowledge of definite rules, is it not then arbitrary? 'How is it decided what is the *right* step to take at any particular stage [of following a rule]?' (*ibid.*, §186). Wittgenstein claims that at some point I must act. I 'leap' from instruction to action, from explanation to employment, without the aid of absolutely authoritative reasons or rules which would provide a cast iron guarantee that *this* continuation is correct: 'my reasons will soon give out. And then I shall act, without reasons'.

Existential decisions

But what if it were otherwise? In my view, the only alternative is no alternative at all. The classical conception interprets 'grasping the rule' as knowledge of a definite rule which (at least for 'central cases') unambiguously dictates or forces a particular continuation on us. But this interpretation evacuates the idea of 'being determined by *rules*' of any content. Rejecting the idea of 'the moment of the leap', our language is pictured as a kind of calculable programme or mechanism on to which we must 'hook' ourselves (see *ibid.*, '§81b, and LI, p. 116). Quite apart from questions as to how we do this,[14] the problem is that it is impossible to conceive the behaviour of someone who is thus 'hooked on', other than as being 'a programmable effect of determinate causes' (LI, p. 116). That is, the forced behaviour of someone hooked on to such a system can only be understood in *causal* terms. There is no room for an assessment in terms of correctness ('the *right* way'), only of an assessment in terms of operational functioning; and hence the idea of a *normative constraint* on behaviour is utterly lost.

It is in the face of this threat that Wittgenstein suggests the following reply to the question, 'How is it decided what is the *right* step to take at any particular stage [of following a rule]?': 'it would almost be more correct to say, not that an intuition was needed at every stage [intuition as the obvious candidate for a 'hooking' device], but that *a new decision* was needed at every stage' (PI, §186, comment and emphasis mine).

Wittgenstein's hesitancy on this issue ('it would *almost be more* correct') has been the subject of some interesting interpretations. Baker and Hacker explain it as a warning against what they consider to be an obviously jejune temptation: 'This line of thought leads in the direction of a kind of logical existentialism' that signifies 'yawning chasms of irrationality beneath our rule-governed activities' (AC, vol. 2, p. 104, p. 106). Their hostility to this line of thought may seem odd given that they accept that the 'ground of grammar' has 'no support' (*ibid.*, p. 106). In their view, however, the jejune line presumes that the ground of grammar stands in 'need' of support from existential decisions (*ibid.*). And this they refuse to countenance. I do not find this convincing. Of course, as I have indicated, it is not the case that someone who is speaking or writing ordinarily faces each 'new decision' as one fraught with anxiety and dread at the possible 'abyss that yawns' before him (PI, §84, quoted above). Indeed, in my view, Wittgenstein's hesitancy is precisely a consequence of the fact that the 'new decision' may 'not be preceded by any deliberation' *at all*, let alone any anxiety (LI, p. 116; cp. BB, p. 143). Any such deliberation would suggest that the foundation of rule-governed behaviour (the leap) was itself a kind of *ratiocination*. And this rationalistic line of thought is definitely opposed to Wittgenstein's own (cp. OC, §475).

This is not simply an issue of correct exegesis. In my view, the 'moment of the leap', the 'new decision', even if it is nothing over and above opening one's mouth to speak or putting the pen to paper (nothing over and above leaping) *cannot* be completely determined or calculated by rational considerations. On the contrary, as I aim to show, only because my action (leap) *exceeds* the calculable can it open the space in which such considerations are possible. This does not mean that the existential leap is *irrational*, as Baker and Hacker suggest; rather, it is ungrounded or structurally abyssal. That is, it is logically prior to a determined rationality (or irrationality).

Rules and inclinations

This interpretation is shared, to a point, by Colin McGinn. He stresses that the reason why it would be misleading but 'more correct to speak of decision than of intuition' is that it

> prevents us from thinking that there must be some consultable authority on how rules are to be followed – some body of reasons – which is independent of how things naturally strike us, i.e. of our natural propensities. Nothing tells us how to go on in applying a sign.
>
> (Colin McGinn, 1984, p. 136)

This reading is, in my view, right and wrong. What is right is that there is nothing, no body of rules, no covenant in reason, which *forces* me to apply a word in the way I do, even though going on in this way 'is something that I do without a smidgen of hesitation' (Pears, 1988, p. 440). As Wittgenstein notes, it is this absence of doubt which first suggests the picture of hooking on to a system of definite rules: 'One follows the rule mechanically. Hence one compares it to a mechanism. "Mechanical" – that means: without thinking. But *entirely* without thinking? Without *reflecting*'. (RFM, VIII-61). McGinn is crucially wrong, however, to conceive of such an unreflective decision (the leap) as a mere (baldly) natural propensity. No doubt most human infants take to their mother tongue like a duck to water. And no doubt, having acquired a language, they find it natural and unavoidable to continue as others do. But this is not and cannot be simply a question of 'how things naturally strike us'. Such an account completely misplaces the nature of our relation to what we call rules. As Wittgenstein notes, the grammar of rules is precisely characterised by the idea that they are regarded as authoritative *independently of how things strike me*: "'As I see the rule, this is what it requires." It does not depend on whether I am disposed this way or that' (*ibid.*, VI-30).

McGinn's treatment of the grammar of rules in terms of going by 'how things strike us' revealingly conflates an important distinction between going by a kind of 'inspiration' or 'inclination' and going by 'a rule'. What is completely missing in the appeal to natural dispositions and propensities is the idea of the objectivity of rule-following. Or, to put it another way, what distinguishes the two kinds of case (following inclinations and following rules) is that only in the latter case can I require *another* to follow in the same way as I do (cp. PI, §232).

The importance of this point should not be underestimated. In this chapter I have been concerned with the question: what meaning is the expression 'the rule by which he proceeds' supposed to have left if we forgo the idea of language as a system of definite rules? In my view, we now have a completely satisfactory answer to this question: a way of behaving of *my own* can be conceived as 'rule-governed' only in so far as I can regard it as authoritative for actions *other than my own*. It is not, and cannot be, merely a question of what is natural for me, even though being able to acquire a language is (baldly) natural for me.

Rules and others

As the following remark from Wittgenstein makes clear, although McGinn has correctly rejected the foundationalist picture, his account necessarily falls short of an account of rule-following behaviour: '"It – for no reason – intimates this or that to me" means: I can't teach you how I follow the line. I make no presumption that you will follow it as I do, even if you do follow it' (RFM, VII-60). As McDowell rightly notes, if we try to establish shared pre-rational natural propensities concerning 'how things strike us' as the basic or bedrock level of linguistic regularities, 'everything normative fades out of the picture' (McDowell, 1984, p. 341).

A central feature of Wittgenstein's account of that behaviour which one can call 'following a rule' is, therefore, the way in which *a relation to the behaviour of others*, and hence a structural *publicness*, is *a priori* implicated by it.[15] A way of behaving of one's own can be (have the status of) 'following a rule' only in so far as one 'knows'[16] that this way of behaving is, essentially, not one's own alone, even if, as a matter of fact, one is isolated.[17]

This thought offers a fundamental insight into the question of how something manifest in the behaviour of the human animal, something 'immanent to the behaviour as such' can, yet, be 'transcendent in relation to the anatomical apparatus'. For what the Wittgensteinian argument suggests is that this is possible precisely when the behaviour is 'in itself' *towards others*. That is, one can only describe the behaviour as the behaviour it is by including in one's description the possibility of a relation to others of the kind indicated above. This is, I suggest, why Wittgenstein's treatment of the phenomenon of language places so much emphasis on what have been called 'normative activities'.[18] Normative activities are ways of establishing for others that '*this* is what is required' and thus exhibit the fundamental difference between rule-governed regularities and regularities of other kinds.[19] So McGinn is right to say that we cannot provide an authoritative body of reasons to provide a foundational justification for such regularities. But this does not mean that the basic or bedrock level is one in which we do not regard our practice and our explanations of meaning as authoritative for correctness. On the contrary, as McGinn notes elsewhere, 'the error is to suppose that I need to turn to anything *else* for guidance' (Colin McGinn, 1984, p. 21, fn 25; cp. PI, §223, §228, §230, §238, and RFM, VI-28).

Of course, we do not acquire all or even most of our mother tongue by having the meanings of individual words or expressions explained to us. Most of it we just pick up as infants from interactions with others. However, even when we are given explanations, nothing special is normally provided; not definite rules, but examples of usage. On this view, in whatever direction we look, '*what is normative [for ordinary use] is ordinary use itself*' (Cavell, 1976, p. 21). Clearly, there is no question of splitting the phenomenon of language here.

According to this argument, what 'the rule' *is* cannot be explained independently of examples of the actual use of language, i.e., independently of actual 'leaps'. Consequently, there can be no rule which provides an ultimate and unambiguous arbiter of what counts as 'a repetition of the same'. This is not to deny that rule-governed behaviour must be identifiable as 'conforming to the rule' (cp. LI, p. 18). But, again, what 'conforming to the rule' *is* is itself constituted on the basis of repetitions which are ungrounded or structurally abyssal. In every case the 'moment of decision' is ineliminable:

> 'I have a particular concept of the rule. If in this sense one follows it, then from that number one can only arrive at this one.' That is a spontaneous decision.
>
> But why do I say 'I must', if it is my decision? Well, may it not be that I must decide?
>
> Doesn't its being a spontaneous decision merely mean: that's how I act; ask for no reason!
>
> You say you must; but cannot say what compels you.
>
> I have a definite concept of the rule. I know what I have to do in any particular case. I know, that is I am in no doubt; it is obvious to me. I say 'Of course'. I can give no reason.
>
> When I say 'I decide spontaneously', naturally that does not mean: I consider which number would really be the best one here and then plump for . . .
>
> We say: 'First the calculations must be done right, and then it will be possible to pass some judgement on the facts of nature.'
>
> (RFM, VI-24, p. 326)

On this approach, recourse to definite rules to explain the phenomenon of language is fundamentally rejected. Through singular, 'spontaneous decisions' which, in each case, necessarily exceed the calculable, one is oneself 'functioning as the instrument of measurement' (Pears, 1988, p. 437):

> Someone asks me: What is the colour of this flower? I answer: 'red'. – Are you absolutely sure? Yes, absolutely sure! But may I not have been deceived and called the wrong colour 'red'? No. The certainty with which I call the colour 'red' is the rigidity of my measuring rod, it is the rigidity from which I start. When I give descriptions, that is not brought into doubt. This simply characterizes what we call describing.
>
> (RFM, VI-35)

The instrument of measurement

According to this argument, it makes no sense to require that what we call 'recognition of the same meaning' presumes that a speaker has a grasp of an ideal identity which is indefinitely repeatable as the same. This is a crucial point and needs to be made as clear as possible. Wittgenstein's treatment of the standard metre at PI §50 provides an extreme but instructive illustration.

At the time Wittgenstein wrote the *Investigations* a certain rod was used as the canonical sample of a metre length in the system of metric measurement. In this practice the rod functioned as a *constant*; it was the 'ideal' metre against which the metric length of all other rods had ultimately to be referred. It was normally treated as the highest court of appeal and definitive authority. The point that I want to emphasise here is that to *use* the rod as a constant in this way is not to make and does not involve any *claim* about its factual constancy – and this is so even if, in the extreme case of a canonical sample such as the standard metre, we might feel that such a claim should also be justified.[20] This explains why Wittgenstein stresses that one cannot claim of the sample that it is either one metre long or not one metre long (PI, §50). The rod functions as, is used as, a canonical constant, this is its 'peculiar role' (*ibid.*). If this is so, however, we cannot, at the same time, use it to ground a factual claim about its own length: it cannot function as a sample for itself, at once both as measure and thing measured.

To use a rod as a constant in the metric system is not to claim to know anything about the constancy of its length. On the contrary, claims to *know* (metric) lengths presuppose it having such a groundless *structural* role. Consequently, even if according to some method of measurement (a technique which need not, in fact, be completely independent of the rod) we judge the rod to be expanding and contracting, and hence we claim of the standard metre rod 'The length of the rod is not constant', this need not ruin its usefulness.[21] The use of the rod as a constant did not claim or entail that it was in fact so, even if 'what we call "measuring" is partly determined by a certain constancy in results of measurement' (*ibid.*, §242).

The analogy with words is this: to 'recognise' a given use of a mark as 'the same' is not to recognise an identity that must, in fact, be constant and unchanging.[22] It does not involve or presume a claim to conform to or know a context-transcendent identity which is 'indefinitely repeatable as the same' – a determinate sense which is carried into every application. Rather, through mastery of a way of behaving which is *in itself* towards others, we are ourselves functioning as a constant. We are ourselves the instrument of measurement of 'the same'.

This argument fundamentally calls into question thinking committed to the ideal of exactness, and hence to the humanist's phenomenon-splitting approach to language. In the next chapter I will present Derrida's attempt to think the phenomenon without splitting it; his attempt to 'think *at once* both the rule and the event, concept and singularity' (LI, p. 119). As we shall see, like Wittgenstein's, Derrida's argument accounts for 'the rule-governed nature of language' not in terms of a speaker's *knowledge* of indefinitely repeatable rules but in terms of the *structural relation to others* that, *in the deed*, a language *is*. As we shall see, this argument will enable us to see that the 'being with others' which belongs to communication in general and the use of a word language in particular is *structural*, not *epistemological*.

7

COMMUNICATION AND ITERABILITY

INTRODUCTION

In the previous chapter it was argued that accounting for the normative nature of meaning required us to turn away from the ideal of exactness and towards an examination of events of the use of signs, events for which 'it would almost be more correct to say' that 'a new decision was needed at every stage' (PI, §186). If we are to take this path, then, instead of acceding to the 'craving for generality' (BB, p. 17), we must learn to 'think *at once* both the rule and the event, concept and singularity' (LI, p. 119). In this chapter, following Derrida, I will propose the concept of *iterability* as the indispensable tool for this task. While the concept of 'family resemblance' is helpful in an empirical ('look and see') refutation of the traditional picture of conceptual idealisation, 'iterability is the ideal concept of the limit of all idealization' (*ibid.*). It thus aims to provide the logical principle of this fact of ordinary language.

As we shall see, 'iterability' is not the concept of the repeatability-of-the-self-same-identity. Rather, it is the concept of the impossibility of any such conceptual purity. That is, in what follows I will explore Derrida's claim that iterability, as the condition for the *possibility* of all conceptual determination and distinction in actuality, is at once the condition for the *impossibility* that such determination be pure or ideal. I will begin, in the first part, by examining the relationship between Derrida's account of the essential iterability of events of the use of signs and more traditional accounts which conceive such events as, in themselves, singular, dateable occurrences. In order to clarify the contrast here I will reconstruct the argument in which Derrida first employs the concept of iterability. Derrida's argument aims to make perspicuous structural features internal to any species of communication whatsoever or 'no matter of what kind' (RFM, VI-34). His strategy is to show that 'the general space of possibility' (LI, p. 19) of the functioning of all signs can be characterised in terms of predicates traditionally restricted to the concept of writing.[1] Setting out the whole field of language in this way thus allows for a strategic generalisation of the concept of writing to cover 'all orders of "signs"' – and, with that, affords a novel account of communication (*ibid.*, p. 9).

REPETITIONS OF THE SAME

A minimal consensus

As I have indicated, the term iterability is introduced by Derrida in the course of an investigation of the limits of any possible idealisation of conceptual identities. Specifically, it is introduced in the course of an account which aims to demonstrate the irreducibility of what we have identified as 'play': that is, in an account which affirms dissemination. Perhaps strangely, however, the term is also capable of finding a use in accounts which are committed to the idea of determining and determinable rules which are, ideally, indefinitely repeatable as the same: that is, in accounts which affirm the ideal of exactness. For example, in his reply to Derrida's reading of Austin's theory of speech acts, Searle is willing to employ the concept in his explanation of the generativity of language (the necessary possibility of using old terms again in sentential contexts that communicate a new sense):

> The performances of actual speech acts (whether written or spoken) are indeed events, *datable singular events* in particular historical contexts. But as events they have some very peculiar properties. They are capable of communicating from speakers to hearers an infinite number of different contents. There is no upper limit on the number of new things that can be communicated by speech acts, which is just another way of saying that there is no limit on the number of new speech acts. Furthermore, hearers are able to understand this infinite number of possible communications simply by recognizing the intentions of the speakers in the performance of the speech acts. Now given that both speaker and hearer are finite, what is it that gives their speech acts this limitless capacity for communication? The answer is that the speakers and hearers are masters of the set of rules we call *the rules of language,* and these rules are recursive. They *allow for the repeated application of the same rule.*
>
> Thus the peculiar features of the intentionality that we find in speech acts require an *iterability* that includes not only . . . the repetition of the same word in different contexts, but also an iterability of the application of syntactical rules. Iterability – both as exemplified by the use of the same word type and as exemplified by the recursive character of syntactical rules – is the necessary presupposition of the forms which that intentionality takes.
>
> (Searle, 1977, p. 208, my emphasis)

That iterability is *in some way* internal to language (and hence also 'intentionality' in general) is not, therefore, in dispute. Indeed, Derrida calls this point of agreement 'the minimal consensus' in the debate with Searle (LI, p. 61). However, a question remains as to the depth or extent of agreement here.

Frank B. Farrell's attempt to clarify Derrida's position on the question of iterability (Farrell, 1988, pp. 53–64) would suggest that the agreement is substantial. Like Searle, Farrell's Derrida is concerned to provide an explanation for the generativity of language. That is, according to Farrell, the concept of iterability is appealed to by Derrida in an account which supposes that a speaker's ability to recognise something as being 'the same word' and 'the same sense' in new contexts is to be explained in terms of the speaker's knowledge of definite 'rules'. Farrell presents Derrida's account in the following way:

> The physical instances of a linguistic expression are never exactly alike. What gives such an instance a stable meaning is that we know what it takes for other physical shapes to count as instances of the same expression. This sort of recognition of what is the same in different instances occurs not only when we see that there may be different tokens of the same type, but also when we see that different utterance-types may have the same meaning and that expressions in different languages may likewise mean the same thing. So a condition for making an expression meaningful is that it be determined, by the conventions of the language, what will count as a repetition of the expression. . . . *The linguistic token* would be meaningless apart from *the system of rules* which fixes what it takes for different utterances to have the same meaning.
>
> (*ibid.*, p. 54, my emphasis)

On this reading, Derrida's use of the concept of iterability aims to explain how, despite empirical differences, identity can be stable both at the level of the appearance of a word and at the level of its meaning. Like Searle, Farrell's Derrida explains the possibility of such persisting stability in terms of rules or 'conventions' which 'fix' which repetitions are to count as actually being and not merely seeming to be 'the same again'. These are those recurrences which conform to the rules. On this view, knowledge of a system of rules underlies and ensures the speaker's recognition of a given use as, objectively, 'the same'.

Note that, for both Searle and Farrell's Derrida, the generativity of language is accounted for by bifurcating the analysis: the phenomenon of language is *split* between a system of rules and their application in singular events of speech, the former explaining the semantic properties of the latter. The existence of indefinitely repeatable as the same ('recursive') rules explains and makes possible the intelligibility of novel events of speech. As I have indicated, on this reading the minimal consensus between Searle and Derrida would appear to be extremely strong. Their differences would then have to be accounted for in terms of the consequences drawn from this starting point. In order to assess this reading, let us consider again the thinking behind the ideal of exactness.

Identity and difference

For simplicity's sake I will start with the idea of recognising 'the same word' without reference to 'sameness of meaning'.

Given that, in various ways, the following marks are *not* the same, what makes it possible to recognise that they *are*, nevertheless, recurrences of 'the same' word?

Same, Same, Same, *Same*, **Same**, SAME, Same, Same.

As we have seen, we are tempted to say: 'These marks count as "the same" because they conform to an identity or rule which is, ideally, indefinitely repeatable as the same in different cases.' Of course, such an ideal is a somewhat 'queer' entity, not quite real, or at least, not quite 'empirical'; it is the *formal essence*, or the repeatable form, of each empirical mark; it is that in which the order of possibilities of the phenomenon can be 'contained' in the present.[2] Thus grasping such a repeatable form explains a subject's ability to anticipate in the present an indefinite number of possible applications on other occasions, each of which would be, despite the empirical variations, *essentially* a recurrence of the same.

It is important to stress that Derrida does not simply affirm the opposite to this account. Specifically, he accepts that a word is something to which we *must* relate as having an identity which is independent of any particular occasion of its application. Thus, he explicitly affirms that the identity of words presumes what he calls 'a minimum of idealization': 'Through empirical variations of tone, voice, etc., possibly of a certain accent, for example, we must be able to recognise the identity, roughly speaking, of a signifying form' (LI, p. 10). With respect to the ideal of exactness, however, the question is: Is what is recognised here something which recurs as the same in each singular event of speech or writing? Something which, despite the differences between the cases, is, in each case, fully present? Derrida argues that it is not. And it is here that we can begin to see how, *pace* Farrell, Derrida's conception of iterability differs dramatically from Searle's more traditional approach:

> The structure of iteration ... implies *both* identity *and* difference. Iteration in its 'purest form' – and it is always impure – contains *in itself* the discrepancy of a difference that constitutes it as iteration. The iterability of an element divides its own identity *a priori*, even without taking into account that this identity can only *determine* or delimit itself through differential relations to other elements and hence that it bears the mark of this difference. It is because this iterability is differential, within each individual 'element' as well as between 'elements' ... that

the remainder, although indispensable, is never that of a full or fulfilling presence: it is a differential structure escaping the logic of presence.

(*ibid.*, p. 53)

No doubt this is rather difficult to follow at present. But a brief elaboration on the (implicit) reference in it to Saussure's 'structuralist' conception of the 'differential' identity of linguistic signs should prove helpful in introducing Derrida's 'post-structuralist' conception of their 'iterability'. Sticking still to words, the Saussurean view is that the basic 'elements' of speech (phonemes) only emerge out of or issue from a system of phonic *differences*. Such a view entails a denial of the intuitive assumption that 'what one hears' when one hears speech is always and simply sounds or properties of sounds: something fully present in the present. The following summarises the central Saussurean *reductio ad absurdum* of the idea of conceiving speech as composed of such substantial 'positive terms':[3]

1   Assume that what can be heard is always a sound, or is composed of sounds or properties of sounds.
2   Articulate, meaningful speech is, by definition, something which can be heard.
3   For articulate, meaningful speech to be possible, a language must contain a number of discriminably different 'units' (call them 'phonemes'). People must be able to discriminate different phonemes if speech is to function as such.
4   The difference between two phonemes is not itself a sound – not an audible 'something'.
5   Therefore, given (1), the difference which establishes speech and lets it be heard is inaudible.
6   But the difference between two phonemes is obviously audible.
7   Therefore one ought to reject (1).

One might feel troubled by this argument. But (5) *does* follow from (4) if we accept (1). So that is the assumption rejected by the Saussurean thesis of differential identity: 'what one hears' when one hears an identifiable phoneme *cannot* be reduced to a sound which is simply present in the present.[4] And that is because, as Derrida puts it in the passage quoted above, its 'identity can only *determine* or delimit itself through differential relations to other elements'. Now, as the same passage indicates, Derrida *also* wishes to affirm, in addition, a differentiality 'within each individual "element" as well as between "elements"'. As we shall see, it is this thought of 'difference within identity' which distinguishes Derrida's conception of iterability, and ruins Farrell's attempt to align it to more traditional accounts of 'repetitions of the same'. In fact, this should have been clear from Derrida's first and most cursory reference to the term:

> In order for my 'written communication' to retain its function as
> writing, i.e., its readability, it must . . . be repeatable – iterable – in the
> absolute absence of the receiver or of any empirically determinable
> collectivity of receivers. Such iterability – (*iter*, 'again', probably comes
> from *itara*, '*other*' in Sanskrit, and everything that follows can be read as
> the working out of *the logic that ties repetition to alterity*) structures the mark
> of writing itself, no matter what particular type of writing is involved.
>
> (*ibid.*, p. 7, my emphasis)

'The logic that ties repetition to alterity'. Paradoxical as it may seem, what has to
be acknowledged here is that Derrida's appeal to the concept of iterability is
made not only because of its connection with the idea of sameness and identity
but also because of its (improbable, etymological) connection with alterity, other-
ness and difference. Roughly, what Derrida aims to show is that alterity and
difference – i.e., what is traditionally conceived as bearing on features which are
essentially 'accidental' or 'external' to 'ideal identities' – are, in fact and in principle, a necessary and universal feature of all idealisation as such. Thus, Derrida
will argue that the recognisability of the 'same word' is, in fact and in principle,
possible only '*in, through*, and even *in view of* its alteration' (*ibid.*, p. 53).

As I have stressed, the view Derrida wishes to defend is that a certain 'play'
within conceptual identities does not threaten the normal functioning of
language but, rather, is an inherent feature of it. In what follows, I will show in
greater detail how Derrida accounts for this feature with reference to the thought
that iterability is 'the positive condition of the emergence of the mark' (*ibid.*,
p. 53). In the demonstration of this thought, the concept of iterability will not be
used in order to explain how, despite empirical differences in the contexts of a
word's use, its sense remains the same. On the contrary, the aim is to explain
how conceptual *identity* is possible only through such contextual *differences*. Clearly,
if this is correct, then the first casualty will be the idea of the rigorous purity of
an indefinitely repeatable ideal identity. The purity of such an identity will be, in
actuality, always already violated.

The Saussurean Circle

The importance of providing a clear defence of Derrida's use of and appeal to
the concept of iterability should not be minimised. As Searle notes, 'iterability
looms large' in all of Derrida's argumentation (Searle, 1977, p. 199). Indeed,
Derrida himself has given the following self-description:

> This is my starting point: no meaning can be determined out of
> context, but no context permits saturation. What I am referring to here
> is not richness of substance, semantic fertility, but rather structure, the
> structure of the remnant or of iteration.
>
> (Derrida, 1979, p. 81)

Clearly, if Derrida's argument in support of this starting point is faulty, then his whole project seems to collapse around it. The question is, therefore, whether it can be given a clear explication.

As I have indicated, in traditional approaches the 'iterability' required by language is identified with the concept of 'repetition of the same', a concept which has been inseparable from the idea of persisting self-identity. On such an approach, communication can occur because a plurality of subjects have a shared knowledge of definite rules which enable them to anticipate an indefinite number of novel applications in unique and singular events of speech. As we shall see, against this view Derrida argues that the 'being with others' that belongs to the use of a language is *structural*, not *epistemological*. That is, according to Derrida, the fact that events of the use of signs can 'communicate' is not to be explained by recourse to knowledge of indefinitely repeatable rules. Rather, 'the rule-governed nature of language' is accounted for in terms of *the mode of being with others that a language **is***. This is not to say that Derrida denies that the use of language is rule-governed. On the contrary, he unequivocally states that the 'first condition of [the] functioning [of any element of a language] is its delineation with regard to a certain code' (LI, p. 10). Nevertheless, he immediately adds that 'I prefer not to become too involved here with this concept of code which does not seem very reliable to me' (*ibid.*). In this section, in order to prepare the ground for an explication of Derrida's conception of iterability, I will explain his caution here.

Derrida's caution with respect to the concept of code, or of a system of rules governing the use of signs, lies precisely in its connection to the traditional tendency to bifurcate or split the phenomenon of language in the manner I have outlined. In Derrida's view, an analysis of the phenomenon of language which begins with a radical distinction between the 'system' and the 'event' of language necessarily deprives itself of the means with which to provide an account of the possibility of what is universally acknowledged to be its 'first condition'.

The claim here can be clarified by considering Derrida's response to what can be called the problem of the 'Saussurean Circle'. I use this title in acknowledgement of its explicit appearance in Saussure's analysis of language in terms of *langue* (language *qua* system of rules) and *parole* (language *qua* event of speech): 'Language (*langue*) is necessary', says Saussure, 'for speech (*parole*) to be intelligible and to produce all its effects; but the latter is necessary for language to establish itself; historically the fact of speech is always prior' (Saussure, 1983, p. 18).

According to Derrida, the problem is that, once one embarks on an analysis of language based on the radical distinction between linguistic systems and linguistic events, the conceptual resources at one's disposal cannot account for the possibility of the very phenomenon it is claiming to delimit. This is because the impossible combination of both the historical priority and the logical posteriority of speech ruins any attempt to provide an internally consistent account of the conditions of possibility for the phenomenon of language:

> If one rigorously distinguishes *langue* and *parole*, code and message, schema and usage, etc., and if one wishes to do justice to the two postulates thus enunciated, one does not know where to begin, nor how something can begin in general, be it language or speech.
>
> (Derrida, 1981, p. 28)

The claim here is not that the Saussurean Circle is vicious in the sense of being a proof which presupposes that which requires demonstration. Rather, it is a 'chicken and egg' difficulty: 'one does not know where to begin'. Thus, Saussure is not really justified in appealing to the historical priority of speech. For 'speech' (*parole*) must be opposed to mere babble, or mere noise production, and this is possible, on Saussure's account, only if 'language' (*langue*) is present. Hence, as soon as one rigorously distinguishes the system from the event of language, these concepts become 'unreliable' when one is concerned with questions concerning the conditions of the possibility for conceptuality in general. And this is Derrida's principle concern.[5]

This point can be made in another way by conceiving the Circle in the form of a regress. As we have seen, if one works within the schema of this distinction, the system of rules is conceived as fixing the sense of words across variations of context of speech. However, if these rules are acknowledged as having a normative role in the use of signs, then it seems clear that, among the 'events of speech', we must be able to identify 'expressions of rules' (cp. PI, §120b). However, on the model under examination, if such 'expressions of rules' are to be intelligible they must be governed by rules, rules which must, if they are to function as such, be expressible . . . and so on.

Derrida does not think that circularity or regress is inevitable here. Rather, treating it as a *reductio* of any attempt to determine the conditions of possibility of language on the basis of a radical system/event or code/message distinction, he concludes that such problems show the necessity of accounting for language in terms which do not split the phenomena of language (see Derrida, 1981, p. 28). As I have indicated, in my view Derrida's primary aim in his investigation of the iterability of signs is to provide just such an account. That is, it constitutes a sustained attempt to overcome the 'chicken and egg' oscillation; a task which, therefore, 'entails the necessity of thinking at once both the rule and the event' (LI, p. 121). It is for this reason that Derrida eschews recourse to the concept of the code or system of rules at the outset of his account of the phenomenon of language.[6]

As noted, Derrida's objection to the Circle does not destroy or annul the use of a distinction between rules of language and events of speech. However, as the regress makes perspicuous, it does imply that an appeal to this distinction in an account of concept formation operates with an uncritical or illegitimately delimited conception of 'events of speech'. It is on this issue that Derrida's appeal to iterability comes to the fore most clearly. Before it is precipitately assumed either that we know what the distinction between rules and events entails or that we know how it must be drawn, we 'should first be clear', Derrida states, 'on what constitutes the status of an "occurrence" or the eventhood of an event . . . that *in itself* can be only . . . iterable in its structure' (*ibid.*, pp. 17–18). In the next section I will turn to a direct examination of Derrida's analysis of this status.

WRITING AND COMMUNICATION

Writing

As the quotation in which Derrida first employs the concept of iterability suggests, the principle context of its use is in an analysis of communication, and in particular of written communication. In this analysis of writing, Derrida attempts to identify in a classical account of communication 'the absence that seems to intervene in a specific manner in the functioning of writing' (*ibid.*, p. 8). As Searle notes, the generalisation of this apparently specific absence to 'every species of sign and communication' is one of the fundamental moves of Derrida's argument (Searle, 1977, p. 199). If we wish to understand Derrida's views concerning the 'eventhood of events' of language, we need to examine this analysis of writing carefully.

Derrida takes his point of departure from the model of communication outlined at the start of Chapter 6. On this model, the use of language is conceived as a means of transport or a transitional medium of a speaker's meaning-to-be-communicated. If we use language, it is because we want or need to convey thoughts or ideas to another. Speech is used to express, externalise, objectify, represent (etc.), thoughts, ideas, contents, meanings (etc.), which precede or accompany but in any case govern the 'outer' event. On this model, 'completely successful communication' is that eventuality in which a thought grasped by one speaker becomes 'fully' known to, or 'fully' understood by, another.[7]

As I have presented it, this conception of communication is characterised by the desire to go beyond interest in the 'signifier' or the 'externalities' of language in the direction of a determinate and indefinitely repeatable 'signified meaning' or definite rule. As we shall see, Derrida's generalisation of the concept of writing is part of a sustained attempt to conceive the nature of communication otherwise than according to this phenomenon-splitting model (cp. LI, p. 5).

Generalised writing

Derrida's criticism of the traditional model of communication focuses on writing, and results in a generalisation of the concept. But what could it mean to say, and how can it be established, that writing is, as John Llewelyn puts it, 'in some strange way presupposed by [both] speaking and writing in the usual meanings of these words' (Llewelyn, 1986, p. 55)?

As we shall see, this generalisation of the 'usual meaning' of writing to cover the entire field of language is defended with an argument which purports to show that 'the traits which can be recognized in the classical, narrowly defined concept of writing' are *necessarily valid* for all signs (LI, p. 9). While this claim to generality does not, for this reason, straightforwardly change the 'usual meaning' of the word 'writing', it does put pressure on what we are inclined to say about the 'usual meaning' of the words of language in general – especially, as Wittgenstein might say, what we are inclined to say when we are doing philosophy.[8]

According to Derrida, on the classical conception of language 'one is compelled to regard [writing] as an especially potent means of communication' (*ibid.*, p. 3). What is the 'potency' that is supposed to be so specific to writing? Derrida cites Condillac as a representative of a tradition of interpretation on this subject for which he claims 'not a single counterexample can be found in the entire history of philosophy' (*ibid.*). According to Condillac's classical interpretation, writing is conceived as a technique or technical instrument for communicating a meaning-content over a far greater distance than is possible by speaking: 'Men in a state of communicating their thoughts by means of sounds, felt the necessity of imagining new signs capable of perpetuating those thoughts and of making them known to persons who are absent' (Condillac, cited *ibid.*, p. 4). The potency of writing is thus found in its capacity to communicate thoughts to addressees who are *absent.* As Derrida notes, this concept of absence is really a 'concept of absence as the modification of presence' (*ibid.*, p. 6). That is, on the classical interpretation, writing emerges as a technical device when the desire or need arises to extend the field of communication to addressees who are present but out of range of the natural voice. Writing thus first appears *in fact* when the space of sociality has changed to the point that we need to send messages to others who are 'not only distant but outside of the entire field of vision and beyond earshot' (Derrida, 1976, p. 281). It is with his interrogation of this concept of absence as the modification of presence that Derrida's analysis challenges the classical model of communication.

Writing and absence

On the classical conception, the absence which specifies writing is conceived in terms of distance in such a way that the absence of the addressee is a modified form of his or her presence – it is, from the point of view of the sender, a distant presence. In his reading of this account, Derrida considers whether in fact and in principle this distance 'must be capable of being carried to a certain absoluteness of absence' if writing is to be possible (LI, p. 7). In short, Derrida's question is whether the absence of the addressee that is supposed to specify writing should be characterised in terms not of communication to those who are currently, *in fact*, absent from me (distantly present) but, rather, in terms of the structural *possibility* of the addressee's radical absence – for example, his or her death.

If we consider again the passage in which Derrida first employs the concept of iterability we can see that Derrida's response to this question is affirmative:

> In order for my 'written communication' to retain its function as writing, i.e., its readability, it must remain readable *despite the absolute disappearance of any receiver, determined in general.* My communication must be repeatable – iterable – in the absolute absence of the receiver or of any empirically determinable collectivity of receivers. Such iterability – (*iter*, meaning 'again', probably comes from *itara*, 'other' in Sanskrit, and everything that follows can be read as the working out of the logic that ties repetition to alterity) structures the mark of writing itself, no matter what particular type of writing is involved.
>
> (ibid., my emphasis)

The central claim is that 'the written mark itself' is only constituted as such – as readable writing – by virtue of its 'iterability'. As I understand it, the idea here is that the readability or recognisability of the written mark is possible on *this* occasion only in view of the possibility of *another* such event;[9] including a repetition in the absolute absence of the 'living presence' of the 'empirically determinable' addressee or receiver.

I write a letter and address it with a proper name. To do this is to write to an empirically determinable receiver or addressee. Of course, it is always possible that, before receiving my written message, this addressee will die. Does this prevent my writing from being read? Of course not. But Derrida does not want the obviousness of this point to be taken to reflect a common sense supplement to Condillac's analysis. On the contrary, with the re-evaluation of the relationship of writing to absence, Derrida aims to transform the conceptual economy which orients the classical interpretation of writing. I will explain this.

Note first of all that Condillac's interpretation of writing does not mention the absence of the producer of the written mark who sends it away to be read elsewhere. It is clear, however, that parallel considerations must hold here too:

> To write is to produce a mark . . . which my future disappearance will not in principle, hinder in its functioning. . . . For a writing to be a writing it must continue to 'act' and to be readable even when what is called the author of the writing no longer answers for what he has written. . . . The situation of the writer is, concerning the written text, basically the same as that of the reader.
>
> (ibid., p. 8)

Derrida is not concerned here with death or writing (in its usual sense) as an empirical eventuality. Rather, his concern is with the logical and not merely the physical possibility that writing can continue to remain readable when the absence of the sender or the addressee is no longer a mode of presence but a radical or absolute absence. And his claim is that the possibility of it functioning again beyond (or in the absence of) the context of its production or its empirically determined destination specifies an essential aspect of what a written mark *is*: to be what it is, all writing must be capable of functioning beyond the death of any empirically determinable sender or receiver. We can thus propose the following 'law' of writing: a mark that is not structurally readable – iterable – beyond the death of the empirically determinable sender and receiver could not be writing (cp. *ibid.*, p. 7).

The general claim is that the *possibility* of 'functioning in the absence of' implied by the classical conception of writing must be capable of being brought to an absolute limit if writing is to constitute itself as such. Any particular event of writing or reading, if it is to take place as such, presumes as its condition of possibility the possibility of another such event in the radical absence of this one. In short, it presumes that the event has an essential iterability. Hence, for any empirically determinable user, his or her current use presumes as its condition of possibility the possibility of an iteration in the absolute absence of his or her current presence.

Derrida emphasises that this holds true even in a case in which I write a note to *myself*.

> The sender and the receiver, even if they were the self-same *subject*, each relate to a mark they experience as made to do without them, from the instant of its production or of its reception on; and they experience this not as the mark's negative limit but rather as the positive condition of its possibility. Barring this, the mark would not function. . . . Either I wouldn't need one or it would be unusable as such.
>
> (*ibid.*, p. 49)

The disjunction at the end here marks two ways in which Derrida attempts to undermine resistance to his account by *reductio ad absurdum*. The first disjunct relates to the superfluity of such marks for a classically conceived 'subject', i.e. for an entity that is supposed to be certain of its presence to itself: Why, if the presence-to-itself of the sender and receiver was as certain as all that, would it bother to make use of or need an *aide memoire*?

The classical objector may then claim that the self-presence in question does not preclude possession of a fallible memory.[10] The second disjunct takes its departure from a case in which memory is not an issue. Take, for example, the extreme case of someone writing something simply in order to read (reread) it a *moment* later (say, for fun). Surely, one might want to say, here we have a case of writing in which the sender and receiver really are present and present to each other. Thus, it is a case in which the possibility of the sender's and receiver's absence is not *essential* to the possibility of communication.

In Derrida's view, however, if it really is a case of pure self-identity of sender and receiver, then it becomes impossible to conceive how the written message could pass or circulate 'between' them.[11] Consequently, the mark 'would be unusable as such'. The written mark is made to supplement an absence of presence that is always possible, and this possibility structures *every* event of writing *a priori*. An event in which this possibility of absence is excluded is, in fact and in principle, not an event of writing or reading.

Public signs

According to the argument of the last section, writing *must* be able to continue functioning beyond the death of *any* empirically determinable user in general. Any written message is such, is what it is, only to the extent that a reader could read whatever a (determinable) sender could write in the radical absence of that sender: *writing can and must be able to do without the presence of the (determinable) sender*. Equally, any message is readable only to the extent that a reader can read whatever the sender could write in the radical absence of the (determinable or destined) receiver's presence: *writing can and must be able to do without the presence of the (destined) receiver*.

These two possible absences 'construct the possibility of the message itself' (*ibid.*, p. 50). That is, *pace* Condillac's classical interpretation, it is *not* the 'permanence' of the written word which makes iterations possible in the absence of the sender or receiver; rather, the written mark is precisely made to make up for these *possible absences*. Or again, writing is not essentially a relation between two present subjects but, in terms of its logical conditions of possibility, it is structured between two possible absences.

It is with this conclusion that the possibility of a strategic generalisation of the term 'writing' becomes forceful. According to Derrida's argument, the absence that characterises writing is not a function of the fact of persistence or permanence but of logically necessary preconditions of its status *as* readable writing. It is true that these preconditions are most perspicuous in the case of writing, but what if these possibilities of absence can be acknowledged to be part of the structure of *every* event of 'communication', no matter of what kind, whatever the 'species'?

The idea here is that a 'singular event' that can 'communicate' (e.g. an event of speech) is possible only on condition of a necessary or structural relation to an iteration that is *another such* 'singular event' which is *not present* at the time of its production or reception. That is, an occasion other than this one which, as a singular event, cannot be conceived as being 'writing' without reference to *another such* event, an occasion other than this one which, as a singular event, cannot be conceived as being 'writing' without reference to *another such* event . . . Numbers are not accumulating here. The limit is only that it is *not once*. This is the differentiality 'within each individual "element"' which is 'the positive condition of the emergence of the mark' (*ibid.*, p. 53). This is what Derrida is insisting upon when he states that the 'unity of the signifying form' that is 'required to permit its recognition' 'only constitutes itself by virtue of its iterability' (*ibid.*, p. 10). The point is that something which could not function in the absence of the current presence of an empirically determinable user *could not be* 'writing' – *no matter of what kind.*[12]

'Writing' (in Derrida's 'no matter of what kind' sense)[13] is, therefore, structurally, for every possible user in general (*ibid.*, p. 8). The space of 'writing' is an intrinsically public space through and through. And hence there can be no 'structurally secret code', no 'writing' which cannot function again and by another (*ibid.*). Even in the case of a language spoken only by a single human being, the possibility of repeating the marks that is entailed by such behaviour (if it is such behaviour) makes it in principle iterable for another in the radical absence of the first (cp. *ibid.*).

On this account, the factual emergence of writing, the eventual emergence of a relatively permanent mark that can do without the current presence of a determinable sender or recipient, is possible because, in principle, the possibility of this absence is part of the logical structure of any linguistic expression in general; part of the conditions of possibility of any 'means of communication' in general. 'Within every sign already, every mark or every trait, there is distancing . . . what there has to be so that it is legible for another, another than you or me' (Derrida, 1987b, p. 29; see also *ibid.*, p. 78).[14]

TRANSFORMING THE TRADITIONAL MODEL OF COMMUNICATION

The intervention of deconstruction

That this structure of distancing is most perspicuous in writing helps the demonstration and provides a strategic *raison d'être* for a generalisation of the old term. However, according to Derrida, this strategy also ensures the most effective intervention into the instituted field of the traditional model of communication.

As we have seen, the traditional model, the model which Condillac inherits and presents, seeks to relegate writing to a position of the (written) representation of a (spoken) representation of signified senses or thought-meanings-to-be-communicated.

On this model, the sense of thoughts, pure idealities, are the inner essence, the 'internalities', of language which can, in the interiority of a subject's own mind, do without their 'externalities', their material 'clothing' – or *almost*. For conceptions of such interiority have always maintained a residual 'clothing' for internal thoughts, namely, as 'silent' or 'inner' *speech*. It is with 'internal speech' that the sign and signified are supposed to be in the closest possible proximity: one 'hears oneself' *at the same time* as one 'understands oneself'. If, however, speech is always a kind of 'writing', this picture of the 'inner' cannot be maintained.[15] Anything 'present in the mind' which is communicable is constituted as such only in virtue of its iterability – and hence is irreducible to an identity that can simply be present in the present (see, e.g., Derrida, 1985, p. 88).

As this point makes clear, the conceptual field of the classical model is fundamentally disrupted by Derrida's generalisation of writing. Derrida describes his deconstructive argument as practising 'a *reversal* of the classical opposition [of speech and writing] and a general *displacement*' of the instituted field of interpretation of communication (LI, p. 21). However, in a certain respect, this deconstruction of the classical model is simply an inflected repetition or 'iteration' of it. That is, Derrida's reading aims to put to work *acknowledged* (but marginalised) predicates *against* the dominant motif of the classical model. This 'active reading' of the classical model is not negative: it affirms what in the classical model itself 'has *always* resisted the prior organization of forces' (*ibid.*). As we have seen, this involves 'liberating' the 'force of generality' (*ibid.*) of certain predicates of writing which are recognised but cannot be done justice to by the classical (phonocentric) model. The idea here is that to do justice to these predicates is, in a certain way, to affirm what we already knew but find it very difficult to realise:[16] writing can and must be able to function *beyond the context of its inscription*; and this is 'no less appropriate to every species of sign and communication' (*ibid.*, p. 7). That is, an event of 'writing', large or small, is necessarily such that 'no context can *entirely* enclose it' (*ibid.*, p.9).

To affirm this generalisation of writing is thus also to affirm dissemination. It is to say that, in fact and in principle, 'writing' will always and interminably be 'offering itself to be read and to be rewritten' (*ibid.*, p. 8). As Derrida notes, 'this does not imply that the mark is valid outside of a context, but on the contrary that there are only contexts without any absolute anchorage' (*ibid.*, p. 12). There is, that is to say, no metacontextual or extra-textual 'outside' which sets a limit to 'play'.[17] Events which *in themselves* can only be iterable are, therefore, at once the condition of possibility for 'writing' in actuality and the condition of impossibility for 'meanings' which attain the ideal of exactness.

Explaining generality

The character of Derrida's affirmation of dissemination can be brought out more sharply if we consider again the role of the concept of iterability in more traditional accounts of language. As we have seen, traditionally, the aim is to provide a general explanation for generality (or generativity) in language. How is it possible for a speaker to apply and recognise words and concepts in an indefinite number of new cases? And the answer was: because the speaker has knowledge of definite rules which are indefinitely repeatable as the same. The rules are 'iterable'. Derrida's argument has a very different character. Iterability does not *explain* generality. Rather, what Derrida's argument from iterability brings to the fore is that it is *inconceivable* that an event of 'writing' might *not* recur in new contexts.[18] Each 'singular event' of 'writing' is not what it is except in view of *another such* 'singular event', an event that is not what it is except in view of *another such* 'singular event', an event . . . And so on. In short, 'what *I* am doing *now*' can only be doing *that* ('writing' something) if I 'know'[19] that '*what* I *do* now' necessarily exceeds, and to that extent is independent of and can do without, my current presence. Consequently, no single context and no element within it ('inner' or 'outer'), conceived in isolation, can give content to the idea that part of it is the occurrence of a 'rule-governed event'.[20] On this account, iterability is not an accidental characteristic of language but its essence: 'In the beginning, in principle, was the post.' (Derrida, 1987b, p. 29). Or, as Wittgenstein puts it, 'what I do is . . . *repeat* an expression. But this is not the *end* of the language-game: it is the *beginning*' (PI, §290).

In Chapter 6 I outlined an important parallel between Wittgenstein and Derrida on the question of conceptual 'looseness' or 'play'. In what follows I will show that the Derridean conception of iterability helps us to clarify two of Wittgenstein's most important but also most telegraphic remarks: 'It is not possible that there should have only been *one* occasion on which someone obeyed a rule' (PI, §199); and 'In order to describe the phenomenon of language, one must describe a practice, not something that happens once, *no matter of what kind*. It is very difficult to realise this' (RFM, VI-34).

The multiple application thesis

The first point to note is that Wittgenstein's emphasis in these remarks is not only on the *possibility* of other occasions on which . . . , but the necessity of *actual* recurrences. This latter aspect (the aspect of itera*tion*) is highlighted in Colin McGinn's reading of these remarks. As the heart of what he calls Wittgenstein's 'multiple application thesis', McGinn argues that the point of these remarks is to insist 'that there must be *some* rules which are multiply obeyed if a person is to grasp *any*' (Colin McGinn, 1984, p. 126). In so far as this formulation warns us against assuming that Wittgenstein's idea is that it is necessary that *every* expression must have occurred more than once, I think McGinn is right.[21] However, I think McGinn is wrong to assume that it makes sense to talk of 'rules' being 'multiply obeyed' in this context. In my view Wittgenstein's remarks are concerned with the conditions in which we can *conceive* of there being 'rules' *überhaupt*, and if this is so then McGinn's thesis cannot be the whole truth. If, not implausibly, we take Wittgenstein's point to be that we cannot conceive of an event being a case of 'obeying a rule' if another *such* event had not, in general, actually occurred, then a very different 'thesis' comes to the fore.

Wittgenstein's remarks can be seen in the right light if we see them as responding to questions of the form: What sort of surrounding must there be for the notions of 'rule' and 'following a rule' to make *sense*? And, in my view, Wittgenstein's central claim on this issue is that we cannot, in general, make sense of an (actual) occasion (singular event) being someone 'obeying a rule' without making reference to the actuality of *another such* event.[22] This is not a thesis about the multiple application of rules, but a thesis concerning the eventhood of an event which is not what it is except against a background of *other such* events. In short, Wittgenstein's thesis is this: in the absolute absence of actual repetitions, in the absence of a *custom*, it is not just the notion of obeying a rule but the notion of a rule itself which has no content.[23]

The emphasis on actuality may seem to distinguish Wittgenstein's account from Derrida's. However, in both cases the concern is to show that the functioning of language presumes, internally, an iterable structure. That is, 'writing' is an institution the 'being-there' of which is constituted only in virtue of its essential iterability. Wittgenstein's stress on the actuality of recurrence ties this point concerning *iterability* to what Derrida calls the 'forms of *iteration*' (LI, p. 18) or 'solid traditions' (*ibid.*, p. 144), which are, *in fact*, in place. Thus the difference between their presentations does not mark, on this point at least, a fundamental contrast. The argument from iterability, as it is presented by both Derrida and Wittgenstein, aims to establish that the 'being there' of 'writing' is, *a priori*, irreducible to anything that can be simply present in the present.[24] On this view, a behavioural event can be a case of 'obeying a rule' not because it represents present thought-meanings-to-be-communicated but, on the contrary, only in so far as 'it implies my absence, if it already detaches itself from me' (*ibid.*, p. 49). It is this logic of 'exceeding current presence' which characterises the publicness which belongs essentially to 'writing'. In what follows I will show that it is this *structural feature* and not shared *knowledge* of rules which marks 'writing' as a mode of being with others.

One man's rule

It may be thought that the approach to the phenomenon of language defended in this chapter and the last leaves us with a 'dark interior'. The complaint here is of the following kind: 'But aren't you neglecting something – the experience or whatever you might call it – ? Almost the world behind the mere words . . . In your language you're only *speaking*' (Wittgenstein, 1968b, pp. 253–4).

My aim has been to show that speaking – or, rather, 'writing' – is quite enough. Marx articulates the basic features of the kind of approach I have been defending in the following claim: 'Language is practical consciousness that exists also for other men, and for that reason alone it really exists for me personally as well.'[25] The claim that language is always already public language is not, according to Marx, to neglect the idea that I, now, can 'mean' or 'understand' something by an expression. Rather, it is to say, at least, that we can make sense of the idea that a linguistic expression is intelligible to *me* only because *in principle* it is not intelligible to *me alone*.

In Marx's writings the idea that language is always public language emerges as a consequence of his materialist treatment of the classical idea that a word-language is a means of communication of consciousness. For Marx, language is public because it is essentially social. On the account of this chapter, however, publicness emerges directly from an examination of the structure of 'writing'.

That is, according to the argument from iterability, 'writing' necessarily entails a *structural* or *internal* relation to others in general; a relation which makes 'writing' *in itself* made to do without one's own presence. 'Writing' is, thus, in principle, 'for every possible user in general' (LI, p. 8).

The connection between this route to publicness and the issue of the sociality of the phenomenon of language can be clarified by considering Wittgenstein's infamously problematic response to the question of the sociality of language in the *Philosophical Investigations*. Wittgenstein's response to the question of the sociality of language is problematic because he explicitly poses it but does not seem to provide a decisive answer to it. Or rather, when he raises the question, he is decisive on a *prima facie* different matter:

> Is what we call 'obeying a rule' something that it would be possible for only *one* man to do, and to do only *once* in his life? This is of course a note on the grammar of the expression 'to obey a rule'. It is not possible that there should have been only one occasion on which someone obeyed a rule.
>
> (PI, §199)

Commentary has tended to polarise around those who do and those who do not think that Wittgenstein is urging a 'social theory of language' in remarks such as this.[26] However, it seems to me that an alternative interpretation has been overlooked, namely, that Wittgenstein's response to the question of sociality is deliberately circumspect. In my view, what we need to see is that the decisive response to the question of recurrence is the thought *through which* we should approach the question of sociality.

The reasoning might run as follows. The concept of a 'rule' is such that a 'rule-governed' event of whatever kind is not what it is except in relation to another such non-present event (other events which, in each case, one must say 'it is not what it is except . . . '). On this account, events as of the use of signs are oriented towards alterity *a priori*. However, the question is: Does this logically *preclude* the possibility that every other such event is, contingently, an event of the behaviour of 'one man alone'? On the account presented in this chapter and the previous one, this idea must strike us as at least problematic. I have argued that what distinguishes 'obeying a rule' from 'obeying an inclination' is that the regularity entailed by the former necessarily introduces the possibility of a definite kind of relation to another in its description, namely, a relation in which it makes sense to 'require another to do the same' (cp. RFM, VI-41–3). But must this *possible* social relation be *actual*? David Pears offers the following case which may be used for consideration of this question:

> It would be quite implausible to argue that it would be impossible for someone who had no contact with other people to take a stick of stan-

dard length with him when he went foraging for firewood, so that he could bring back logs that would fit his fireplace.

(Pears, 1988, p. 384)

This example suggests that we *can* make sense of 'one man obeying a rule', and hence, can conceive rule-governed practices without recourse to *actual* sociality. Does this show that the question of recurrence has no impact on the question of sociality whatsoever? I do not think so. Indeed, I think that Pears's example tends to disguise the facts it aims to describe. Specifically, what we need to see is that it is part of the structure and functioning of the stick-using behaviour that a possible relation to others pertains to it *necessarily*. That is, in order to describe it as 'obeying a rule' at all, the possibility of a definite kind of relation to others *must* enter into the description of the behaviour of this individual. The behaviour at any time will only be as of 'one man obeying a rule' (rather than, say, 'one man following his inclinations') in so far as the essential iterability of some aspect of his current behaviour, as it were, 'detaches' it from his behaviour conceived as something simply present in the present (LI, p. 49). The behavioural event, *in itself iterable*, is thus, in essence, iterable by another, by any user in general: in Crusoe's act, the *eventuality* of Friday's 'service' is already implicated, as *possibility*, in its structure. Thus, both in principle and in fact, at the moment of its occurrence the 'what he is doing now' of his stick-using behaviour is necessarily deported beyond the presence of this isolated individual. Indeed, it implies the possibility of his absence: the stick-using behaviour is, *a priori*, 'made to do without him' (*ibid.*). This is the impact of the decisive answer to the question of recurrence on the question of sociality: when we conceive 'one man obeying a rule' we are *already obliged* to conceive this in terms which necessarily imply *more than one*.[27]

Leaping towards others

According to the argument of this chapter, the possibility of repeating a linguistic element in new contexts, its *iterability*, is not to be explained by recourse to an indefinitely repeatable 'form' that we must learn to recognise and re-identify. Rather, the claim is that 'this "form" only constitutes itself by virtue of its iterability' (*ibid.*, p. 10). The argument here is not simply that words or concepts are repeatable. Rather, it concerns the very 'eventhood' of an event of language use; namely, that its description entails a necessary reference to *other such* events. The idea that a bit of behaviour, conceived in isolation, could *be* an event as of a use of signs is, therefore, empty.

On this view the recognition of such an event is, *eo ipso*, to recognise something which is made to do without one's presence; something capable, in principle, of occurring again and in one's absence. Of course, this does not imply that what is recognised here is something which sustains itself independently of contexts. On the contrary, the whole thrust of the argument thus far is

125

that there are *only* contexts of use. That is, the very same principle which accounts for the necessary independence of the identity of an expression from any single context of its use (the principle of iterability) also excludes the possibility that this independence could ever be absolute or pure. There is 'nothing outside contexts' (*ibid.*, p. 136), nothing transcending our actual 'forms of iteration' (*ibid.*, p. 18) that limits or dictates the iterability of linguistic elements.

This way of rejecting what one might call 'objectivity of meaning' has often been interpreted as the idea that 'anything goes', and hence as a straightforward denial of the normativity of meaning. But, as we have seen, the argument is not that 'any amount of "play" is permissible' but, rather, that it is inconceivable that words in general have a 'meaning' which escapes the principle of iterability. For an event to *be* a use of language does not presuppose that it possesses a univocal sense or is used in accordance with definite rules, but only that it is 'identifiable as *conforming* with an iterable model' (LI, p. 18).

The idea that such models or patterns are, essentially, 'made to do without one's presence' perhaps explains what John McDowell somewhat obscurely refers to as the necessary 'ratification independence' of the patterns of use of our concept-words (McDowell, 1984, p. 326). If the preceding account is correct, however, then it should be clear that any such independence is something which must be established and maintained by our own efforts. To adapt an idea from David Pears, each 'moment of the leap' both maintains the stability of linguistic regularities and helps to set the standard of the stability that it maintains (see Pears, 1988, p. 434). My behaviour has, one might say, an irreducibly 'performative' dimension.[28]

As should be clear, this conclusion is nothing other than an accounting for language in which one can 'think at once both the rule and the event'. 'Writing', that is to say, is the 'root' of the 'two stems' – language-as-structure and speech-act:[29] in the performance of an iterable model, which has no instituted *end*,[30] one is oneself functioning as the instrument of measurement of 'the same'.[31]

Conceiving the use of signs along these lines constitutes a massive complication to the concept of language-use as the communicable representation or expression of determinate senses. Rigorously speaking, when one attempts to say, against this tradition, that 'only the text signifies' (Derrida, 1981, p. 34), or that 'whatever accompanies the sign would for us just be another sign' (BB, p. 5), one is necessarily transforming the values of 'signifier'/'signified' ('externality'/'internality'). For, if one is attempting to understand these terms in their classical determinations, one will have to say that 'the text is insignificant' (Derrida, 1981, p. 34) or that 'meaning drops out of language' (PG, I-3; cp. PI, §120b).

As Derrida stresses, this kind of transformation of the 'relation idea/sign' 'necessitates, obviously, a rigorous and renewed analysis of the value of presence to others' (LI, p. 49). We have already begun to touch on this issue, and in the next and final chapter I will focus explicitly on it. In doing so I will also return to the issue which first oriented this line of thinking. For, as should be becoming more clear, the foregoing examination of the iterability of events of the use of signs enables us to resist conceiving them either as the 'outward surface' of 'present acts of consciousness' (the metaphysics of the subject) or as something reducible to the 'mere behaviour of an animal organism' (bald naturalism). Indeed, it will enable us to affirm a fundamentally non-humanist and non-sceptical approach to being with others: in virtue of one's familiarity with behavioural events which are, in themselves, iterable, what can be manifest when one perceives the behaviour of living things need not fall short of the 'being there too' of 'those among whom one is too'.

8

READING THE OTHER

INTRODUCTION

In the previous chapter it was argued that, in every case, one *must* regard any event of 'writing' of one's own as capable of functioning in one's absence and hence as having an identity which is independent of, or 'detachable' from, one's current presence. This 'must' does not derive from anything outside the use of language. Rather, relating to an event as of the use of a word is, *eo ipso*, to relate to it as something which is capable, in principle, of recurring in one's absence. An 'anonymous publicity' (Derrida, 1992, p. 260) belongs to it essentially: as 'writing', it detaches itself 'from every empirically determined "subject"' (LI, p. 8). According to this argument, in conceiving 'writing' we need to take into account the general point that its identity is irreducible to *either* a pure occasion-transcendent ideality *or* a pure behavioural event which is simply singular and dateable. As I suggested at the end of the previous chapter, this conclusion has important consequences for our thinking about behavioural events (linguistic or otherwise) which can 'communicate'. For what we can see is that events which, like 'writing', are *in themselves* iterable, have an identity which is *at once* both 'transcendent in relation to the anatomical apparatus' and 'immanent to the behaviour as such' (Merleau-Ponty, 1962, p. 189). In this chapter I aim to show how this conception of 'writing' provides the basis for a fundamentally non-humanist and non-sceptical approach to being with others. The view I will defend is that, by conceiving behavioural events of *others* as essentially a kind of 'writing' (or akin to 'writing' in having an identity which is irreducible to what is simply present in the present), we can affirm the Wittgensteinian thesis that to see the behaviour of a living thing is to see its soul (PI, §357).

CRITERIA AND OTHER MINDS

Criteria and certainty

Throughout this book I have been working towards an account of being with others which enables us to understand how what is disclosed in our perception of certain living things does not fall short of the perception of 'the soul' of another. In this chapter I will explain how Wittgenstein's notion of 'criteria' can help us to achieve such an understanding.

In previous chapters I have argued against the view that significant behaviour should be conceived in terms of singular events governed by definite rules. In my view, Wittgenstein's work on behavioural criteria outlines an approach to the behaviour of others which respects this conclusion. I will argue for an interpretation which conceives them neither as (general) rules nor as (singular) behavioural events, but as *iterable traits*. As I hope to show, this interpretation of Wittgenstein's notion will make plausible the following conception of being with others: the perception of a 'soul', being open to a living thing *as* another, is a matter of *reading* the behaviour of a living thing; a matter of being at home with its iterable traits.

This approach may seem to be making heavy weather of a topic for which there is already a relatively straightforward and significant consensus. Criteria in Wittgenstein's sense are, surely, the 'outward' behavioural grounds or reasons for judging the existence or presence of something 'inner'. To employ a phrase of Stanley Cavell's to which I will return, criteria are criteria for something's '*being so*' in the sense that they are ways of telling how things *are* (Cavell, 1979, p. 45). This is, indeed, the orthodox view. Selectively quoting from what have been the most influential readings, we find the following claims:

> The satisfaction of the criterion of y establishes the existence of y beyond question ... It will not make sense for one to suppose that another person is not in pain if one's criterion of his being in pain is satisfied.
>
> (Malcolm, 1966, p. 543)

and

> If a kind of behaviour is a criterion, in Wittgenstein's sense ... for the use of the word 'toothache' ... his so behaving may be taken to decide the question whether he has toothache or not: he does.
>
> (Albritton, 1966, p. 249)

and

> If p is C-related to q, then q is made certain by the truth of p.
>
> (Baker, 1974, p. 162)

and

> The entailment [between outward behaviour X and inner state Y] would hold . . . between X *plus* a statement of the results of an as yet uncarried-out conceptual analysis of the concept in question on the one hand, and Y on the other.
>
> (Canfield, 1974, p. 82)

and

> If the criteria for q are *satisfied* . . . then it is certain that q.
>
> (Hacker, 1986, p. 315)

In each case the general aim is to establish a relation between one ('outer') event or condition and another ('inner') event or condition such that the presence of the first is the non-empirical basis or ground (perhaps 'in certain circumstance') for certainty concerning the presence of the second. On this reading, the appeal to criteria can provide a clear and devastating response to the threat of scepticism: criteria are logically adequate ways of telling, from the 'outer' state of another, how things *are* with his or her 'inner' state.

In the midst of familiar scenes of exegetical diversity one might think that such a consensus of readings suggests that something like this must be what Wittgenstein's notion implies. But what is at issue here? What does this agreement concern? Clearly, each of the readers cited above sees Wittgenstein's use of the notion of criteria as part of a sustained attack on scepticism concerning other minds. Furthermore, this attack is understood as one which ultimately shows such scepticism to be in some way 'refuted'. By this I mean that these readers hold that Wittgenstein's reflections on criteria enable us to insist that, *pace* the sceptic, one *can* know or be certain of the existence or presence of other minds through or via the behaviour of other bodies. The promise held out by such readings is obviously attractive. However, in my view it misconceives Wittgenstein's use of, and appeal to, the notion of criteria. In the first half of this chapter I will show that, when being with others is conceived as founded on a relation of knowledge (criteria as 'ways of telling how things are'), our criteria will always be found wanting and the threat of scepticism always pressing. In doing so another, and in my view much more fruitful, interpretation of criteria will emerge.

Ordinary and Wittgensteinian criteria

The notion of criteria undoubtedly plays a central role in Wittgenstein's investigations of 'expressions of life in the language' (LWI, §121). But what are 'Wittgensteinian criteria'? As Cavell notes, a glance at Wittgenstein's references to them suggests that 'the bulk of [his] rhetoric in manipulating the term . . . is just the rhetoric of the ordinary word' (Cavell, 1979, p. 7). Thus, for example, in the course of the *Investigations* it is suggested that criteria are the kind of thing:

1   which are ours (p. 203);
2   which we fix (§322);
3   which we accept or adopt or have (§182, §141);
4   which we can apply (§165);
5   of which there are usual, ordinary ones (§185);
6   of which we can introduce completely new ones (p. 222);
7   which can be much more complicated than might appear at first sight (§182);
8   to which we can have our attention drawn (p. 181).

This list is not exhaustive but they are significant instances which display the way in which the grammar of 'Wittgensteinian criteria' is usual or ordinary. To see this, let us take an everyday case of the use of criteria: i.e., let us follow (8) in a real example. In the *University of Oxford Examination Decrees and Regulations* for 1995 (p. 11) we find the following statement:

> No person shall be permitted to reside as a student or scholar of the University . . . unless such person
>
> i   has been admitted to a college or other society;
> ii has been admitted to matriculation within fourteen days after such admission or permission to reside.

The Decree continues through five further conditions and their respective provisos. Of any person, if they fulfil or satisfy these conditions, he or she can (*usually* – see (5)) 'reside as a student or scholar of the University'. Who is thus permitted is determined by *applying* (see (4)) these conditions and assessing whether a person fulfils or satisfies them. Whether he (or, *nowadays*, he or she (see (6)) does or does not satisfy the conditions is not a property of this person but a matter of definition or convention – it has been *fixed* (see (2)), laid down or decreed by the appropriate *authorities* (see (1)). Criteria are the measure, not the measured, and in this case one cannot tell just by looking at someone whether he or she satisfies them. Indeed, when one looks at the conditions for 'studenthood' on the one hand and studenthood on the other, point (7) seems particularly apt. In summary we might now say: the Decree provides criteria or rules with which one can judge, assess and settle whether someone has the status of (counts as) someone permitted to reside as a student or scholar of The University of Oxford.

If we grant the similarity between the grammar of ordinary and Wittgensteinian criteria, it should remain surprising that the kinds of thing with respect to which Wittgenstein talks of criteria are not the kind of thing which we would ordinarily think of as having criteria at all. That is, it is not the way he uses the term which is odd but in respect of what he claims them. The kinds of thing which we can count as 'having criteria for' for Wittgenstein include the following:

(a) 'fitting', 'being able to', 'understanding' (§182, §146);
(b) mastery of the series of natural numbers (§185);
(c) demonstrating a capacity (p. 181);
(d) 'inner states' (p. 181, §580, §572);
(e) the truth of a confession (p. 222);
(f) saying someone is seeing a drawing three-dimensionally (p. 203);
(g) someone's being of such and such an opinion (§573);
(h) the identity of pains etc. (§253, §288, §322);
(i) the sameness of two images (§377);
(j) personal 'identity' (§404);
(k) looking at something but not seeing it (p. 211);
(l) the way a formula is meant (§190, §692);
(m) reading (§159, §160, §165).

To say that these are strange things to have criteria for marks the difference between ordinary cases in which criteria are appealed to and Wittgenstein's cases. Items (1)–(8) in the first list seem to have clear and natural application to the Oxford Decree. What it means, e.g., to fix, apply, accept, introduce, etc., criteria is unproblematic in such cases. But what does it mean to do any of these things in Wittgenstein's cases? When and why did we *fix* them? And did *we* fix them? Did I have a hand in this? Did you? If I want to draw your attention to an official decree I can at least show you the book. Where are Wittgensteinian criteria laid down? And if we do 'have' them and 'apply' them, why do I seem to be ignorant of this fact?

P. M. S. Hacker states: 'We fix criteria by laying down grammatical rules' (Hacker, 1986, p. 310). But what does this mean in the kinds of cases Wittgenstein considers? Every term in this sentence strikes me as deeply problematic. One might rather write: 'We' 'fix' 'criteria' by 'laying down' 'grammatical' 'rules'. But I still do not know what is being said. Really I want to say: How can it seem so *un*problematic? While I understand why Oxford University requires and needs to establish criteria to assess and settle whether someone has a particular status (or counts as a certain kind of thing) it is none so clear why we need criteria in the kinds of cases Wittgenstein considers. For example, Wittgenstein claims at PI §404 that 'there is a great variety of criteria for personal "*identity*"', and yet in the examination of the Oxford Decree I used the terms 'person', 'he or she', 'particular person' without a second thought. I did not stop to consider whether we might need criteria to settle identity here. If concepts like these need criteria, *any* concepts will.

Criteria and identity

Before I attempt to resolve these issues a specific contrast between the ordinary and Wittgensteinian cases needs to be highlighted. Return to items (1)–(3) in the list of characterisations of the grammar of 'criteria'. These relate to what we can call the 'authority' or 'source of authority' in the ordinary case. With ordinary criteria there is usually an acknowledged or determinable source. This feature does not hold in Wittgenstein's cases. Wittgenstein's cases seem always to presume a 'we' of some indeterminate kind. They are 'mine' because they are 'ours'. And this indeterminate community's 'criteria' is Wittgenstein's point of departure in his investigation of the use of psychological concepts and the language of personal experience.[1]

But note: such a starting point is completely intolerable from the perspective of the traditional problem of other minds. The sceptic (and indeed his opponent, his refuter) claims precisely that the existence or presence of the other must be or is capable of some kind of demonstration. Starting with an appeal to a 'we', however indeterminate, begs every epistemological question. If Wittgensteinian criteria are never one's own alone, how can they be construed as the starting point for a refutation of scepticism concerning other minds? Bluntly, I believe they cannot be so construed. But this needs defence to be convincing. Let us return to the comparison of ordinary and Wittgensteinian criteria.

It was noted that ordinary criteria are rules with which we assess or judge an object as having a certain status, as entitled to a particular title. Criteria are the measure with which we establish the identity of a thing. That is, criteria are *criteria of identity*, of counting as 'the same'. For example, with respect to the criteria laid down in the Oxford Decree, one can imagine a list of names being compiled and a college official going down the list and ticking off (i.e. making *the same mark* against the name of) each individual who has satisfied the criteria. Or again, one can imagine a telephone conversation in which one official reads out names and another says 'Yes' each time the name of a candidate who has satisfied the criteria is read out. As I have indicated, because of the everyday and unexceptional nature of the 'objects' concerned in the case of Wittgenstein's investigations, 'criteria' in his work appear to function as rules for judgements of identity – rules, as it were, for 'Yes: same'-saying – *überhaupt*.

As a provisional approximation I think that this is acceptable. However, as should by now be expected, I want to resist the assumption that Wittgensteinian criteria can be given expression in the form of definite, ideally exact, rules. Indeed, as I have presented his arguments thus far, this is the central conclusion of Wittgenstein's 'grammatical investigations' of our concepts in general. In my view, his appeal to criteria is not exceptional in this respect. Note how, in the following remarks, Wittgenstein uses the interrogative form in addressing the issue of our criteria:

What in particular cases do we regard as criteria for someone's being of such-and-such an opinion? When do we say: he reached this opinion at that time? When: he has altered his opinion? And so on.

(PI, §573)

and

What is the criterion for the sameness of two images? What is the criterion for the redness of an image?

(*ibid.*, §377)

and

Expectation is grammatically a state . . . But in order to understand the grammar of these states it is necessary to ask: 'What counts as a criterion for anyone's being in such and such a state?'

(*ibid.*, §572)

It is not accidental that these remarks are posed as questions (see LWI, §150). This form of account forces us to 'look and see'. And the result of such an inquiry will not be a list of hitherto unremarked yet definite rules of judgement of identity. On the contrary, 'you will find it difficult to hit upon a convention; at least any that satisfies you' (PI, §88). What we imagine or recall in response to being asked: 'What, in what particular cases, do we regard as criteria for . . . ?' do not form a formal unity. We cannot codify our criteria in terms of a system of definite rules or conventions, and no single example can provide a paradigm or protocol for such a code:

The systems that occur to him are inadequate, and he seems suddenly to find himself in a wilderness instead of in the well laid out garden that he knew so well. Rules occur to him, no doubt, but the reality shows nothing but exceptions.

(RPPI, §557)

As we have seen, the ordinary logic of concepts (repetitions of *the same*) constantly invites us to conceive the patterns of life's textile as if it approximates a fixed or rigid structure or system. But these patterns *cannot* be adequately captured with the idea of a system or structure of definite rules. What structure there is exists only *in der Tat*, in the actuality of interweaving forms of iteration. And this is a weave which 'can be learned purely practically, without learning any explicit rules' (OC, §95).

Of course, none of this is to deny that there is a rough regularity in the use of words. But this indefinite constancy should not be conceived on the model of the ideal of exactness – as if the actuality of our concepts entails a less than ideal exactness. Following Derrida, I have suggested that we can picture this through the idea of 'the play of the world'. This idea may seem to retain the metaphysical desire to 'say the essence' of the world. However, by constantly plunging us back into actuality, the argument from iterability which informs it outlines, in fact, an ultra-mundane (if not baldly naturalistic) position. The 'form of the world' is not a structure of 'purest crystal' (PI, §97; cp. TLP, 5.5563). Rather, what is being suggested is 'the play of the world' internally related to the rough regularity in the patterns of iteration which permeate human lives.[2] On this view, conceptual identity is precisely *not* opposed to the complexity and variety of differences exhibited in the 'hurly burly' of actual life (Z, §567):

> Seeing life as a weave, this pattern (pretence, say) is not always complete and is varied in a multiplicity of ways. But we, in our conceptual world, keep on seeing the same, recurring with variations. That is how our concepts take it. For concepts are not for use on a single occasion.
>
> And one pattern in the weave is interwoven with many others.
>
> (Z, §§568–9)

This approach challenges the fundamental assumptions of humanist metaphysics, both in terms of its rejection of the ideal of exactness, and in the way it embeds human conceptuality into a naturalistic setting. In my view, the 'fix' of Wittgensteinian criteria must be seen in this naturalistic light, too. 'Being at home' with 'criteria of the inner' is not to have knowledge of definite rules which are recognised to be satisfied or unsatisfied in particular cases. Rather, it is to be seen in terms of one's familiarity with the *iterable traits* of living things. Thus, on this approach, to 'recall criteria' is not to recall rules of judgement, but, rather, unreflective 'leaps', occasions of 'Yes: same'-sayings. And these, I want to argue, just are: occasions in which the perception of a living thing does not stop short of the perception of a soul.

The idea of a perception of a living thing 'not stopping short' of the perception of another's 'soul' may be thought to have some *prima facie* plausibility in cases of what McDowell has called 'transparent modes of expression' of life such as 'the verbal expression of thoughts' (McDowell, 1983, p. 473, fn. 1). However, one might think that it is quite implausible with respect to the expression of sensations. Here, surely, the expression is, as it were, 'opaque': there remains a subjective side which is baldly internal and private to the subject who has it, something with respect to which perception inevitably 'stops short'.[3]

So the question is: In what sense is another's pain not a blankly external fact or, what comes to the same thing here, not baldly internal and private to the other? In what follows I will explain how the idea of the perception of another's 'soul' is applicable to this troublesome case. For reasons which will become clear shortly, my account will be developed by taking its lead from the account of criteria developed by McDowell.

McDOWELL ON OTHER MINDS

Satisfied criteria

While there is much to admire in McDowell's approach to the problem of other minds, there is a feature of it which, in my view, prevents it from providing a satisfactory response to scepticism. And that is his commitment to the assumption that Wittgensteinian criteria are 'ways of telling how things are'. I have suggested that this kind of interpretation will always leave the threat of scepticism intact. In this section I will show why this is so.

McDowell develops his view by way of contrast to one which supposes that the circumstances which constitute the satisfaction of a criterion do not guarantee that the claim to know it warrants it true. Thus, it might be thought, for example, that 'if . . . *further* circumstances are unfavourable, we still have a case of a criterion being satisfied, but the support that it affords the claim is defeated' (McDowell, 1983, p. 463). The presence of satisfied criteria thus constitutes a 'highest common factor' in cases of the real or merely apparent presence of the 'inner' state (*ibid.*, p. 471). On that view, therefore, the 'reach' of perception *always* stops short of the facts. For, even if one sees a behavioural display of the right kind, and so criteria for thinking that a particular individual is, say, in pain are satisfied, that individual might still be, for example, only feigning pain.[4] Criterial knowledge about how things are with a person is accordingly understood to fall short of that person's true inner state because *what is known* in such a case is compatible with the person not being in that state at all.

I think McDowell is right to argue that this 'defeasibility' feature is a function of an epistemology that merely proposes 'an alteration of detail within the sceptic's position' (*ibid.*, p. 469). For, on the view being considered, any situation which *seems* to reveal the inner state of another might, so far as one *knows*, always be the mere simulation of such a state. Given the analysis of this problem in Chapter 1, it should be clear that the threat of scepticism is, on such a view, completely unavoidable.

McDowell does not take this argument to show that the problem of 'reach' is an intractable feature inherent in the very idea of behavioural 'criteria'. Indeed, he continues to suppose that reflection on our criteria can quiet the sceptic. I will explain this.

As I have indicated, McDowell, like the other readers of Wittgenstein with which I began, defends the view that criteria are 'ways of telling how things *are*' (*ibid.*, p. 470). It is for this reason that McDowell supposes that a satisfactory conception of criteria should provide a satisfactory response to the sceptic. Of course, once one takes the path of this construal of criteria one will be forced (or happy) to concede that propositions which simply describe the *behaviour* of someone in pain do not logically imply the truth of the proposition 'N.N. is in pain'. McDowell accepts (or urges with the others) that progress requires that we acknowledge 'that criterial knowledge depends on circumstances' (*ibid.*, p. 492); a point which he claims 'is obviously faithful to Wittgenstein' (*ibid.*). Let us follow this line of faith.

McDowell agrees with the 'highest common factor' view that criteria are related to circumstances. However, he conceives this relation in an unusual manner. On the more orthodox view, criteria are a behavioural condition the presence of which warrants a claim to know or confers certainty on such a claim. According to McDowell, Wittgenstein's remarks on criteria outline a rather different interpretation than that presumed by that view: whether something is a criterion for something *at all* depends on the circumstances. McDowell cites PI §164, in which Wittgenstein suggests that what is a criterion for a person 'reading' in one sort of circumstance is not a criterion for a person 'reading' in another sort of circumstance. The more orthodox view is then revised by McDowell in the following way: what can, on some occasion, be a case of the satisfaction of criteria is never merely the presence of a behavioural condition but the presence of behaviour-in-circumstance.

McDowell is then faced with the problem that leads the more orthodox view to add the *'favourable* circumstance' rider. The problem is that it would still seem possible for one's criterion for pain to be satisfied and yet the subject *not* be experiencing pain. According to McDowell, however, this is not so. More specifically, it would only be so if we construed 'criteria' as 'a basis for a judgement . . . on which we have a firmer cognitive purchase than we do on the judgement itself' (*ibid.*, p. 471). So McDowell rejects this assumption: knowledge of the inner states of others requires no *epistemic* mediation as is proffered by the orthodox criterion. Thus, with respect to the issue of the 'reach' of criteria, McDowell can bite the bullet: if the criteria for *p*'s being the case (e.g. that *someone is expressing pain*) are satisfied then one knows that *p*. But, now, given that one cannot know that *p* if *p* is not the case, what is McDowell to say about cases of deception (e.g. pretence)? McDowell's response is simple: if it is not the case that *p* then, equally, the criteria only *appear* to be satisfied.[5]

The disjunctive conception

Either the criteria for its being the case that *p* are satisfied, *or* they only appear to be. Thus, McDowell's account of our knowledge of other minds is disjunctive. In the former case what is given to experience does not stop short of the circumstance that *p*. In the latter case it is a mere appearance that *p*. Granted, there can be deceptive cases experientially indistinguishable from non-deceptive cases. But we are no longer required to infer some substantial indistinguishability.[6] This is the essence of McDowell's response to the sceptic:

> But suppose we say – not at all unnaturally – that an appearance that such and such is the case can be *either* a mere appearance *or* the fact that such and such is the case making itself perceptually manifest to someone. As before, the object of experience in the deceptive cases is a

mere appearance. But we are not to accept that in the non-deceptive cases too the object of experience is a mere appearance, and hence something that falls short of the fact itself. On the contrary, we are to *insist* that the appearance that is presented to one in those cases is a matter of the fact itself disclosed to the experiencer.

(McDowell, 1983, p. 472, final emphasis mine)

According to McDowell's disjunctive conception, appearances may be *either* mere appearances *or* manifestations. In the latter case, the facts themselves are present to the mind, and in the former case mere appearances are present to the mind. And now, since the satisfaction of criteria need not be defined so as to cover both cases, then we need no longer suppose that, in cases where the criteria *are* satisfied, where one is *not* misled, what one observes is merely an appearance which falls short of the facts. On the contrary, we are free to affirm that, in such cases, what one is observing is that p (e.g. that *someone is expressing pain*). *That* fact (and no substitute) is manifest to one.

In summary, McDowell's argument aims to make plausible the idea that facts in the world, including facts about others, are not, as he puts it, 'blankly external' to perception (McDowell, 1983, p. 474): what is perceptually manifest to one is, when one is not misled, that things are thus and so. The fallacy which we have observed McDowell root out in the 'highest common factor' view is a conception of behaviour which serves as a ubiquitous *interface*, interposing itself between subject and subject. The nerve of this fallacy is an epistemological presupposition, the defeasibility feature, which states that beliefs about what we experience are at best defeasibly connected to the truth about what we experience.

McDowell offers the disjunctive conception as an alternative to the interface model; accepting his reasons for preferring this alternative depends upon agreeing with him that the interface model is philosophically unattractive because intolerably sceptical. For McDowell, criteria *need not* and therefore *should not* be conceived as an interface or a bridge between subject and subject. On the unsatisfactory 'highest common factor' conception, knowledge of behavioural criteria is self-standing and autonomous and, consequently, one's grasp on the inner state of others is intrinsically insecure and problematic. McDowell's use of the disjunctive conception aims to defend an account in which the threat of scepticism no longer arises. That is, it aims to give us a conception of experience and its objects which cannot be exploited by sceptical doubts. It thus aims to give us 'an intellectual right to shrug our shoulders at sceptical questions' (McDowell, 1994b, p. 143).

The return of the threat

The question I want to pursue is this: Does McDowell's account provide a coherent motivation for the realist claim he asks us to insist upon? That is, can McDowell give us 'an intellectual right' to '*insist* that the appearance that is presented to one in those [non-misleading] cases is a matter of the fact itself disclosed to the experiencer'? If he cannot, then, as a response to the sceptic, his 'insistence' will be no less dogmatic than the more orthodox view which he rightly rejects.

In fact, in my view there is an aspect of McDowell's account which does betray a too conciliatory and deeply problematic relation to what he calls the 'dominant contemporary philosophy of mind' (McDowell, 1983, p. 478, fn. 2). The most salient symptom of this is his acceptance, at the level of experience itself, of a version of the interface model. That is, his allowing 'what is given to experience in the two sorts of case [namely, deceptive and non-deceptive perceptions] to be the same *in so far* as it is an appearance that things are thus and so' (*ibid.*, p. 475).

The central feature of this model of experience is that it clings to the assumption that 'enjoying an experience' has a distinctive first-personal character. That is, it is committed to the idea that there is 'something that it is like' to enjoy an experience and that 'what it is like to enjoy access or apparent access' is the same (McDowell, 1986, p. 149).[7]

The inclusion of this conception of the subjective character of experience is not deemed problematic by McDowell. Nor, of course, is it deemed so by adherents to the orthodox 'interface' conception. Here, I think, one can see a significant yet silent agreement between McDowell's conception of subjectivity and the more traditional, broadly Cartesian, conception. Specifically, both assume as coherent a particular interpretation of what it is for a living human being to be a 'subject of experience', namely, an interpretation conceived in terms of its potential for a distinctively first-personal, 'inside take' on its own states, its presence to its own experiences.

The conception of our 'subject' character as something 'constantly present-at-hand both in and for a closed realm' has been the focus of quite general criticism throughout this book. However, the worry at this point can be spelled out as follows. McDowell accepts that, for a 'subject', 'what it is like to enjoy access or apparent access' is the same. The disjunctive conception is then introduced to foreclose 'the characteristically Cartesian willingness to face up to losing the external world with the inner for consolation' (*ibid.*, p. 149). But there is no reason to suppose that such a 'subject' should find any consolation from the introduction of the disjunctive conception at all. We are to suppose that this 'subject's' best theory of his or her current perceptual standing (the appearance that such and such is the case) is that it is *either* a mere appearance *or* the fact that such and such is the case making itself perceptually manifest. *But no sceptic need deny this.* The sceptic's conclusion is only that, in every case, one must suspend judgement as to *which*. And my view is that McDowell's adherence to a version of the interface conception of experience leaves him without the resources for answering such a question. For, on the basis of any given 'subject's' perceptual standing (i.e., on the basis of 'what is given' to its 'experience'), there is no way for it to provide any adequate grounds for 'insisting' that either option is, in each case, in fact true, and so, ultimately, it is nothing but a dogmatic insistence to say that any are.

The inescapable conclusion is that McDowell has not established the right to insist upon what he asks us to insist upon. That this is so is evident in his recourse to plainly and unsatisfactorily sceptical responses when the viability of necessarily subjective foundations to support a deceptive/non-deceptive distinction are challenged. For example, when challenged with the question 'Which?' (deceptive or non-deceptive), McDowell is willing to admit as a possible response the idea that 'there is nothing here to exclude the ancient [sceptic's] option of living comfortably in the world without aspiring to know it' (*ibid.*, p. 150). On any account such a response must seem weak. However, beyond its intrinsic weakness as a retreat from the ordinary practice of making and sustaining claims to know, it is not even clear that McDowell can help himself to such ancient comfort: it is arguable that the attempt to 'live comfortably' in a 'world of appearances' would lead us only to 'entangle ourselves in our most common-place assertions' (Kant, 1933 [1781] A378). And that is not ancient but cold comfort.

McDowell also attempts more robust responses to the fact that his account provokes the sceptical 'Which?'. For example, having accepted that 'in a given case one cannot tell for certain whether what confronts one is one or other of [a mere appearance or a fact made manifest]' (McDowell, 1983, p. 475), he claims that we should be satisfied by the thought that the factual difference itself makes a difference: 'when someone has a fact made manifest to him, the obtaining of the fact contributes to his epistemic standing on the question' (*ibid.*, p. 476). But this response is, *for such a subject*, no advance at all. In each case, one will have to say: this is *either* a case of a fact contributing to my epistemic standing *or* the mere appearance that it does. Again, entanglement is inevitable.

McDowell concedes to the tradition that he 'can allow what is given to experience in the two sorts of case [non-deceptive and deceptive] to be the same *in so far* as it is an appearance that things are thus and so' (McDowell, 1983, p. 475). My view is that the italics do not prevent his account from conceding *too much*. For, *from this point of departure*, it is impossible to avoid the threat of scepticism. At this point it may be being thought that there is no way one can avoid this problem. In the next section I will introduce a conception of criteria which shows that there is.

ON BEING WITH OTHERS

Lifting the humanist restriction

It is important to stress that, while I do not accept McDowell's account, I am not entirely hostile to everything in it either. Indeed, he *aims* to affirm a similar picture of openness to others as I do:

> Shared membership in a linguistic community is not just a matter of matching in aspects of an exterior that we present to anyone whatever,

but equips us to make our minds available to one another, by confronting one another with a different exterior from that which we present to outsiders. . . . A linguistic community is conceived as bound together, not by a match in mere externals (facts accessible to just anyone), but by a capacity for a meeting of minds.

(McDowell, 1984, pp. 350–1)

The idea of 'insiders' and 'outsiders' (facts not accessible to just anyone) that this suggests clearly resonates with the ideas about reading that I aim to defend: if the behaviour of a living thing must be read to be manifest as another soul, then the other's soul can be conceived as something manifest but not thus manifest 'to just anyone'. Merleau-Ponty provides a clear illustration of the kind of account of being with others which this entails in the more 'opaque' case of emotions:

Faced with an angry or threatening gesture I have no need, in order to understand it, to recall the feelings which I myself experienced when I used these gestures on my own account. I know very little, from inside of the mime of anger so that a decisive factor is missing for any association by resemblance or reasoning by analogy, and what is more, I do not see anger or a threatening attitude as a psychic fact hidden behind the gesture, *I read anger in it*. The gesture does not make me think of anger, it is anger itself. However, *the meaning of the gesture is not perceived as the colour of the carpet*, for example is perceived. If it were given to me as a thing, it is not clear why my understanding of gestures should for the most part be confined to human ones. I do not 'understand' the sexual pantomime of the dog, still less of the cockchafer or the praying mantis. I do not even understand the expression of emotions in primitive people or in circles too unlike the ones in which I move.

(Merleau-Ponty, 1962, p. 184, my emphasis)

As a kind of preface to the argument that follows, it is worth noting that, in the passage quoted above, McDowell's identification of 'the circles in which I move' (those with a capacity for a meeting of minds) is only considered with respect to those who are 'members of a linguistic community', membership of which requires 'knowledge of shared commitments' (McDowell, 1984, p. 349). In short, with respect to human beings. I have already explained why being with others in language should not be conceived as founded on shared knowledge of rules ('commitments'). But I also think that his limitation of 'insiders' to human beings at least threatens McDowell's account with the kind of humanist idealisation which characterises the Heideggerian conception of Being-with. Of course, I have not claimed that the Being-with between human beings and other animals is equivalent to that between human beings and other human beings (and, as Austin and Wittgenstein point out, one should not conceive *that* as homogenous either). Nevertheless, the general thrust of the argument against the ideal of

141

exactness suggests that it is a mistake to assume that the insider/outsider distinction can be used to save (at least the concept of) an ideal purity or ideal *telos* of 'mutual intelligibility'. As I have stressed, this is not intended to 'cover up ruptures and heterogeneities' (Derrida, 1991, p. 116) between, for example, different species or, for that matter, different cultures. Rather, it is to stress that 'human language, as original as it might be, does not allow us to "cut" once and for all where we would in general like to cut' (*ibid.*, pp. 116–17). In this case (to paraphrase Wittgenstein), there is not one genuine proper case of 'mutual intelligibility', the rest being just vague, something which awaits clarification, or which must just be swept aside as rubbish (cp. PI, p. 200). The way this point lifts the threatened humanist restriction can be tied to the problem of Wittgensteinian criteria with an example.

There is (what I definitely want to call) a game I used to play with my mother's dog Sophie, in which we would run around a small pond. My aim was to catch her; hers to avoid being caught. Sometimes we would find ourselves facing each other, almost motionless, on either side of the pond, each of us watching the other for movements indicating a direction of pursuit or flight. I would try faking a movement; starting to the left but running to my right. Sophie would sometimes be foxed, but would always correct her run when she saw me coming the other way.

Sophie has a lot of Collie in her and I never caught her. But one day while we (*we*) were playing this game I slipped as I tried to change direction too quickly on damp grass. Almost immediately Sophie ran straight up to me. I was unhurt, but she licked my face anyway.

I do not see why this cannot be counted as a case of 'mutual intelligibility'. The dog could see my distress and I could see her sympathy.[8]

Reading iterable traits

But had the criteria for my being in distress been *satisfied*? Didn't Sophie come just a bit too quickly? After all, only my pride was hurt. And was that really 'sympathy'? Were we not both hasty and presumptuous in our judgements and ascriptions?

Of course, the truth is, Sophie did not wait for the nod of 'satisfied criteria'. She did not wait for anything at all. Equally, I could see that her whole manner and demeanour was (in the dog way) concernful. It may make sense to say that both Sophie and I were (in an uncanny, non-matching way) 'satisfied' about these things; but it strikes me as crazy to say that either of us saw or recognised that criteria were satisfied.

In general I find the recurrent talk of the 'satisfaction of criteria' extremely unenlightening. It suggests that we have at our disposal rules of some kind which the facts fit or fail to fit. But this is not how things are, nor how it could be. I will explain this.

In the literature, 'criteria' are often conceived as behavioural conditions of some type.[9] And in a sense that is correct. However, in my view, what is in question here is never simply a case of the presence of some typical condition which *then* elicits some typical response. On the contrary, the behavioural condition in question is not something that can be established to obtain independently of one's response.[10] That is, the identification or 'recognition' of such a behavioural condition is *already* a response. The 'presence' of a criterion, or what I want to call the 'being there' of an *iterable trait*, is not a 'blankly external' fact.[11] But now, by this I do not mean that 'what is given' here is not 'blankly external' to the perceiving 'subject' but that it is not blankly external to a human being's (or non-human being's) response to the behaviour of a living thing. The claim here is not that this response is 'projected' back on to the object responded to; we are not seeing something in the world that we put there. Rather, the idea is that it is not a property of or fact about the 'object' which is, to use the now familiar expression, available to just anyone you please; the behavioural condition in question is manifest only to a creature that responds in this distinctive way.

This account identifies and highlights a crucial feature of Wittgenstein's appeal to criteria; namely, that I am implicated in the 'what' of what is recalled when I recall criteria. As Wittgenstein puts it, 'my relation to the appearance here is part of my concept' (Z, §543). On this account, in each case, *what I recognise* (for example, 'a wince' of pain rather than 'a smirk' or 'a frown') is not a blankly external feature of the behaviour of a living thing: the *identity* of an iterable trait is not something which can be established independently of its recognition, its reading.

It is with this thought that we can begin to see how the idea of reading the behaviour of a living thing can develop into a non-sceptical, non-humanistic, conception of being with others.

There are two claims that I want to highlight with the notion of reading the behaviour of a living thing: first, a claim concerning the identity, the 'what', of 'inner states and processes'; and second, a claim concerning the identity, the 'who', of their owner or possessor. Taking these in order, the first claim is that the ways in which we respond to the behaviour of a living thing are integral to the 'what' of sentient states. Christopher Cherry makes the first step towards this claim when he argues that 'there are as many responses as there are sentient states responded to' (Cherry, 1991, p. 21). My claim is that this is because these responses to the behaviour of a living thing are integral to the 'what' of the sentient states they respond to. The second claim is more difficult to articulate in an unproblematic way. Like any identity constituted in virtue of its iterability, the possibility of another repetition is internal to the identity of a behavioural trait. It must, therefore, maintain a certain independence from what occurs in a particular context. This is what confers on the trait an intrinsically *public* intelligibility. The problem is, as I have indicated, that it also confers on it a structural *anonymity*. In my view, this anonymity is ineliminable, and any reading-response must *pass through* it. However, as should be clear, such anonymity is also *limited*;

there is no absolutely anonymous trait. Like any recognition of an iterable model, a reading-response always assumes a non-calculable 'moment of the leap' (a 'Yes'-saying) with a singularity of its own (even if one which is structured by an internal relation to other times). And my claim is that, in the context of a reading-response, such a 'leap' is *eo ipso* an identifying but ungrounded turn towards a living thing *as* an other. *It performs a leap to a 'we'.* The second claim can thus be put like this: Responding to the behaviour of a living thing by, among other things, returning a psychological concept-word, is always also to identify a 'subject' of such states and processes.[12] I will further explore and explain this second claim shortly. For the moment I will focus primarily on the first claim.

Feigning pain

In the examination of McDowell's appeal to criteria we found ourselves back in a position which is vulnerable to the threat of scepticism. We can, I think, rescue the situation here simply by resisting the assumption that McDowell shares with the more orthodox view, namely, that criteria are 'ways of telling how things *are*'. In my view the correct answer to the question: 'When is an event a (satisfied) criterion of *p*?' is simply: 'When it is an occasion of response as to an expression of *p*'. McDowell is, it seems to me, on the right track when he insists that 'behaviour' should not be thought of as a surface which hides the facts. However, I think he is wrong to conceive cases of, say, pain-behaviour without pain (pretence etc.) as cases in which criteria only *appear* to be satisfied. For such cases are still ones in which, among other things, we respond or, as I want to say, *read-respond* to behaviour as of someone, for example, feigning *pain*, acting as if in *pain*, simulating *pain*-behaviour, pretending to be in *pain*, etc. And my claim is that this cannot be understood unless we conceive these cases as ones in which we are responding (again) as to an occasion of the expression of *pain* (and not some other state). If we want to use the word, we can say: In all such cases the criteria are satisfied. For this just means: We are responding (again) with, among other things, *this* concept-word. We return it. Or, as Cavell neatly puts it, we 'retain' it (Cavell, 1979, p. 45).

This approach should remove any temptation to say that the answer to the question 'When are criteria for *p* unsatisfied?' must be of the form 'When it is not the case that *p*'. Rather, we should answer 'When we do not respond to the behaviour as *p*'. For example, a peculiar clearing of the throat may, in certain contexts, look and sound just like someone groaning in pain, but we do not normally respond to this behaviour as an expression of pain (see Z, §§532–4).

Such reading-responses must, in my view, be seen as our *primary* way of being with others. And, *pace* McDowell (1983, p. 404), it is not a matter of knowing something which 'makes it right to say' *p*, because *it is not a matter of knowing at all*.

Against both McDowell and the more orthodox view, then, my claim is that criteria are not ways of telling how things *are*. Rather, they are what we recall when we are answering questions concerning *what* things are. As Cavell has felicitously put it, 'criteria are "criteria for something's being so", not in the sense that they tell of a thing's existence, but of something like its identity, not of its *being* so but of its being *so*' (Cavell, 1979, p. 45). On this view, the 'satisfaction' of criteria does not establish or determine the certainty of statements or knowledge of some circumstance. Wittgensteinian criteria are criteria for the *identity* of inner states and processes. They are, therefore, what are elicited when we are asked to recall or imagine occasions in which we return/retain a psychological concept-word; i.e., contexts in which the behaviour of a living thing is read in this special way.

On this view, one will not say that a case of pretence pain-behaviour (i.e., a 'mere repetition' of an iterable trait) is a case of 'unsatisfied criteria'. On the contrary, it is a kind of paradigm of a criterion's satisfaction. In fact, the notion of 'unsatisfied criteria' does not really have an obvious place in *ordinary* life at all. It should, rather, be reserved for cases in which, in the face of the behaviour of a living thing, *one is altogether lost for words*. In such cases one cannot read-respond to (cannot recognise an iterable trait in) what one sees. The behavioural occurrence or happening is unintelligible. And hence, on the approach I am defending, one does not perceive the soul of a living thing. A radically extreme case in which 'no criteria are satisfied' would be one in which the behaviour of a living thing is not part of a life-textile in which one is remotely at home. Living things of this kind are what one might call 'radical aliens'.

The return of the subject

One can imagine circumstances in which one is at sea with the behaviour of one's own body in a *somewhat* comparable way.[13] But this is not normally the case. However, this is not because one is so familiar with one's own behavioural traits. Rather, it is because, *in der Tat*, one rarely *reads* one's own behaviour at all. In the case of personal experiences, for example, 'what I do is not, of course, to identify my sensation by criteria: but to *repeat an expression*' (PI, §290, my emphasis; cp. *ibid.*, §377).

In one's own case, in so far as nothing is read, one is essentially not identifying anything by criteria. Thus, the work of reading, the 'criterial identification' of inner states and processes ('being *so*'), is fully and wholly entrusted to the third person. This is why, in his famous formulation of this thought, Wittgenstein places the 'what' that is identified in inverted commas: 'An "inner process" stands in need of outward criteria' (*ibid.*, §580).[14] These are not scare quotes – as if what is identified is not *really* 'inner'.[15] Rather, with their use he is drawing attention to the fact that what the outward criteria are bound up with is the identity (being *so*) and not the existence (*being* so) of the process: its being, say, a 'pain' or an 'expectation' (and not some other thing). This is why the language of the inner is necessarily, and through and through, 'not one intelligible to me alone' (*ibid.*, §261). And this is also why the identificatory 'what' of sentient states fundamentally 'stands in need' of a reading-response:

> Do I say in my own case that I am saying something to myself, because
> I am behaving in such-and-such a way? – I do *not* say it from observa-
> tion of my behaviour. *But it only makes sense because I do behave in this way.*
>
> (*ibid.*, §357, my emphasis)

The perhaps paradoxical consequence of this logic is that one has no (identifying)
relation to oneself 'that is not forced to defer itself by passing through the
other . . . who is supposed to send his signature back to me' (Derrida, 1985, p. 88).

This 'returned signature' is the 'standing in need of the reading-response'
which characterises the 'what' of inner states and processes. However, the idea of
an authorising signature, or attesting countersignature, also suggests something
like the leap to a 'we' which I introduced earlier. It is here that the second,
possessor claim that I wish to defend comes to the fore. For, in one's own case, in
so far as nothing is read, one is not only not identifying, say, a sensation by
criteria but also, essentially, not identifying an owner or 'subject' which *has* it:
'the experience of feeling pain is not that a person "I" has something' (PR, §65).
As Wittgenstein goes on to note, this means that the first personal repetition of
an expression cannot be the end of the story: 'what sort of thing would a pain be
that no one has? Pain belonging to no one at all?' (*ibid.*). In my view, what we
have to see is that it is not just the identity of inner states and processes (the
'what'), but also the identity or individuation of the subject *of* such states and
processes (the 'who') which 'stands in need' of a reading-response.

As indicated, my suggestion here is that the context of a reading-response must
be seen as being, *eo ipso*, a turn towards a living thing *as* another. For example, if
the response is as to a 'pain in a hand' 'one does not comfort the hand, but the
sufferer: one looks into his face' (PI, §286). In short, the reading-response is always
also a singular identifying response to a 'soul'. I will explain this.

As we have seen, in reading the behaviour of a living thing one is *already caught*
responding or 'recognising criteria'. My claim is that such a response (even if it is
in the phenomenal form of a decisive 'No!') is necessarily one in which, here and
now, a 'we' is . . . – A 'we' is what? Discovered? Produced? Performed?
Chanced? Risked? I would suggest that the reading-response is best conceived as
a *spontaneous* or *originary* apostrophe. That is, it is a turn to a living thing *as*
another *in advance* of evidence or reasons which might *ground* it. Performing '(Yes:)
p', responding to the behaviour of a living thing by, among other things,
returning/retaining a psychological concept-word is, 'here and now', to leap to a
'we'.[16] This leap, the returned signature, does not *constitute* the other as other.
Rather, it is what *assigns* to a living thing the *position* of a subject, it is what 'opens
up the position' of the 'I' as subject (Derrida, 1992, p. 300). This is why the individuation of a subject of experience, the 'who', 'stands in need' of a
reading-response:

> 'When I say "I am in pain", I do not point to a person who is in pain,
> since in a certain sense I have no idea *who* is.' And this can be given a

146

justification. For the main point is: I did not say that such-and-such a person was in pain, but 'I am . . . ' Now in saying this I don't name any person. Just as I don't name anyone when I *groan* with pain. Though someone else sees *who* is in pain from the groaning.

(PI, §404)

On this approach, the 'who' is not something which, in one's own case, can be individuated without being 'forced to defer itself by passing through the other'. Thus, one is not, to oneself, 'constantly present-at hand', rather, and crudely, 'only our bodies are the principle of individuation' (PR, §60).[17] Or perhaps better, in each case, we *are* what we *do*. On this approach, the behaviour of a living thing is not a *scene* as of, say, 'a subject experiencing pain', except in its structural relation to a reading-response – even if the 'subject' is, in fact, isolated, and even if it is, in fact, 'oneself' who is in pain.

Another like myself

In the opening chapters of this book I drew special attention to the way in which an objectifying conception of subjectivity sustains the threat of scepticism. This metaphysical framework is focused on a compelling interpretation of the purity – and unique dignity – of the self-relation:

> Reference in this case [namely the use of 'I' as subject], unlike any other type of reference, is immune to error through misidentification. This is not because it is an encounter with an unmistakeable thing, but because reference in such a case does not denote an encounter at all. It does not denote a self-encounter but self-presence.
>
> (Chapter 1, p. 13)

On the approach I have been defending, however, the reason why this use is immune to error is not because it denotes self-presence but because it does not denote at all.[18] That is, if the foregoing argument is sound, then the use of 'I' as subject begins not with a self-present subject, but in a scene of an ungrounded reading-response (a 'Yes: same'-saying) which leaps to a 'we'. According to this argument, there is no openness to a living thing *as* another which is not caught in such a reading-response. And, again, this must be seen as our *primary* relation to others. That is, in being open to others, we are not first given a type of behaviour which will then *ground* an attribution of psychological properties – rather, *in advance of such evidence*, through the spontaneous and originary apostrophe of a reading-response 'the other appears as such' (Derrida, 1988b, p. 634).

The case of a 'radical alien' is, on this account, an entity with respect to which, while suspecting signs of life, we *hold in suspense* this reading-response. Unable to read-respond, unable to identify an iterable trait with which I am remotely at home, I may be said to see nothing but the behaviour of an organic body or of an anatomical apparatus: something fully (or merely) present in the present. But with a human being and what resembles a human being, this is not the normal case: 'we have begun to respond' (*ibid.*).[19] And, in such a context, one can say: 'if one sees the behaviour of a living thing, one sees its soul' (PI, §357). And one can say it of a dog.

On this view, 'encountering another' does not involve coming across an entity present-at-hand in the world which is discriminated and apprehended as being, like oneself, a subject that has experiences and entertains ideas. Rather, others are 'like oneself' just in so far as they, too, are at home with the 'writing' of living things; just in so far as they, too, exhibit a non-inferential familiarity with the *iterable traits* of living things. It is in these terms that we must conceive the 'being there too' of 'others'. That is – and lifting the humanist restriction which governs Heidegger's analysis – it is in these terms that we must conceive 'those from whom, for the most part, one does *not* distinguish oneself – those among whom one is too' (BT, p. 118).

CLOSING REMARKS

Since we are back to where we were, the argument is over. However, some closing remarks are in order – mainly to tie up some loose ends; but also to make one.

Constitutional uncertainty

The perspective in which the reading-response is, in theory at least, persistently held in suspense is, of course, the perspective of the sceptic. In this section I will sharpen my claim that the orthodox interpretation of Wittgensteinian criteria remains within the compass of this sceptic's framework.

According to the sceptical argument, the 'real presence' of the other's 'inner' life seems vulnerable to doubt. The orthodox interpretation of Wittgensteinian criteria is an attempt to argue that the notion of criteria can help us to dispel this doubt. As I have indicated, in general the aim of such approaches is to exhibit a relation between one ('outer') event or condition and another ('inner') event or condition such that observation of the presence of the first can confer certainty on judgements concerning the presence or existence of the second. My basic objection to such approaches should be clear. There is and could be no code or codification of behavioural conditions the satisfaction of which confers certainty or knowledge that *p* (e.g., that someone is expressing pain). The misplaced expectation concerning our criteria is clearly brought out by Wittgenstein in the following remark, a remark which demolishes the idea that he thinks that the notion of criteria is a resource with which to refute scepticism:

> The following is true: I can't give criteria which put the presence of the sensation beyond doubt; that is to say *there are no such criteria*. – But what

sort of fact is that? A psychological one, concerning sensations? Will one want to say that it resides in the nature of sensation, or the expression of sensation. I might say, it is a peculiarity of our language-game. – But even if that is true, it passes over a main point: In certain cases I am in some uncertainty whether someone else is in pain or not, I am not secure in my sympathy with him – and no expression on his part can remove this uncertainty.

(RPPI, §137, my emphasis)

The supporters of the criterial response to scepticism conceive the presence of criteria as something which will *ground* my response to the other. It is at this point that the refuters of the sceptic are at one with the sceptic: the 'being there' of criteria are conceived as blankly external to our reading-responses. On the approach taken in this chapter, however, there are no criteria that do not *already* implicate a regularity of singular reading-responses of and to the behaviour of living things. For this reason alone it is illegitimate to appeal to criteria to refute scepticism. As a refutation of scepticism, recourse to criteria will always beg the question. With their identification we will have already been caught responding to the other *as such*. And hence a 'we' will *already* be in play.

The account of criteria I have presented does not preclude the possibility of uncertainty in particular cases. However, in so far as the authenticity or sincerity of an expression is 'unpresentable', this is not because it relates to a subjective character which is necessarily hidden. Rather, it is part of the structure of iterable traits that it is *a priori* possible to repeat and hence *mimic* them. This structural possibility might be called the truth of scepticism. But the 'uncertainty' in question here does not relate to readings in particular cases. The uncertainty is 'constitutional' (RPPI, §141). The peculiarity of the logic of an iterable trait is that it prevents it being the case that one could 'give criteria which put the presence of the sensation beyond doubt'. However, since the 'moment of the leap' necessarily exceeds the calculable, this uncertainty does not affect reading-responses in particular cases (see Z, §555). That is, the uncertainty in question here does not threaten hesitations beyond the ordinary.

Bald naturalism and classical humanism

At the start of this book I distinguished two responses to the question whether 'all there is to others is events of behaviour'. It can now be seen that the two notional philosophers that I was responding to both 'split the phenomenon of significant behaviour' – each taking different sides in an unresolvable drama between bald naturalism and classical humanism.

The first (baldly naturalistic) philosopher is one who treats the concept of behaviour in terms of bodily events conceived as singular and dateable occurrences. In essence this is also the perspective of the sceptic. Here, behaviour is construed as something with respect to which 'we are holding in suspense all attributions of psychological properties' (McDowell, 1983, p. 469). According to the argument of this book, this means that the sceptic is the picture of someone who, faced with the behaviour of a living thing, refuses to read it and hence (tries, pretends to) see a 'radical alien'. To this philosopher I said and say again: 'No, it is not the case that all there is to others is events of behaviour'.

The second (classical humanist) philosopher recognises that such an approach leaves the idea of access to the soul of another in total darkness. In response to the sceptical (baldly naturalist) construal, this second philosopher insists that there must be something else present, something which lies 'behind' or 'in' the events of behaviour. It is towards this philosopher that the bulk of the argumentation of this book has been directed. This is the philosopher who wishes to thicken 'mere behaviour' by reference to the agency of a 'self-present subject'. To this philosopher I said and say again: 'Your "subject" cannot do the work of "thickening" that you suppose it can. It is a fiction. If we wish to avoid both scepticism and behaviourism then let us first be clear on what constitutes the status or eventhood of an event in such a case.'

In this book I have set out to provide a clarification of this crucial point. This has been a 'slow cook' response to scepticism concerning other minds. I have not attempted to refute scepticism but to reframe it. This reframing has taken the form of targeting investigation upon questions of the following form: What is it about human beings that makes them maintain an interpretation of themselves which sustains the threat of scepticism? Beginning with the Heideggerian identification of the traditional, objectifying conception of the subject character of a human being, my claim has been that the threat of scepticism has its source in an interpretation of the structure and functioning of *human language* – an interpretation which splits the phenomenon between singular events of speech and occasion-transcendent rules. Through an examination of the essential iterability of events of the use of signs, I have argued that a behavioural event (linguistic or otherwise) can be conceived as a case of 'communication' only if its identity is, *in itself*, iterable, and hence *at once*, both 'transcendent in relation to the anatomical apparatus' and 'immanent to the behaviour as such'.

The classical conception of communication

The classical interpretation of communication has been characterised as one in which there is a need or desire of one subject to give material ('outward') expression to thoughts (experiences, ideas, attitudes, feelings, etc.) so that they can be entertained, shared or understood ('inwardly') by another subject. Derrida summarises this conception in the following terms:

> Communication presupposes subjects (whose identity and presence are constituted before the signifying operation) and objects (signified concepts, a thought-meaning that the passage of communication will have neither to constitute, nor, by all rights, to transform). *A* communi-

cates *B* to *C*. Through the sign the emitter communicates something to a receptor.

(Derrida, 1981, pp. 23–4)

At a certain level this picture looks indisputable. Surely, if a case of communication were to be successful, it would have to involve a speaker who said what he meant and a listener who understood what he said. On the view I have been defending, however, expressions such as 'saying what one means' do not and cannot refer us to the presence of a determinate 'thought meaning' or 'intention-to-say' alongside the speaker's 'outward emission' of in themselves insignificant words. Hence, to borrow John McDowell's recommendation, if, when doing philosophy, one is still inclined to affirm the indisputability of the formulation '*A* communicates *B* to *C*', 'one must search one's conscience to be sure that what one has in mind is not really after all' the idealised phenomenon-splitting picture (McDowell, 1984, p. 345).

We have to be careful not to misrepresent this warning. I have argued for the view that the tension between the actual structure and functioning of language and the metaphysics of the subject is also a kind of complicity. The logic of ordinary language *enjoins* us to misunderstand it. On this view there is no question of excluding sentences like 'She expressed her thought very well' from ordinary use, just because of the confusions to which it can lead when we philosophise. As Wittgenstein stresses, to try to legislate in this way 'would cut out a very important part of our lives' (Wittgenstein, 1988, p. 53). Nevertheless, as long as such sentences do play an important part in our lives, the metaphysical experience will live on, too. Derrida makes the point in response to a question concerning the possibility of 'surpassing expressivism':

> On the one hand, expressivism is never simply surpassable, because it is impossible to reduce the couple inside/outside as a simple structure of opposition. . . . The representation of language as expression, as expressive re-presentation, a translation on the outside of what was constituted inside, is not an accidental prejudice, but rather a kind of structural lure. . . . On the other hand, and inversely, I would say that if expressivism is not simply and once and for all surpassable, expressivity is in fact always already surpassed, whether one wishes it or not, whether one knows it or not.
>
> (Derrida, 1981, p. 33)

On this account, the actual logic of language both destroys and invites the classical conception of communication, destroys and invites the humanist metaphysics of the subject. I have argued that resistance to this metaphysics requires the affirmation of dissemination. On this view, 'meaning', in the sense of a determinate sense, 'drops out of language'. In always singular cases, 'writing' is read.

151

Kripke's reading of Wittgenstein on other minds

I have argued that that way of responding to living things which reads iterable traits performs an originary, apostrophic 'leap' to a 'we'. This is what Derrida calls 'a friendship prior to friendship' (Derrida, 1988, p. 636) and Wittgenstein calls 'an attitude towards a soul' which is 'not an *opinion*' (PI, p. 178; see also Wittgenstein, 1977, §301). On this account, no 'epistemic-bridge' from one 'subject' to another is necessary in order to *ground* being with others. Any such bridge comes too late.

These ideas have, to a degree, been recognised by Saul Kripke in his reading of Wittgenstein:

> The correct interpretation of our normal discourse involves a certain inversion: we do not pity others because we attribute pain to them, we attribute pain to them because we pity them. (More exactly: our attitude is revealed to be an attitude toward other minds in virtue of our pity and related attitudes.)
>
> (Kripke, 1982, p. 142)

My reading of Wittgenstein on this point diverges from Kripke in two important respects. First, while I fully agree that this idea is continuous with ideas in Wittgenstein's earliest writings,[20] it is, on my account, clearly wrong to suppose that it is 'a strand in Wittgenstein's argument' that should be separated from and 'explained without resort to the notion of a criterion' (*ibid.*, p. 120). Second, once we do see its connection to this notion, it becomes clear that Kripke is wrong to suppose that my attitude requires an empathic move in which, for example, 'I, who have myself experienced pain and can imagine it, can imaginatively put *myself* in place of the sufferer' (*ibid.*, p. 140). Kripke does not, at this point, sufficiently respect his own observation that the kind of account he is examining 'involves a certain inversion [of the traditional interpretation]' (*ibid.*, p. 142). That a living human being has the kind of subject position or subject character described by Kripke *presupposes* and cannot explain being with others. As Heidegger puts it '"empathy" does not first constitute Being-with; only on the basis of Being-with does "empathy" become possible' (BT, p. 125; see Z, §§540–2).

The interminability of reading

Since the eventhood of an event of 'writing' is riven by iterability, there is never just one 'proper reading' of a 'text'; another reading is *always possible*. 'Writing' is such that it always offers itself to new readings, new responses – and, hence, new *responsibilities*. This rhythm of reading, and the ineluctable responsibility which it implies, is inescapable. It is a rhythm that does not end. Or barely, for example, ~~now~~.

NOTES

INTRODUCTION

1 The notion of 'bald naturalism' is John McDowell's name for the philosophical 'opt out' which conceives of human life as fully explicable in the terms of natural science (McDowell, 1994b, p. 67).

1 THE THREAT OF SCEPTICISM

1 See, e.g., BB, pp. 4–6.
2 All page references to *Being and Time* in this book are to the pagination of the German edition, as indicated in the margins of the Macquarrie and Robinson translation.
3 Wittgenstein, 1969, p. 5
4 The argument that follows is indebted to many philosophers, especially, although in different ways, to Descartes, Kant, Wittgenstein, Gareth Evans and Marie McGinn. In order to maintain the intimacy of a first-personal narration, indebtedness will, for the most part, be indicated in notes rather than direct quotation. NB: *none* of the notes should be thought of as provided by the sceptic. They are, as it were, my 'editorial' annotations on the sceptic's text.
5 This schema derives from Wittgenstein (BB, p. 66).
6 The existence of animals (and human infants) clearly introduces a sort of disorder into the sceptics categories. However, the sceptic does not stop to reflect on this limitation. Later we will see that this oversight is not accidental.
7 Wittgenstein, NB, p. 80.
8 Evans, 1982, p. 220.
9 Frege's lovely line: 'Someone can have sympathy for me but still my pain always belongs to me and his sympathy to him. He does not have my pain and I do not have his sympathy' (Frege, 1967, p. 28).
10 In the following argument the sceptic presents what is, in fact, a *solipsistic misreading* of Wittgenstein's *reductio* at PI, §293.
11 This paragraph includes a modified version of an argument from P. M. S. Hacker (1986, p. 220) and fragments of PI §294 and PI §283.
12 This conception of the Sceptical Predicament is indebted to Marie McGinn's reading of scepticism (1989, pp. 1–13). I come back to McGinn's account in the next section of this chapter.
13 The sceptic imagines an android as a machine which is programmed to *represent* or *depict* a (real) human being in a manner analogous to the way an actor represents or depicts a (fictional) character in a play. Of course, the sceptic assumes that there is 'nothing that it is like' to be the machine-that-depicts-persons. For a clear defence of

this conception of androids see Cherry, 1991, pp. 11–25. For an alternative conception, in which the android is conceived as a sentient but 'unnatural kind', see Dick, 1968, *passim*.

14 Descartes, 1968 [1641], p. 100.
15 Descartes, 1980, p. 110.
16 The significance of this split will become a central theme in my diagnosis of the threat of scepticism. In this paragraph the sceptic construes the split in terms derived from Evans, 1982, pp. 157–8.
17 Descartes, 1980, p. 131.
18 Descartes, 1980, p. 114.
19 This argument connects to Bernard Williams's treatment of Descartes's attempt to argue that knowledge is possible (Williams, 1978, ch. 7).
20 The final sentence is derived from Nagel (1986, p. 20), which is itself derived from Wittgenstein (PI, §302).
21 McGinn, 1989, p. 4.
22 The phrase 'contours of a subjectivity' is from McDowell, 1993, p. 222.

2 REFRAMING SCEPTICISM I

1 See Austin, S&S, pp. 1–5. Austin's statements of this view are quoted and examined in the next section.
2 Austin's most sustained defence of this claim is at 1979, pp. 181–5.
3 See also 1979, p. 76 and p. 182.
4 For typically Austinian statements of this intention see, e.g., Austin, 1979, p. 181, and S&S, p. 5.
5 See G. E. Moore, 'Proof of an External World', *Proceedings of the British Academy*, Vol. XXV, 1939; also 'A Defence of Common Sense', in *Contemporary British Philosophy, 2nd series*, ed. J. H. Muirhead, 1925. Both papers are in Moore, *Philosophical Papers*, 1959.
6 This follows the same movement of thought pursued by the sceptic. As we saw in the last chapter, the sceptic's doubts are prompted by a recognition that he often hesitates and makes mistakes about the psychological states of Others. Austin's typically roguish examples of cases in which he is inclined to hesitate include 'the feelings of royalty, or fakirs, or bushmen or Wykehamists or simple eccentrics' (OM, p. 104).
7 Austin stresses that, in general, recognition of a thing *as* the thing that it is is not something which can be done 'by anybody you please' (OM, p. 85). In the case of other people you have to be a certain kind of insider to see their behaviour as the display that it is.
8 It is worth noting that '*Gleichschaltung*' has had, since the 1930s, an irreducibly political connotation and that, like '*Führer*', is now rarely used. Metaphorised by Hitler, '*Gleichschaltung*' was the watchword for the (forced) integration of various previously autonomous bodies under the control of the National Socialist Party (e.g. trade unions, the police, the civil service, the media). The word was subsequently appropriated and its meaning further displaced by anti-Nazis to refer to those who became intellectually integrated into the Party, particularly the intellectual elite (such as Heidegger). '*Gleichschaltung*' has, and certainly had at the time Austin was writing, strong overtones of a mind-set which, in the name of purity, forges order by force. Austin's deployment of this word in a philosophical context serves, as it were, as a monogram of his conviction that 'simplifying' ways of going on in philosophy are a species of shackled and shackling thinking.
9 See Austin, 1980, p. 151.
10 See Austin, 1979, p. 108, p. 280, p. 282.

11 This point is stressed by Austin at 1979, p. 284; see also *ibid.*, pp. 283–4, fn. 2. Austin's most explicit statement of this identification of ordinary action with intentional action is at 1980, p. 21. I will return to this.

12 Frege famously includes interrogatives among the class of sentences which can communicate something. With sentence-questions, he states, 'we expect to hear "yes" or "no". The answer "yes" means the same as an indicative sentence, for in it the thought that was already completely contained in the interrogative sentence is laid down as true' (Frege, 1967, p. 21). Again, the important point with respect to the notion of force is that, for Frege, it applies only to events of speech in which thoughts are laid down as true. That is, it does not seem to be intended to highlight a component of sentences which is variable between sentences that can express the same thought. As the quotation indicates, strictly speaking it is the answer 'yes' and not the interrogative sentence itself that can possess force.

13 Since the conditions of felicity that Austin considers are conventional, it is at best misleading of Cavell to say that infelicitousness is a matter of failing to be 'adequate to reality' (Cavell, 1994, p. 81). However, he is right to criticise Derrida for supposing that, for truth, Austin 'at times' substitutes 'the value of force' (Derrida, 1988a, p. 13). This being admitted, we must not overlook the fact that, if (like Austin) we aim to lift the Fregean restriction, what the special infelicities (those which Austin 'excludes from current consideration') affect would be, precisely, the force of the utterance.

14 In the terms of his own (restricted) analysis, Frege makes the same point very clearly: 'Where [the indicative sentence] loses its assertive force the word "true" cannot put it back again . . . It must still always be asked . . . whether it really contains an assertion. And this must be answered in the negative if the requisite seriousness is lacking. It is irrelevant whether the word "true" is used here' (Frege, 1967, p. 22). I am simply adding that it is equally irrelevant whether the words 'I am serious' are used either.

3 REFRAMING SCEPTICISM II

1 This qualification will turn out to be crucial in outlining the problems with Heidegger's analysis. As with the presentation of Austin, however, I will let the problems ride for a while in order to show those aspects of his account which offer the most powerful reframing of scepticism.

2 Derrida, 1982, p. 38. As I have indicated, this is not to say there are no difficulties with Heidegger's approach. These will be considered in the next chapter.

3 An inquiry into the Being of a (type of) entity is termed 'ontological', and contrasts to 'ontical' inquiries into (types of) entities themselves (i.e., the kinds of inquiries which characterise the various sciences). This contrast runs roughly parallel to the Kantian contrast between transcendental and empirical investigations.

4 See note 1 to Introduction, p.153.

5 Perhaps, louder still than the word 'mind', we hear today the praises sung of the mechanisms of the 'brain' in constructing 'models' and 'maps' of reality 'outside' it.

6 In Kantian terms, one might say that an entity which 'exists' or has Dasein as its kind of Being is an entity for whom 'metaphysics' is a 'natural disposition' (Kant, 1933 [1787], B22).

7 It is worth noting that this distinction, Heidegger's basic dualism, exactly parallels the distinction drawn up by the sceptic in Chapter 1.

8 Ominously, like the sceptic, Heidegger does not stop to consider the Being that belongs to *animals* at this point and within this opposition of categories and existentialia. As will be seen in the next chapter, like the sceptic, and for similar reasons, he will find great difficulty doing so.

9 This theme is developed, *passim*, in Mulhall, 1996 (see especially Mulhall's Preface, p. xi).

10 Of course, if we conceive what it is to be human in categorial terms, this looks absurd. But, as we have seen, the phenomenon of Being-in-the-world cannot be reduced to the taking place of a relation between two discrete entities (a subject and a world). Being-in-the-world is not itself a kind of knowing. Indeed, knowledge of entities presumes Being-in-the-world and cannot give it any support.

11 Heidegger explores the concept of 'understanding', like Wittgenstein, through its relation to the concepts of 'being able to' and 'being competent to'. The competence in question in the current context is not, of course, over a (categorial) 'what' but Dasein's 'Being as existing' (BT, p. 144).

12 Of course, encountering entities in their mere presence-at-hand is still a mode of Being-in-the-world. But Heidegger's argument is that it cannot be our primary mode. On the contrary, it is a 'deficient' mode: a mode in which Dasein must 'hold back' from its concern with the 'in-order-to' which is constitutive for the entity in its readiness-to-hand (BT, p. 61).

13 Heidegger suggests that it is only 'lit up' (i.e., in some sense present-at-hand) when the structure of involvements is, in certain ways, interrupted (e.g., when the hammer breaks) (BT, pp. 72–6).

14 Conceptions such as this were identified in Nagel's work in Chapter 1 and in Austin's in Chapter 2.

15 That Heidegger's account includes a crucial distinction between the 'they-self' ('the Self of everyday Dasein') and the authentic self ('the Self which has been taken hold of in its own way') should not lead one to conclude that the authentic self inhabits a private world. As Heidegger stresses, 'authentic Being-one's-Self does not rest upon an exceptional condition of the subject, a condition that has been detached from the "they"; it is rather an existentiell [i.e. "lived"] modification of the "they" – of the "they" as an essential existentiale' (BT, p. 131). The point is that the 'self-relation' is always already a mode of Being-with others.

4 THE HUMAN ANIMAL

1 Much more could be said about Heidegger's appeal to 'experience' to identify human beings alone as the singular 'example' of Dasein. As I will indicate in the next section, Heidegger links having Dasein's Being very closely to the capacity for language, and claims, trenchantly and confidently, that animals 'lack language' (LH, p. 230). This supposed lack of language (I will explain my reticence here in the final section) is also used to disqualify animals from being such that they 'can have the hand': 'Only beings who can speak, that is, think, can have the hand or be handy . . . Apes, for example, have organs that can grasp, but they have no hand' (Heidegger, 1968, p. 16). (Note that this alone suggests that animals are disqualified from inhabiting a world of the ready-to-*hand*.) A similar disqualification is registered in Heidegger's distinction between dying and perishing, the former of which is denied the animal: 'Animals cannot do this. But animals cannot speak either' (Heidegger, 1971, p. 107).

2 As Heidegger stresses in 'The Letter on Humanism', the conception of the essence of human existence which is proposed in *Being and Time* is not intended to imply that 'man is that entity through which Being is first fashioned'. On the contrary: 'Being is illumined for man in the ecstatic projection. But this projection does not create Being' (LH, pp. 240–1).

3 Krell suggests that the extent to which the question of life dominates the second part of the course is partly explained by the fact that Heidegger was 'oppressed by the

sense of his earlier failure [in *Being and Time*] to confront the problems of *Lebensphilosophie*' (Krell, 1992, p. 104).

4 For the procedural parallel, see, e.g., BT, p. 55: 'The issue is one of *seeing* a primordial structure of Dasein's Being. . . . We shall again choose the method of contrasting it with a relationship of Being which is essentially different ontologically.' Just as this method aims, in *Being and Time*, at an ontological clarification of Dasein, so it is employed in the 1929–30 lectures to conceive 'the essence of the animality of the animal' and 'the essence of the humanity of man' (FCM, p. 179).

5 For detailed examinations of Heidegger's account of animal drives, and the way in which Heidegger problematises (but never abandons or refutes) the initial 'comparative' theses, see Krell, 1992, pp. 119–30; and Franck, 1991, pp. 138–44.

6 This line of interpretation has been taken up by many readers of Wittgenstein, most notably by David Pears (1971, ch. 9), Bernard Williams (1982), Jonathan Lear (1984), and John McDowell (1994b).

7 Wittgenstein's early humanism is rarely remarked upon. But it really is fundamental to his early metaphysics of the subject (Wittgenstein, 1961a, 5.62–5.641). See also Wittgenstein, 1961, pp. 80–89: 'The willing subject exists. If the will did not exist, neither would there be that *centre of the world* which we call the I' (p. 80); 'It is true: Man *is* the microcosm' (p. 84).

8 The Wittgensteinian view that 'to see the behaviour of a living thing is to see its soul' (*PI*, §357) is, of course, one which I aim to defend in this book. I do not take the preceding discussion to have established this view, and will return to it in detail in the final chapter.

9 The central features of such a re-evaluation of the naturalistic assumption are outlined in Gibson, 1986, *passim*. For a realistic naturalism which suggests that the attribution of perceptual content at the level of the animal is *not* 'as if' talk, see McDowell, 1994a, *passim*.

10 See Wittgenstein, 1981, §§540–5.

5 PHILOSOPHY AND THE IDEAL OF EXACTNESS

1 That is, that living thing whose Being is essentially determined by the potentiality for '*logos*' (discourse, understanding, reason).

2 As should be clear, I am wholly sympathetic to resistance to the idea that the natural sciences exhaust what can be said about human life. But, as I have explained, this is partly because I am resistant to this idea with respect to all animal life in general. (A slogan: Neither bald naturalism nor another humanism.)

3 I am not at this stage including Heidegger's analysis of Dasein within what Derrida calls the 'closure' of humanism. However, as I hope to make clear, the 'magnetic attraction' identified in the previous chapter remains powerfully operative, particularly, as we shall see, in relation to the Heideggerian conception of the 'as such' which marks Dasein's access to the world.

4 Cp. Wittgenstein's suggestion that his investigations, like traditional philosophy, can be called 'analysis', 'for the process is sometimes like one of taking a thing apart' (PI, §90).

5 For a clear discussion of Derrida's erasure of the distinction between 'reading' and 'doing' philosophy, see Bennington, 1988, pp. 83–5 and, with this in mind, Gasché, 1986, pp. 121–47.

6 Such an exclusion (the exclusion of 'non-serious' utterances) was seen to be a central feature of Austin's attempt to isolate the 'happy' performative.

7 This is not intended to suggest that the expression 'Mary possessed a young sheep', unlike 'Mary had a little lamb', has a *unitary* sense which is 'carried with it into every kind of application' (PI, §117).

8 Again, the thought is that no text has the kind of *unitary* sense or meaning which is 'carried with it into every kind of application' (PI, §117). As I indicated in Chapter 2, this must not be taken to imply that *any* or *every* reading is 'correct' (on this, see, e.g., LI, pp. 142–50). This gross *misreading* of Derrida's views is still quite prevalent. The irony is, I suppose, that Derrida is consistently concerned to show how such misreading arises and is possible.

9 The place to examine Heidegger on this issue is the difficult concept of Dasein's 'horizonal leeway' [*Spielraum*] (BT, p. 145, p. 355, pp. 367f); literally, 'space (or room) for playing'.

10 See PR, Foreword.

11 It should be noted that this is not a speculative interpretation of the central concern of the *Investigations*. On the contrary, that the question of clarity about the essence of language is *the* principal theme is in fact quite clearly marked by Wittgenstein, At PI, §65 he explicitly identifies the '*great question* that lies behind *all* these considerations' with the attempt to discern 'the essence of language'. And again: 'We *too* in these investigations are trying to understand the essence of language' (PI, §92).

12 These are brought out extremely neatly by Peter Winch (1987, ch. 1).

13 Derrida, 1993, pp. 145–6: 'Haven't all the differences [in the history of philosophy] taken the form of a going-one-better in eschatological eloquence, each newcomer more lucid than the other?'

14 'In the course of the lectures in 1930–3 Wittgenstein claimed that philosophy as he was now practising it was not merely a stage in the continuous development of the subject, but a new subject. . . . Wittgenstein declared that with the emergence of his new style of philosophizing there was a "kink" in the evolution of philosophy' (Hacker, 1986, pp. 146–7).

15 Derrida notes (1976, p. lxxxix) that in his work he has 'concerned [himself] with a *structural figure* as much as a *historical totality*'. While one cannot say of the latter that it will ever come to an end, in terms of the former we can 'outline its closure' (*ibid.*, p. 14).

16 Not least a sense of piety to his favourite Christian saint.

17 Malcolm, 1986, p. 106.

18 'Perhaps paradoxically', but not really: where else could this conception come from?

19 It is in view of this assumption that Derrida calls traditional philosophy 'logocentric' (Derrida, 1976, p. 3).

20 Wittgenstein's attitude towards the *Confessions* extract has two major aspects; a 'positive' and a 'negative' assessment of it. On the one hand, Augustine's picture is accepted as a description of language which is 'correct for a simpler language than ours' (BB, p. 77; PI, §2). It is a simplification which can be used to help us achieve clarity when we are struggling with philosophical difficulties: 'When we look at such simple forms of language the mental mist which seems to enshroud the ordinary use of language disappears' (BB, p. 17; PI, §5). On the other hand, Wittgenstein's interest in Augustine's picture is also motivated by its being the expression of a conception of the essence of language which invites us to idealise the idea of 'meaning'. It is this tendency to idealise the ordinary use of language which is 'a primitive idea of the way language functions', and which *is* the mental mist of unclarity (PI, §5).

21 This view recalls the Heideggerian conception of the world (the structure of significance) outlined in Chapter 3. For further discussion of this comparison see Mulhall, 1990, pp. 147–51. The limits of this comparison reside in Wittgenstein's rejection of

the idea that 'the world as such' has the kind of unity presupposed by Heidegger's analysis of Dasein.

22 Wittgenstein does not claim that we all *must* succumb to this tendency to idealise 'meanings': 'If I am convinced that a mouse cannot come into being from [grey rags and dust] then this investigation will perhaps be superfluous.' (PI, §52)

6 RULES AND EVENTS OF LANGUAGE

1 This conception of the nature of the problem is, as Derrida acknowledges (1981, p. 33), formally related to the Kantian doctrine of 'transcendental illusions'. According to Kant, such an illusion is not of the sort 'in which a bungler might entangle himself through lack of knowledge'; rather, it 'continually entraps' thinking into aberrations 'ever and again calling for correction and hence will not cease'. The illusion (fiction) is structural (grammatical) and not, as is the case with fallacious reasoning, a consequence of 'a lack of attention' (Kant, 1933 [1787], A297–8, B354; cp. PI, §307).

2 A clear presentation of Wittgenstein's arguments against such accounts of communication is in Hacker, 1986, pp. 255–75.

3 NB: 'Communication is never anything *like* . . . '

4 No doubt such a split strongly suggests a 'realm of the inner' in which such 'meanings' are held or apprehended.

5 Wittgenstein states that 'the concept of language *is contained in* the concept of communication' (PG, p. 193). My view is that the latter cannot be limited to or by the former. The quotation in the sentence to which this note is attached is from McDowell (1984, p. 351). I will refer to and critically examine McDowell's account of communication in the final chapter.

6 Conceiving concepts in terms of rules can be traced, at least, to Kant: 'a concept is always, as regards its form, something universal which serves as a rule' (Kant, 1933 [1787], A106).

7 This is the strategy pursued by Searle presented in the last chapter. It is also the strategy pursued by Austin in his isolation of 'happy' performatives.

8 See PI, §108 and §81. Derrida, too, insists that 'to [the] oppositional logic, which is necessarily, legitimately, a logic of "all or nothing" and without which the distinction and limits of a concept would have no chance, I oppose nothing, least of all a logic of approximation, a simple empiricism of difference in degree.' (LI, p. 117).

9 This is not to say that the desire for ideal exactness is *completely* unrelated to other expressions of the desire for purity. For example, in politics and ethics, what is the logic of 'Ethnic Cleansing', or of 'Virginity'?

10 This is a simplification which avoids the complications arising from explanations involving ostensive gestures. Wittgenstein's claim is that the situation is fundamentally the same in both kinds of case (PI, §28). This is also, of course, one of the central implications of the thought that 'there is nothing outside the text'.

11 As is shown in Chapter 7, Derrida affirms the same point in his analysis of writing.

12 RPPII §§401–2: 'But what this really amounts to is that consistently following a series can only be shown by example. And here one is tempted again and again to talk more than still makes sense. To continue talking where one should stop.'

13 The expression 'instant talisman' is from Pears, 1988, p. 209. On the classical conception, this talisman is always only hinted at in explanations by example. In giving examples, 'you get him to guess the essential thing' (PI, §210). Pears notes (1988, p. 209), correctly in my view, that the idea of an instant talisman is not biased towards subjectivism (psychologism, empiricism) or objectivism (Platonism, Fregeanism).

14 Pears explores this in some detail (1988, pp. 468–70).

15 'The word "agreement" and the word "rule" are *related*, they are cousins. The phenomena of agreement and acting according to a rule hang together.' (RFM, VI-41; cp. PI, §224).

16 I use the term 'knowing' here simply to designate the relations which each one of us *necessarily* maintains with the kind of structure that belongs to language.

17 This point raises the important distinction between 'an individual conceived in isolation' (who may therefore be in a crowd) and 'an isolated individual' (a Crusoe). As is shown in Chapter 7, there is no contradiction in conceiving a language in the latter case. The former case is far more problematic. I will argue that it is in principle inconceivable.

18 '"Normative activities", viz. teaching, explaining, justifying and criticizing, evaluating and defining rule-governed activities' (AC, vol. 2, p. 47).

19 In Wittgenstein's terms it is a *criterion* for judging, for example, 'whether someone meant such-and-such [by a mathematical formula for the expansion of a series] that he taught *someone else* the expansion of a series in the usual way' (PI, §692; cp. RFM, VI-41-2). An interpretation of Wittgensteinian criteria is proposed in the final chapter.

20 I am indebted to conversations with Stephen Law for this paragraph.

21 Cp. RFM, VII-35: '"But surely this isn't ideal certainty!" – Ideal for what purpose?'

22 Throughout his post-Tractarian career Wittgenstein argued that there are two ways of looking at, two senses of 'recognition' (see, e.g., PR, §19; BB, p. 88 and p. 130; Z, §§202-3; RPPI, §120, §295; PI, §§602-7). In general, Wittgenstein's consistent point is that recognition does not always involve being struck by a similarity between one thing and another. We must acknowledge a mode of 'recognition' which can consist *wholly* in my acting with respect to the 'what' of objects and events without hesitation. For example, he states: 'One must distinguish between the experience of recognizing something again and recognizing, which is simply a being-familiar-to-me' (LWI, §547). It is this latter sense of recognition which is normally in question when we talk about 'understanding a word' in terms of 'recognising the same sense'.

7 COMMUNICATION AND ITERABILITY

1 This point should make it a little more clear why Derrida is willing to talk about 'texts' in reference to phenomena which are not 'written' in the usual or narrow sense of this word.

2 It is irrelevant to this claim whether this form is considered as being immanent in (Aristotelianism) or transcendent of (Platonism) the empirical marks.

3 This argument is a version of that presented by Derrida (1982, p. 5).

4 This argument recalls the Heideggerian claim that readiness-to-hand cannot be apprehended by attending to what is merely present-at-hand and its properties.

5 This is not to claim that a system/event distinction is of no value at all. Indeed, Derrida is perfectly willing to accept that it can profitably (reliably) be employed in order to 'demarcate a linguistics of language and a linguistics of speech' (1981, p. 28) for a *determined* language. The objection is, rather, that an account grounded on this distinction cannot determine the logically necessary or structural conditions of its own possibility, the possibility of its own conceptual (oppositional) logic.

6 This point defuses an important objection to Derrida's argument posed by John Llewelyn. Llewelyn argues (1986, p. 46) that Derrida's attempt to draw a necessary conclusion from the problem of the Saussurean Circle is a *non-sequitur*: 'Could it be that both historically and logically language and speech – speech as opposed to babble – are equiprimordial?' This objection cannot stand, since this is basically what the argument from iterability is intended to show. The point is that, in order to

remove the problem of chicken and egg, one is compelled to achieve a perspective on language in which the two apparently opposing terms can be seen as abstractions from a single structure or practice. This cannot be done if one *begins* with a bifurcated account.

7 The idea of 'fully' understanding must be understood in the sense outlined in the last chapter; i.e., an understanding for which every possible ambiguity has been removed.

8 As I have tried to stress, Derrida's argument is not made with the view to a future *revision* of the ordinary functioning of words, including the word 'writing'. On the contrary, he is attempting to transform the habitual logical space which prevents clarity about the ordinary functioning of language in general. That is, the generalisation must be seen to be strategic and local, not revisionary and general.

9 This claim is, in my view, connected to Wittgenstein's remarks on multiple applications at PI, §199 and RFM, VI-34. This connection is examined directly at the end of this chapter.

10 Cp. Locke's criterion for personal identity (1964 [1690], p. 213).

11 Cp. PI, §268.

12 Thus, for example, the possibility of the *recitation* of speech is not an eventuality which can possibly be excluded from an analysis of the functioning of ordinary language. On the contrary, its possibility specifies an essential part of its structure and should be acknowledged as such. This is, of course, Derrida's basic claim in his reading of Austin.

13 Hereafter in the text I will distinguish Derrida's generalised 'writing' from writing in the narrow sense by the use of quotation marks.

14 The point about 'distancing' is that anything I might do which is *so dependent* on my subjectivity that it could not do without my presence could not be a case of my 'using signs'.

15 In virtue of the way in which it privileges speech, Derrida calls such thinking 'phonocentric'.

16 Cp. PI, §89 and RFM, VI-34.

17 'The phrase which for some has become a sort of slogan, in general so badly understood, of deconstruction ("there is nothing outside the text" [*il n'y a pas de hors-texte*, literally "there is no outside text"]), means nothing else: there is nothing outside context' (LI, p. 136).

18 Stanley Cavell makes a similar point in his reading of Wittgenstein (1979, p. 188). I return to a comparison of Derrida's views with Wittgenstein's in the next section of the chapter.

19 Again, 'know' is being used here to designate relations which one 'necessarily entertains with the object being constructed' (LI, p. 49).

20 Think here of the difference between a blink and a wink. Only in the latter case is a relation to an iteration at another time implicated in the structure of the event *a priori*.

21 It should be noted, however, that according to Wittgenstein, an eventuality in which an expression is, in fact, only used once is only possible against a background in which *similar* expressions *are used* (see RFM, VI-32).

22 That is, again, an occasion other than this one which, as a singular event, cannot be conceived as being a case of 'obeying a rule' without reference to *another such* event, an occasion other than this one which, as a singular event, cannot be conceived as being a case of 'obeying a rule' without reference to *another such* event . . . Again, the crucial point is: '*not once*'.

23 This point is also made by Marie McGinn (1984, pp. 25–6).

24 This conclusion leads Derrida to thought-provoking (or, for some readers, merely provocative) claims such as this: 'Writing, if there is any, perhaps communicates, but certainly does not exist. Or barely, hereby, in the form of the most improbable signa-

ture' (LI, p. 21; this text is followed by the reproduction of Derrida's signature). I offer the following translation of this sentence for the bemused, confused or frustrated: We might say that 'writing' is (if we can talk about it in the present tense without confusion) 'a means of communication'. But let us first be clear about what constitutes the eventhood of an event of 'writing'. For these terms, 'writing' and 'communication' invite, and are embedded in, systems of interpretation which sustain interminable confusions. 'Writing' is not simply a physical externality of language, the representation of speech, the outward expression of sense, and is irreducible to anything simply present in the present. Or rather, it is of course *in some sense* present (the use of an expression is in some sense present when we use it). But even the most explicit expression of its authenticity as 'writing', for example an appended signature, is *by itself* insufficient evidence of authenticity. For what holds for the 'writing' holds, *a fortiori*, for the signature too.

25 Marx, cited in Norman, 1983, p. 181. The idea of language as 'practical consciousness' is affirmed by Wittgenstein with the thought that language is not the communicable representation of consciousness but can itself be the 'vehicle of thought' (PI, §329).

26 This polarisation of views is clearly presented in Malcolm, 1989, pp. 5–28. David Pears is a notable exception to this pattern (see Pears, 1988, ch. 14).

27 'Inasmuch as it is essential and structural, this possibility is always at work marking *all the facts*, all the events, even those which appear to disguise it' (LI, p. 48). Again, the crucial distinction is between 'conceiving of an isolated individual' and 'an individual conceived in isolation'. It is fairly clear, I think, that the latter is only amenable to a description in baldly naturalistic terms. So much the worse for bald naturalism.

28 This term is obviously intended to connect this conception to Austin's notion of a performative utterance. However, the performative is not examined by Austin as a feature of the logic of *locutions in general*, as I am urging here.

29 'There are two stems of human knowledge, namely, sensibility and understanding, which perhaps spring from a common, but to us unknown, root' (Kant, 1933 [1787], A15 B29). The sensibility/understanding opposition is the name Kant gives to the relationship between singularity (intuition) and generality (concepts). The argument here is that such a distinction is rooted in the (pre-oppositional) logic of iterability.

30 By 'end' I mean limit, *not* purpose.

31 This is, I think, the crucial lesson of Wittgenstein's *reductio* at PI §§201–2, and the idea that 'there is a way of grasping a rule which is not an interpretation'. This conclusion points to a further, and in my view decisive, reason for treating the concept of a code or calculus of rules with caution. It is difficult to rely on it to account for the phenomenon of language because it suggests that 'meaning' or 'understanding' an expression is primarily a matter of encoding or decoding it. As Derrida also puts it, 'writing is read; it is not the site, "in the last instance", of a hermeneutic deciphering, the decoding of a meaning or truth' (LI, p. 21; cp. PI §81).

8 READING THE OTHER

1 See RFM, VI-19: 'We talk and act. That is already presupposed in everything that I am saying.' I return to this point in the first Closing Remark at the end of this chapter.

2 'If a pattern of life is the basis for the use of a word then the word must contain some amount of indefiniteness. The pattern of life, after all, is not one of exact regularity' (LWI, §211; see also Z, §374).

3 Some philosophers are unwilling to concede the publicity claim even in the case of 'intentional acts of consciousness' such as thinking. Nagel, for example, states that

'not only raw feels but also intentional mental states – however objective their content – must be capable of manifesting themselves in subjective form' (Nagel, 1986, pp. 15–16). The argument that follows, which focuses on sensations, should be seen as pertinent to Nagel's cases too.

4 See, for example, Wright (1993, p. 97): 'a claim made on the basis of satisfaction of its criteria can subsequently be jettisoned consistently with retention of the belief that criteria were indeed satisfied.'

5 The contrast between McDowell's account and the 'highest common factor' (HCF) view can be summarised as follows. McDowell: Groaning-in-certain-circumstances is either a satisfied or merely apparently satisfied criterion of pain. HCF: Groaning is a criterion of pain that confers certainty only in certain circumstances.

6 I am indebted to Max de Gaynesford for this way of putting McDowell's view.

7 It is noteworthy that McDowell presents his advocacy of this idea as an explicit *concession* to the Cartesian conception of subjectivity as a 'region of reality' or 'realm of fact and knowledge'. McDowell describes his alternative account as maintaining a position which stops 'short of the fully Cartesian picture' (McDowell, 1986, pp. 149–50). As will become clear, in my view McDowell's account does not stop short enough.

8 Cp. Frege, 1967, p. 28.

9 In Chapter 2 it was noted that Austin calls such types 'behavioural syndromes'.

10 This approach is related to that defended by McDowell (see 1983, p. 462).

11 It should be stressed that the notion of an iterable trait cannot be captured in terms of a type/token distinction such that criteria are type-conditions of which the behavioural facts are tokens. As should be clear, such a distinction necessarily involves an idealisation of a 'type' which splits the phenomenon.

12 I use 'return' here as in 'returning the book I borrowed', or 'returning the compliment'. However, as we shall see, the return in question here is, in a crucial sense, originary. As the 'moment of the leap' in which there is a 'leap' to a 'we', it must be given *in advance* of any exchange which 'we' may enter into.

13 Think of Gabriel Conroy's puzzlement (in James Joyce's *Dubliners*: Joyce, 1993, p. 281) at his own outward appearance: 'As he passed in the way of the cheval-glass he caught sight of himself in full length, his broad, well-filled shirt-front, the face whose expression always puzzled him when he saw it in a mirror . . . '

14 See also Z, §548.

15 If that was what was at issue, he would have placed them around 'outward' too.

16 As I indicated above, as an event which is, in itself, iterable, the 'here and now' of this response, its singularity, is at once deported beyond itself towards other, non-present, times.

17 Compare this to the early Wittgenstein's assumption that '*my world* is adequate for individuation' (NB, p. 89).

18 For further arguments on this point, see the articles by Kenny (1979) and Malcolm (1979).

19 It is perhaps worth stressing at this stage that, in the case of the behaviour of living human beings, what is manifest on the basis of this response is: What they say and do.

20 This is something I have been unable to stress sufficiently in this book. I refer the reader to Kripke's essay as a point of departure on this issue.

BIBLIOGRAPHY

Albritton, Rogers (1966) 'On Wittgenstein's Use of the Term "Criterion" ', in G. Pitcher (ed.), *Wittgenstein: The Philosophical Investigations*, Macmillan, London.

Arrington, Robert L. (1975) 'Can There Be a Linguistic Phenomenology', *The Philosophical Quarterly*, vol. 25, no. 101.

Austin, J. L. (1962) *Sense and Sensibilia*, Oxford University Press, Oxford.

—— (1979) *Philosophical Papers*, Oxford University Press, Oxford.

—— (1980) *How To Do Things With Words*, Oxford University Press, Oxford.

Ayer, A. J. (1956) *The Problem of Knowledge*, Penguin Books, Harmondsworth.

—— (1967) 'Has Austin Refuted the Sense-Datum Theory?', *Synthèse*, vol. 17.

Baker, G. P. and Hacker, P. M. S. (1983) *Analytical Commentary on the 'Philosophical Investigations': Wittgenstein: Meaning and Understanding*, vol. I, Basil Blackwell, Oxford.

—— (1984) *Scepticism, Rules and Language*, Basil Blackwell, Oxford.

—— (1985) *An Analytic Commentary on the 'Philosophical Investigations': Rules, Grammar and Necessity*, vol. II, Basil Blackwell, Oxford.

Baker, Gordon (1974) 'Criteria: A New Foundation For Semantics', *Ratio*, vol. 2.

Bennington, Geoffrey (1988) 'Deconstruction and the Philosophers (The Very Idea)', *The Oxford Literary Review*, vol. 10, no. 1–2.

—— (1989) 'Outside Language', *The Oxford Literary Review*, vol. 11, no. 1–2.

Bennington, Geoffrey and Derrida, Jacques (1993) *Jacques Derrida*, trans. Geoffrey Bennington, The University of Chicago Press, Chicago.

Canfield, John (1974) 'Criteria and Rules of Language', *The Philosophical Review*, vol. 83.

Cavell, Stanley (1976) *Must We Mean What We Say*, Cambridge University Press, Cambridge.

—— (1979) *The Claim of Reason: Wittgenstein, Skepticism, Morality, and Tragedy*, Oxford University Press, Oxford.

—— (1988) *In Quest of the Ordinary: Lines of Skepticism and Romanticism*, University of Chicago Press, Chicago.

—— (1994) *A Pitch of Philosophy*, Harvard University Press, Cambridge MA.

—— (1995) *Philosophical Passages: Wittgenstein, Emerson, Austin, Derrida*, Basil Blackwell, Oxford.

Cherry, Christopher (1991) 'Machines As Persons?', in D. Cockburn (ed.), *Human Beings*, Cambridge University Press, Cambridge.

Child, William (1992) 'Vision and Experience: The Causal Theory and the Disjunctive Conception', *The Philosophical Quarterly*, vol. 42, no. 168.

Culler, Jonathan (1983) *On Deconstruction: Theory and Criticism After Structuralism*, Routledge & Kegan Paul, London.

Derrida, Jacques (1976) *Of Grammatology*, trans. G. C. Spivak, The Johns Hopkins University Press, Baltimore.

—— (1979) *Spurs*, trans. B. Harlow, University of Chicago Press, Chicago.

—— (1981) *Positions*, trans. Alan Bass, The Athlone Press, London.

—— (1982) *Margins of Philosophy*, trans. Alan Bass, The Harvester Press, Brighton.

—— (1985) *Otobiographies: The Ear of the Other*, trans. Avital Ronell, University of Nebraska Press, Lincoln.

—— (1987a) *Of Spirit: Heidegger and the Question*, trans. Geoffrey Bennington and Rachel Bowlby, The University of Chicago Press, Chicago.

—— (1987b) *The Postcard: From Socrates to Freud and Beyond*, trans. Alan Bass, The University of Chicago Press, London.

—— (1988a) *Limited Inc*, North Western University Press, Evanston.

—— (1988b) 'The Politics of Friendship', *The Journal of Philosophy*, vol. LXXXV, no. 11.

—— (1991) '"Eating Well", or The Calculation of the Subject', in Eduardo Cadava *et. al.* (eds), *Who Comes After the Subject*, Routledge, London and New York.

—— (1992) *Acts Of Literature*, Routledge, London and New York.

—— (1993) *Aporias*, Stanford University Press, Stanford.

Descartes, René (1968) *Meditations*, trans. F. E. Sutcliffe, Penguin Books, Harmondsworth.

Dick, Philip K. (1969) *Do Androids Dream of Electric Sheep?*, Grafton, London.

Evans, Gareth (1982) *The Varieties of Reference*, Clarendon Press, Oxford.

Farrell, Frank B. (1988) 'Iterability and Meaning: The Searle–Derrida debate', *Metaphilosophy*, vol. 19, no. 1.

Franke, D. (1991) 'Being and the Living', in Eduardo Cadava *et al.* (eds), *Who Comes After The Subject*, Routledge, London and New York.

Frege, Gottlob (1967) 'The Thought: A Logical Enquiry', in P. F. Strawson (ed.), *Philosophical Logic*, Oxford University Press, Oxford.

Gasché, Rodolphe (1986) *The Tain of the Mirror: Derrida and the Philosophy of Reflection*, Harvard University Press, London.

Gibson, James J. (1986) *The Ecological Approach to Visual Perception*, Lawrence Erlbaum Associates, Hillsdale.

Glendinning, Simon B. (1996) 'Heidegger and the Question of Animality', *International Journal of Philosophical Studies*, vol. 4, no. 1.

Hacker, P. M. S. (1986) *Insight and Illusion: Themes in the Philosophy of Wittgenstein*, revised edition, Clarendon Press, Oxford.

Haugeland, John (1992) 'Dasein's Disclosedness', in H. Dreyfus and H. Hall (eds), *Heidegger: A Critical Reader*, Basil Blackwell, Oxford.

Heidegger, Martin (1962) *Being and Time*, trans. John Macquarrie and Edward Robinson, Basil Blackwell, Oxford.

—— (1968) *What is Called Thinking*, trans. F. D. Wieck and J. G. Gray, Harper, New York.

—— (1971) *On the Way to Language*, trans. P. D. Hertz, Harper, New York.

—— (1977) *Basic Writings*, trans. David Farrell Krell, Routledge, London.

—— (1995) *The Fundamental Concepts of Metaphysics*, trans. W. McNeill and N. Walker, Indiana University Press, Bloomington.

Joyce, James (1993) *Dubliners*, Wordsworth Editions, Ware.

Kant, Immanuel (1933) *Critique of Pure Reason*, trans. Norman Kemp Smith, The Macmillan Press, London.

Kenny, Anthony (1979) 'The First Person', in C. Diamond and J. Teichman (eds), *Intention and Intentionality*, The Harvester Press, Brighton.

—— (1992) *The Metaphysics of Mind*, Oxford University Press, Oxford.

Kerr, Fergus (1991) 'Getting The Subject Back Into The World: Heidegger's Version', in D. Cockburn (ed.), *Human Beings*, Cambridge University Press, Cambridge.

Krell, D. F. (1992) *Daimon Life: Heidegger and Life Philosophy*, Indiana University Press, Bloomington.

Kripke, Saul A. (1982) *Wittgenstein On Rules and Private Language: An Elementary Exposition*, Basil Blackwell, Oxford.

Lear, Jonathan (1984) 'The Disappearing "We"', *Proceedings of the Aristotelian Society*, vol. LVIII.

Leiber, Justin (1976) 'How J. L. Austin Does Things With Words', *Philosophy and Literature*, vol. 1, no. 1.

Llewelyn, John (1986) *Derrida on the Threshold of Sense*, Macmillan, London.

Locke, John (1964) *An Essay Concerning Human Understanding*, Collins, Glasgow.

Malcolm, Norman (1966) 'Wittgenstein's "Philiosophical Investigations"', in G. Pitcher (ed.), *Wittgenstein: The Philosophical Investigations*, Macmillan, London.

—— (1979) 'Whether "I" is a Referring Expression', in C. Diamond and J. Teichman (eds), *Intention and Intentionality*, The Harvester Press, Brighton.

—— (1986) *Wittgenstein: Nothing Is Hidden*, Basil Blackwell, Oxford.

—— (1989) 'Wittgenstein on Language and Rules', *Philosophy*, vol. 64, no. 247.

—— (1993) *Wittgenstein: A Religious Point of View*, Cornell University Press, Ithaca.

McDowell, John (1983) 'Criteria, Defeasibility, and Knowledge', *Proceedings of the British Academy*, vol. lxviii.

—— (1984) 'Wittgenstein On Following A Rule', *Synthèse*, vol. 58.

—— (1986) 'Singular Thought and the Extent of Inner Space', in P. Pettit and J. McDowell (eds), *Subject, Thought, and Context*, Clarendon Press, Oxford.

—— (1994a) 'The Content of Perceptual Experience', *The Philosophical Quarterly*, vol. 44, no. 175.

—— (1994b) *Mind and World*, Harvard University Press, London.

McGinn, Colin (1984) *Wittgenstein on Meaning: An Interpretation and Evaluation*, Basil Blackwell, Oxford.

McGinn, Marie (1984) 'Kripke on Wittgenstein's Sceptical Problem', *Ratio*, vol. XXVI, no. 1.

—— (1989) *Sense and Certainty: A Dissolution of Scepticism*, Basil Blackwell, Oxford.

Merleau-Ponty, Maurice (1962) *Phenomenology of Perception*, trans. Colin Smith, Routledge, London.

Moore, G. E. (1959) 'A Defence of Common Sense' and 'Proof Of An External World', in *Philosophical Papers*, Allen and Unwin, London.

Mulhall, Stephen (1990) *On Being in the World: Wittgenstein and Heidegger on Seeing Aspects*, Routledge, London.

—— (1996) *Heidegger and Being and Time*, Routledge, London.

Nagel, Thomas (1986) *The View From Nowhere*, Oxford University Press, New York.

Nietzsche, Friedrich (1992) *Ecce Homo*, Penguin, London.

Norman, Richard (1983) *The Moral Philosophers*, Clarendon Press, Oxford.

Pears, David (1971) *Wittgenstein*, Fontana, Glasgow.

—— (1988) *The False Prison: Study of the Development of Wittgenstein's Philosophy*, vol. II, Clarendon Press, Oxford.

Sartre, Jean-Paul (1948) *Existentialism and Humanism*, trans. Philip Mairet, Methuen, London.

Saussure, Ferdinand de (1983) *Course in General Linguistics*, trans. R. Harris, Duckworth, London.

Savigny, Eike von (1991) 'No Chapter "On Philosophy" in the "Philosophical Investigations"', *Metaphilosophy*, vol. 22, no. 4.

Sayers, Sean (1985) *Reality and Reason: Dialectic and the Theory of Knowledge*, Basil Blackwell, Oxford.

Schatzki, Theodore R. (1992) 'Early Heidegger on Being, The Clearing and Realism', in H. L. Dreyfus and H. Hall (eds), *Heidegger: A Critical Reader*, Basil Blackwell, Oxford.

Searle, John R. (1966) 'Assertions and Aberrations', in B. Williams and A. Montefiore (eds), *British Analytical Philosophy*, Routledge & Kegan Paul, London.

—— (1969) *Speech Acts: An Essay in the Philosophy of Language*, Cambridge University Press, Cambridge.

—— (1983) *Intentionality: An Essay in the Philosophy of Mind*, Cambridge University Press, Cambridge.

Staten, Henry (1985) *Wittgenstein and Derrida*, Basil Blackwell, Oxford.

Strawson, P. F. (1959) *Individuals: An Essay in Descriptive Metaphysics*, Methuen, London.

Williams, Bernard (1978) *Descartes: The Project of Pure Enquiry*, Penguin Books, Harmondsworth.

—— (1982) 'Wittgenstein and Idealism', in *Moral Luck*, Cambridge University Press, Cambridge.

Winch, Peter (1987) *Trying to Make Sense*, Basil Blackwell, Oxford.

Wittgenstein, Ludwig (1961a) *Notebooks: 1914–1916*, trans. G. E. M. Anscombe, Basil Blackwell, Oxford.

—— (1961b) *Tractatus Logico-Philosophicus*, trans. D. F. Pears and B. F. McGuinness, Routledge & Kegan Paul, London.

—— (1968a) *Philosophical Investigations*, trans. G. E. M. Anscombe, Basil Blackwell, Oxford.

—— (1968b) 'Wittgenstein's Notes for Lectures on "Private Experience" and "Sense Data"', *The Philosophical Review*, vol. LXXVII.

—— (1969) *The Blue and Brown Books*, Basil Blackwell, Oxford.

—— (1974) *Philosophical Grammar*, trans. A. Kenny, Basil Blackwell, Oxford.

—— (1975) *Philosophical Remarks*, trans. R. Hargreaves and R. White, Basil Blackwell, Oxford.

—— (1977) *Remarks on Colour*, trans L. L. McAlister and M. Schättle, Basil Blackwell, Oxford.

—— (1978) *Remarks on the Foundations of Mathematics*, trans. G. E. M. Anscombe, Basil Blackwell, Oxford.

—— (1979) *On Certainty*, trans. D. Paul and G. E. M. Anscombe, Basil Blackwell, Oxford.

—— (1980a) *Remarks on the Philosophy of Psychology*, vol. I, trans. G. E. M. Anscombe, Basil Blackwell, Oxford.

—— (1980b) *Remarks on the Philosophy of Psychology*, vol. II, trans. C. G. Luckhardt and M. A. E. Aue, Basil Blackwell, Oxford.

—— (1981) *Zettel*, trans. G. E. M. Anscombe, Basil Blackwell, Oxford.

—— (1982) *Last Writings On The Philosophy of Psychology*, vol. I, trans. C. G. Luckhardt and M. A. E. Aue, Basil Blackwell, Oxford.

—— (1988) *Wittgenstein's Lectures on Philosophical Psychology 1946–47*, notes by P. T. Geach, K. J. Shah, A. C. Jackson, ed. P. T. Geach, Harvester Wheatsheaf, London.

Wright, Crispin (1993) 'Realism, Truth-Value Links, Other Minds and the Past', in C. Wright, *Realism, Meaning and Truth*, Blackwell, Oxford.

INDEX

Made in the USA
Middletown, DE
13 July 2022

69215557R00104